Grooming to Win

How to Groom, Trim, Braid, and Prepare Your Horse for Show

Third Edition

SUSAN E. HARRIS

WILEY

Wiley Publishing, Inc.

D0888332

Table of Contents

FOREWORD   V

PREFACE   VII

1   Horse Management: Conditioning to Win   1

2   Skin and Hair Care   34

3   Grooming and Daily Care   41

4   Grooming Tools and Supplies   60

5   Mane and Tail Care   74

6   Bathing, Bandaging, and Other Procedures   102

7   Trimming and Clipping   128

8   Blankets and Horse Clothing   163

9   Final Touches   175

10 The Show Hunter   187

11 Sport Horses: Turnout for Dressage,
    Show Jumping, Eventing and Driving   220

12 The Western Show Horse   242

13   The Pleasure and Versatility Breeds   256

14   Other Breeds   266

15   The Saddlebred, Walking Horse, Parade Horse
     and Other Set-Tail Horses   275

16   Grooming at Horse Shows   290

APPENDIX I Trimming Styles by Type And Event   324

APPENDIX II Trimming Styles by Breed   334

INDEX   339

Foreword

It's hard to believe thirty years have passed since I wrote the foreword to Susan Harris's classic stable management book, *Grooming To Win*. Susan and her work have certainly stood the test of time. She is a passionate, devoted, and totally committed horse-person and has been for a very long time.

Before one can talk about riding a horse, let alone training or owning one, one must consider caring for the horse. Unfortunately, due to this age of specialization, many riders know how to compete, but they certainly don't know how to care for, manage, and present their animals.

This third edition of *Grooming To Win* has stood the test of timeless, basic principles of horse management, yet it has kept us up to date and brought us into the 21st century. Nothing is really new in today's age; we just do things better and quicker. The great beauty of this book is that it not only covers the essentials of caring for a horse at home, but goes into detail about every sophisticated nuance of preparing the show horse for the ring.

This book is needed more today than ever before. Stable management is a dying, almost lost, art. Thanks to Susan Harris and her prolific writing (as well as her enormous influence) perhaps this art will live to see another day.

GEORGE H. MORRIS
Wellington, Florida

Preface

It has been years since the last edition of *Grooming to Win* appeared, and I'm glad to have the chance to bring it in line with current show ring practices. In the horse show world, new styles, trends, and methods keep emerging like new channels in an old river. Some changes are fads of the moment; other reflect a more basic change in the type of horse, the way he is shown, and how we can best present him.

The more things change, the more they stay the same—technology and show ring glitter will never supplant the discipline, daily routine, attention to detail, and horsemanship that go into the making of a champion. A true horseman always puts the horse's welfare first, ahead of his own convenience, the current fashion, and even his desire to win. The more demanding the specialty in which you compete, the more important true horsemanship is to the success of both horse and rider. Those who prepare their horses for the challenge of competition, weather the demands of the show circuit, and keep their horses sound, healthy, and happy in there are good horsemen and women indeed, and they deserve our respect along with their winnings—so does anyone who keeps their own horse fit, clean, healthy, and happy, whether they ever compete or not.

In the new edition of *Grooming to Win,* there's an increased emphasis on conditioning and the physiology that under lies the conditioning process. A real "show glow" comes from within, not from a bottle, and understanding how this happens helps keeps us on the right track.

As the level of competition and the pressures of showing increase, we must consider the horse's mental health, attitude, and his relationship with people along with his physique and his looks. We must be aware of how we handle horses and use good judgment about how far to follow a fashion. Some things that are done to show horses in the name of winning are uncomfortable, unhealthy, or downright inhumane. We must be sensitive to each horse's attitude, needs, and reactions when grooming, conditioning, training, or showing, and do what we can to make his lot a happy one. Please groom your horse with feeling, listen to what he tells you as you work with him, and let your horse be a horse, even if it means you must brush off some mud later!

This book can never be the final word on grooming, as the subject is constantly evolving, yet I hope it will bring out some new and practical ideas while keeping the best of the old, traditional methods. If you have a grooming tip or a different way of doing things, I'd love to know about it, and if your horses are shiny, healthy, and happy, you must be doing it right.

Susan E. Harris
Cortland, New York

Chapter 1

Horse Management: Conditioning to Win

Since we are responsible for our horses' well-being, we must find a sensible balance between the horse's natural ways; the requirements of riding, showing, and training; and the needs of each individual animal. Show horses are not self-sufficient; we have a heavy responsibility to take the best possible care of them. The success we have in producing and keeping horses healthy, sound, and fit to show their best depends on how much time, knowledge, and effort we are willing to put forth for them.

When horses live as nature intended, they are usually fit, healthy, and self-sufficient as long as they have adequate range, forage, and water. Equine systems, habits, and behavior have evolved over fifty million years to help horses function and survive in a herd, constantly grazing and moving over a wide territory. It is only when we remove horses from their natural environment and use them for our own purposes that they need special care and management.

A horse "in the rough" is adapted to withstand harsh weather and fend off flies. The natural oils of the ungroomed coat prevent rain from soaking through, and his long winter coat keeps him warm even in bitter cold. The long mane and tail and the hair inside the ears protect him from flies, while long hair on the legs, face, and fetlocks keeps those parts warm and allows water to run off. Ranging over large areas and varying terrain toughens his feet and wears them down into a natural shape, and he grooms himself by rolling in dust or sand.

FIGURE 1. *The natural horse.*

Horses kept in domestic pastures are adapted to living outside but usually are more sedentary and less physically fit than range horses. Some develop overgrown feet, which can crack and chip and may cause stumbling, sprains, or gait abnormalities. Some pastures do not supply sufficient nutrition, while others have such lush grass that some animals are in danger of obesity and grass founder. Horses prefer to graze clean grass; but in small, overgrazed, or high traffic areas the grass becomes contaminated with manure and the eggs and larvae of internal parasites. The smaller the field and the more horses that use it, the more severe the internal parasite infestation is likely to be.

In conditioning pleasure and show horses, we are asking a horse to adapt to an artificial lifestyle. He may be confined to a stall or small paddock and expected to perform demanding gaits and paces instead of roaming and grazing at will. He may be fed a concentrated diet high in energy instead of the constant grazing she prefers. We may shorten his coat artificially by keeping him blanketed in a warm stable but make him more vulnerable to chills. His work may demand athletic performance, travel, and stress on her mind and body that his natural life never would.

Domestic horses used for sport or pleasure riding need care and management that their wild ancestors would neither need nor tolerate. Some horses, through selective breeding, have become so refined and sensitive that they would suffer and deteriorate if placed under range conditions or even a lower standard of care. In this chapter, I give you some guidance on how to successfully keep your horses healthy, sound, and fit so that they can show their best.

FIGURE 2. *The confined horse being conditioned for show must adjust to stable life and restrictions on behavior and environment.*

Stabling

The ultimate use of the horse may dictate the type of stabling, care, and management. For instance:

- A saddle-bred show horse with built-up feet and a set tail must be kept stabled, meticulously cared for and exercised, and can seldom be turned out safely.

- Endurance horses often do best kept in a field and seldom stabled.

- Pleasure horses used for occasional showing can usually be kept as they would be for ordinary riding, with a little extra attention to show details.

- A stall with an adjoining field, so the horse can be allowed to go freely in and out or kept in when necessary, is an excellent arrangement for horses whose owners work or go to school.

Try to permit your horse the most natural lifestyle possible. Don't impose procedures on her that limit his lifestyle (such as blanketing or body clipping) unless they are necessary; if you do, you must be conscientious about such details as changing blankets according to the weather.

A horse kept stabled full time requires more time and daily work. When a horse is kept stabled, you need to pay attention to several details:

- His stall must be cleaned and picked out more often to keep him clean.

- He needs plenty of bedding to cushion his legs and so that he can lie down in comfort.

- Feed and water buckets must be scrubbed out daily and clean, fresh water always available.

- Fly control is important because show horses' manes and tails may be shortened, tied up, or otherwise altered; and many have fine coats and skin that are extremely sensitive to fly bites. Some fly-control measures include:

  Screened stalls

  Fly sheets

  Ear covers and fly masks

  Meticulous stall cleaning and manure disposal

  Use of fly repellents, insecticides, and automated fly spray systems

  Turning horses out at night instead of during the day

- He needs exercise every day—nothing is worse for a horse than standing in confinement, particularly when she is fit. Allow him access to a pasture or paddock as often as you can, or graze him on a lead line when turnout is impossible.

- Let your horse "be a horse" by rolling and playing; no matter how dirty he gets, you can always clean him up!

Organization and Planning

If you're planning to show your horse, you should consider your goals and resources. Are you a pleasure rider who wants to show at a few local shows, or are you campaigning pursuit of major breed or national awards? When is your first competition, and how long will it take to prepare your horse? Must he be fit for athletic events such as jumping, reining, or barrel racing, or in "halter condition"? Most important, how much daily time and effort can you devote to conditioning, exercise, grooming, and other care?

Your show schedule impacts your day-to-day management because you have to balance your conditioning plans with other essential tasks:

- Major competitions and prep shows should be marked on a calendar so that you can plan to bring your horse into peak condition at the right time.

- No horse can maintain peak condition indefinitely, and the greater the physical demands on a horse, the more important it is to allow some rest time at home.

- Routine but essential procedures such as shoeing, deworming, inoculations, and dental care must be scheduled so that they are taken care of well in advance of shows and travel.

To make sure you don't miss a beat, the following sections help you chart your way to success so that you make plans for conditioning as well as day-to-day management tasks.

CHARTS, CALENDARS, AND KEEPING RECORDS

Charts, calendars, and records can help in planning, managing your horse, and going to competitions. You should assemble the records and documents you need before the show season and keep them up to date. A zippered binder with photocopies of all required papers can be taken to shows. Some horsemen prefer to keep shoeing, deworming, work schedules, and similar information on a chart in the barn. You may need some or all of the following:

- Registration papers (extra photocopies)
- Individual health records, including:

  Veterinary Health Certificate (if required for shows or interstate travel)

  Coggins test (extra photocopies)

  Inoculation records; proof of rabies inoculation (extra photocopies)

Normal vital signs (temperature, pulse, and respiration rates)

Veterinary record (exam and treatment notes, illnesses, injuries, allergies, sensitivity to medications, etc.)

Dental record (dates and notes on dental work)

Deworming schedule, including dates and product used

Shoeing notes; special shoeing requirements

- Insurance policy (if horse is insured), with contact information in case of a claim

- Contact information and emergency phone numbers for veterinarian, farrier, equine dental specialist, and other professionals

- Membership cards, USEF numbers, and owner/trainer information, as required for shows and competitions

- FEI passport (if horse competes in FEI classes)

- Calendar with show dates, plus scheduled dates for shoeing, deworming, inoculations, dental work, etc.

- Daily notes on training, condition, feeding, vet or farrier visits, etc.

YOUR PROFESSIONAL TEAM

No one produces a winner single-handedly. Here's a list of some of the professionals show horse owners may work with:

- An instructor or trainer

- A stable manager

- A groom

- A regular veterinarian

- A good farrier

- An equine dental expert

- An equine massage practitioner

All are important members of the team who contribute to the effort of getting the horse healthy, sound, fit, and ready to show. Everyone who works with the horse needs up-to-date information about his training program, his health, his soundness, fitness, and attitude, and should communicate about any problems or major changes.

Keeping notes or a logbook can make sure that important things are not missed. Jot down daily progress notes on work and training, occurrences such as heat in a leg or a loose shoe, or any significant changes. This can help in keeping track of progress, or health, fitness, or training issues.

Before You Begin

To bring a horse from pasture to show condition, you must prepare her system for the new demands to be made on it. His digestive system must gradually become accustomed to more concentrated energy-producing food. His muscles, legs, and cardiovascular system must be conditioned for more strenuous work and his immune system prepared to meet the challenges of stress and exposure to disease. His feet need proper shoeing for his best movement, and his coat and skin must be conditioned for best appearance and to cool and dry efficiently as he works. All this takes time, so you must start to prepare a horse well before his first show. A horse that's only slightly out of shape might take a month to condition; an unfit horse may need three months or longer to reach peak condition. Before you begin your conditioning regimen, you need to first assess your horse to see whether you're beginning with an unfit horse or a slightly out-of-shape horse.

Assessing Weight and Condition

You'll need to evaluate your horse's present condition and decide on conditioning goals. Is he overweight, lacking muscle tone, or too thin? While you cannot change his conformation, you can get him into the shape that shows him off best. Show horses look better with a *little* fat—just enough to round their body contours a bit and produce an overall "bloom." Judges discriminate against horses that look thin, which gives a poor impression of their management.

Assessing Weight

You should know your horse's current weight, for feeding purposes as well as for evaluating his condition. This can be found by weighing the horse on livestock or truck scales or estimated by using a weight tape around the heart girth.

Assessing Condition

You need to evaluate your horse's condition coupled with his weight. The Henneke Body Condition Scale classifies horses from 1 (emaciated) to 10 (obese), based on body fat. Ideal show condition falls in the middle range (5 to 6), along with indications of health and fitness such as good muscle tone; a healthy, shiny coat; clean, tight tendons and ligaments; clear eyes; a good appetite; and an alert attitude.

WHERE TO BEGIN

Fat horses are soft, lack endurance, are easily injured, and are prone to problems such as laminitis and colic. While show fashions, particularly in halter classes, have sometimes favored overfed, overweight, and under-exercised horses, this is an unhealthy trend that has cost horses their show careers and even their lives. It is better to condition for optimal muscle development and the health and stamina to do the job in the show ring; the results are lasting and worth the effort. Happily, more judges are selecting well-conditioned horses over excessively fat "feed 'em and lead 'em" types.

If your horse is used to being on pasture all the time, you could bring him into the stable during the day and turn her out at night for the first couple of weeks. While inside, he can have hay and a small feed of grain twice a day, can be groomed, trimmed, shod; and can begin her exercise program. Eventually he may be kept stabled with daily turnout, and hay will replace the grass in her diet. A horse's grain intake must be carefully balanced against her work and all changes made gradually.

When you first begin to work an unfit horse, start at a walk for about half an hour, just long enough to make the horse sweat under the saddle. Gradually increase the time and amount of exercise (see The Conditioning Process, p. 17).

FIGURE 3. Condition—obese, show condition, poor condition.

Always groom before riding, warm up and cool out gradually, groom or rinse the horse clean after work, and put him away clean, dry, and comfortable. Tack (especially girths, harness, and saddle pads) must be kept clean, soft, and supple to prevent rubs and galls. He should get a good daily grooming, with attention to feet, mane, and tail as well as cleaning and grooming the coat.

Prepping and Caring for the Hooves

The farrier should check your horse's feet and shoes, note their condition, wear, alignment, and angles, and evaluate her movement before trimming or shoeing. Tell your farrier what kind of work your horse is doing, and about any problems such as stumbling or forging. Major changes in shoeing should be made gradually, so as not to stress the structures of the feet and legs.

The horse's feet must be trimmed so that they are balanced and the bones of the hoof and pastern are correctly aligned according to her conformation. Sometimes showmen try to camouflage conformation faults by having the feet trimmed with excessively low heels, or having large feet pared down to make them appear smaller. Such practices can contribute to lameness and conditions such as navicular disease and may make it impossible for the horse to move athletically.

Feeding the Show Horse

The right feeding program is a vital factor in producing and maintaining a fit and healthy horse and in conditioning for competition. All horses require energy, protein, fiber, vitamins, minerals, salt, and water in the right amount and balance to meet their individual needs. The kind and amount of feed a horse requires depend on many factors—his age, weight, condition, body type, and temperament; work intended; and any special nutritional needs. Nutrition is important, but it is too large a subject to be covered in depth in this book, which can only give you some basic guidelines on feeding show horses.

Each horse must be fed as an individual; the amount of feed must be adjusted for her condition and work. It is more accurate to feed by weight than by amount; weigh a container of grain and an average flake of hay so that you know how many pounds of each your horse gets per feeding.

Balancing a ration means determining a horse's nutritional requirements and the kind and amount of hay, grain, and supplements that will meet her needs. Balancing a ration requires nutritional charts and a little math; it can save money and ensure that your feeding program meets all her nutritional needs without deficiencies or dangerous overfeeding. You can get help in balancing a ration and other nutritional advice from your county agricultural agent or a feed company representative.

All feed and hay should be of the best quality and must be properly stored to avoid dampness, mold, or contamination.

WATER, SALT, AND ELECTROLYTES

Horses need clean, fresh water at all times—they may drink a minimum of five to eight gallons of water a day and often more, especially in hot weather. It is important to know how much a horse is drinking daily, as failure to drink enough water leads to dehydration, which can have serious consequences. Some horses need extra buckets hung in their stall. If a fussy horse refuses to drink unfamiliar water away from home, an old trick is flavoring her water with Kool-Aid, peppermint, or another flavor he likes, then adding the same ingredient to water at a show to make it taste "just like home."

A simple test for dehydration is the "pinch test." If you pinch the skin on the horse's shoulder into a tiny "tent", it should fall back into place almost immediately when you release it. If the skin remains raised for a second or so or subsides slowly over several seconds, the horse is dehydrated and needs water immediately.

Horses need salt, especially in hot weather. They cannot replace salt and other essential minerals lost when they sweat, unless they have access to a salt block or salt is added to their feed. Supplementary electrolytes (a mixture of salts and potassium) may be required when horses sweat heavily, especially during hot weather. These can be given in water, in feed, or as oral paste.

SUPPLEMENTS

Many show horses receive some or all of the following types of nutritional supplements:

- *Vitamin supplements:* single or multivitamin supplements

- *Mineral supplements:* to balance calcium and phosphorous and supply necessary trace minerals

- *Coat supplements:* usually contain fats or oils, flaxseed or rice bran, plus vitamins and biotin to promote hair growth and increase the shine of the coat and richness of the color

- *Hoof supplements:* formulated to promote healthy hoof growth, usually contain biotin

- *Joint supplements:* promote development of healthy cartilage and synovial fluid in joints; may help some arthritic horses

- *Iron or blood builders:* contain iron to treat and prevent anemia

- *Weight builders:* contain proteins, fats, oils, rice bran, and vitamins to promote weight gain

- *Calmatives:* include magnesium supplements and some herbal products intended to promote healthy nerves and a calmer attitude

Some horse owners overfeed and oversupplement in their zeal to achieve perfect show condition. Too many calories can make a horse too energetic or too fat; excess protein is either converted into fat or excreted through the kidneys; and overfeeding most vitamins is simply a waste of money. Feeding a single supplement according to directions may be beneficial, but feeding excessive supplements is not only a waste of money but may even be harmful. Always check the ingredients of any supplement to be sure it does not contain a forbidden substance that could result in a positive drug test.

GOOD FEEDING PRACTICES

All changes in feed must be done gradually. The horse's digestion depends on the action of certain beneficial bacteria in the gut. It takes ten days to two weeks for these bacteria to adapt to a different kind of feed, so any change should be made gradually over this period, or colic may result.

Horses' grain intake must be carefully balanced against their work and condition. Although feed changes should be made gradually, grain can be cut back or even withheld completely without causing harm, and it is safer to err on the side of too little than too much. If a horse must be kept in without exercise, his grain should be cut to half or less than half the usual amount to avoid azoturia or *tying-up syndrome.*

Health and Veterinary Care

INITIAL EXAMINATION

Conditioning should begin with a veterinary check of condition and general soundness. A blood count may be done as part of the initial evaluation; if a horse is slightly anemic, this should be corrected, and the test gives a baseline for later comparison.

This is a good time to take and record your horse's vital signs (resting pulse rate, temperature, and respiration rates). You should know what is normal for your horse in order to tell if he is running a slight fever, showing signs of stress, or is otherwise off color.

INOCULATIONS

Show horses must be inoculated against contagious diseases, because they are exposed to large numbers of horses while their resistance may be lowered by the stress of travel and showing. Most horsemen inoculate against tetanus, Eastern and Western encephalomyelitis (sleeping sickness), influenza, and rhinopneumonitis (equine herpesvirus or EHV). Some also vaccinate against rabies, strangles, West Nile virus, Potomac horse fever, or other diseases, depending on the veterinarian's advice and which diseases pose a threat. You also need to know how long immunity lasts for inoculation and when booster shots should be scheduled. Since inoculations may cause a mild reaction or some stress, they should not be given right before shipping or competition.

The veterinarian should also draw blood for a Coggins test for equine infectious anemia. Most states, shows, and stables require a negative Coggins test within a certain time period in order to transport horses, enter a show, or stable at a facility.

Coggins tests, health certificates, and/or proof of inoculation may be required for some shows. If your horse competes in FEI (Federation Equestre Internationale) classes or competitions, a veterinarian must help you complete the identification information for the horse's FEI passport, which is required for such competitions.

Conditioning Problems

AZOTURIA (EQUINE RHABDOMYELOSIS) OR TYING-UP SYNDROME

Azoturia, or tying-up syndrome, is a metabolic disorder that may occur when fit, grain-fed horses are kept in without exercise for a day or two without cutting the grain ration. When the horse starts back to work, she may suffer muscle cramps and then partial paralysis of the muscles of the hindquarters; in severe cases, muscle tissue may break down and be excreted in the urine, which would become as dark as coffee. Signs of tying up include:

- Sweating and trembling, especially in the hindquarters

- Tight, corded hindquarter muscles

- Short, crampy steps, leading to inability to move

- Muscles that tighten until the horse appears to stand on tiptoe or knuckle over on the hind legs

There are various degrees of tying up, which is a syndrome rather than a disease. If you suspect that a horse may be tying up, walk him slowly to help relieve the muscle cramps. If the symptoms are severe or he appears to get worse, stop her from moving and call a veterinarian. Blanketing the

FIGURE 4. Azoturia.

hindquarters and applying heat and massage to the affected muscles may give some relief, but veterinary treatment is necessary.

Azoturia, or tying up, is more common in fit, heavily muscled horses doing hard work; some veterinarians believe it is associated with deficiency of selenium, vitamin E, or thiamine. (Similar symptoms may occur in horses afflicted with HYPP or PSSM, and there are other possible causes.) A horse that has had one attack is more prone to have another.

GASTRIC ULCERS

Show horses are at risk for equine gastric ulcers. The stress of training, confinement, travel, concentrated feed, certain medications and lack of free grazing are contributing factors. Studies have shown that as many as 80 percent of show horses may have gastric ulcers, which can affect their health, comfort, performance, and attitude.

Signs of ulcers include: dull coat, weight loss, diarrhea, recurrent colic, failure to perform up to potential, altered eating behavior, and a dull or cranky attitude. If a horse's performance deteriorates, she no longer cleans up her feed, or a normally pleasant horse frequently pins her ears back or begins biting or kicking, ulcers may be the cause. Ulcers can be diagnosed and treated, and there are preventative anti-ulcer medications.

DEWORMING PROGRAM

Your veterinarian can perform a fecal parasite count to determine what kind and how many internal parasites your horse may be carrying, and can advise you on a deworming and parasite control program. No horse can respond to conditioning if he is loaded with internal parasites, and fatal colics have been linked to parasite damage. Show horses are usually dewormed at least every two months; some veterinarians recommend deworming more often, and rotating the type of dewormer periodically. Along with regular deworming, it is important to keep feed and hay from becoming contaminated by manure, and to mow, drag, and pick up manure in paddocks regularly.

DENTAL CARE

A horse's teeth should be checked by an equine dental specialist once or twice a year, or if he is underweight or shows signs of mouth trouble.

Dropping wads of partially chewed hay ("quidding") or allowing food to fall out of the mouth while chewing are signs that his teeth need attention. Horses develop sharp edges or "hooks" worn into their molars by their natural chewing motion, and some have mouth abnormalities, which can cause abnormal wear. Expert "floating" (filing) can improve a horse's condition, comfort, and attitude, especially if he is given a "performance float," which smoothes the premolars to make it more comfortable for him to carry the bit.

Turnout

Horses are freedom-loving creatures by nature; their most natural setting is a pasture, and some freedom to graze, play, run, roll, and just "be a horse" is good for their mental health. Show horses are sometimes deprived of turnout because of lack of a safe turnout area, because of special shoeing that could lead to injury if they ran and played, or because they are too valuable to risk injury. That a horse will get dirty is *not* a valid excuse for denying him turnout—he can wear a turnout rug or sheet and can be cleaned up afterward.

The first requirement is a safe turnout area, safely fenced so that the horse cannot get out and is safe from injuring herself. Since a show horse may be spirited and full of himself, bell boots and splint boots or polo wraps are standard turnout precautions to protect his legs and prevent her from pulling a shoe. If the halter is left on during turnout, it should have a breakaway safety crownpiece. Blanketed horses should wear a turnout rug or sheet with leg straps to keep it in place when she rolls or bucks.

Some horses are unhappy when turned out alone; they may settle down if they have a quiet and compatible turnout buddy. For valuable horses, no more than two should go out together. Turn out the more dominant horse after his mate is already out, and bring him in first.

Show horses usually have fine coats and may be extra sensitive to fly bites. They need fly repellent and shade or shelter to escape flies and should not be turned out during the buggiest times of day. It may work better to turn horses out at night to avoid flies, which also prevents their coats from being bleached by the sun. Protective turnout clothing includes fly masks, fly sheets, and anti-fly leggings that prevent flies from biting their legs, making them kick and stamp. Avoid turnout during the hours of strongest sunlight, and use equine sunscreen ointment on horses with extensive white face markings.

If you cannot turn a horse out, take him out to walk and graze on a lead line as often as possible. This is a good way to help him relax and get used to the sights at a horse show, and the grazing is good for both his digestion and his peace of mind.

The Conditioning Process

Conditioning is the process by which the body becomes stronger and more efficient—in short, body-building. While most people think of conditioning as building muscle, it involves the whole body and all its systems. Good conditioning not only makes a horse look better but also, more importantly, makes him healthier, stronger, and able to work with less fatigue and less chance of injury.

One of the advantages of good conditioning is that you can improve your horse's shape, muscle development, and movement by proper work. Horses that travel with a high head and a hollow back are not only unattractive and difficult to ride but are also weak in the top line and abdominal muscles; they develop a bulging under-neck and a saggy belly. By training a horse to move in a round frame with long, swinging, and rhythmic strides, you can develop his neck, back, loin, top line, and hindquarter muscles, and tone up his abdominal muscles. This cannot be forced by head-setting devices; good riding and an understanding of equine movement are needed to develop the "circle of muscles," while most devices only teach the horse to carry her head in a certain way. Riding in well-balanced working gaits, frequent transitions, working up- and downhill with long, free-moving gaits, and cavaletti work can contribute to the muscle development that make a horse look more attractive as well as help him move better.

THE SCIENCE BEHIND CONDITIONING

Conditioning really takes place at the cellular level. When a system or part of the body (such as a muscle) is stressed by more work than it is used to, the body responds by strengthening that part. This is called the "training effect." Muscle fibers become larger and stronger, bones and joints strengthen, the heart and lungs develop more capacity to pump blood and take in oxygen, and the circulation develops more capillaries to deliver oxygen and nutrients and carry off waste products. We see the result in bigger muscles, increased endurance, greater strength, and a faster recovery rate after work. Other benefits are a shiny coat, extra energy, and a spirited, zestful attitude.

The stress that triggers this process must be just enough, but not too much. Too little work will not activate the training effect. Too much stress, especially without rest, depletes the body's resources and eventually results in injury. Conditioning a horse requires just enough exercise to tire him, but not enough to cause injury or wear him down. Excessive stress that burns up a horse's resources is called overtraining; this leads to a thin, nervous horse that is chronically fatigued, sour, and difficult to train. Too much exercise at once, especially on an unfit horse, can cause sore muscles, tendon injuries, or other damage.

The conditioning process is fueled by essential nutrients—carbohydrates, fats, protein, vitamins, and minerals—and by oxygen, all of which are delivered to the cells by the blood. Circulation improves with exercise; an unfit horse cannot deliver as much oxygen to the cells as a fit horse— that's why he huffs and puffs when he works.

SAFELY IMPROVING YOUR HORSE'S CONDITION

All horses need exercise every day. When deprived of exercise, the muscles, circulation, and other systems deteriorate, causing a horse to become first unfit and eventually unhealthy. Conditioning a horse requires regular, consistent exercise five or six days per week, increasing gradually as he becomes fitter, with turnout or walking exercise on rest days. To maintain a basic level of fitness, he should be worked at least three times per week, with turnout on the other days.

However, to improve condition, work must be balanced against rest. Rest gives the body time to clear away waste, deliver nutrients to the cells, and build tissue. Rest doesn't mean standing idle—it can mean dropping back to a slower gait or changing to an exercise that works different muscles. If you trot for five minutes, walk for five minutes, and then canter, you are working and resting different muscles. Injuries happen most often to tired horses at the end of a ride, just as human athletes are most likely to get hurt on the last ski run or late in a game.

Tendons, ligaments, joints, and feet condition more slowly than muscles. This can be a problem if a horse muscles up quickly but his rider forgets that his other tissues are still unfit; strenuous work too soon can easily pull a tendon or sprain a ligament. If you start with a sufficient base of long, slow distance work before doing fast work, sharp turns, or jumping, tendons, joints and other structures have time to strengthen and are less likely to be injured.

The hoof can adapt to the demands placed on it by extra work and the ground it works on, but this takes time. Exercise pumps more blood through the inner structures of the foot, increasing circulation and hoof growth and keeping the foot flexible to absorb shock. Lack of exercise can contribute to contracted heels and unhealthy feet. However, overwork on hard surfaces or rough ground can cause sole bruises or damage the sensitive structures of the foot, causing lameness.

RECOVERY RATE

The pulse recovery rate is used as a measure of a horse's cardiovascular fitness; it can help you determine how much work your horse can handle. To check the recovery rate, the horse is worked at a certain speed, distance, and length of time. For instance, trot steadily for five minutes. Then stop and immediately take the pulse, rest and walk for ten minutes, then take the pulse again. The difference between the two pulse rates is the recovery rate. The pulse may be taken at the lower edge of the jawbone or by using a stethoscope on the side of the ribs over the heart; some trainers use on-board heart-rate monitors to monitor pulse and recovery rates more accurately during training and rest periods.

A fit horse's pulse will drop back to nearly normal very quickly even if it has gone very high during exercise; an unfit horse's pulse remains elevated for much longer. Heat and humidity have a great effect on heart rate and respiration, so the recovery rate will be slower on hot, muggy days. A wise trainer will take it easy in such conditions, anyway.

Exercise

Various exercise methods are used for different types of horses. Some exercise methods train the horse in the skills he will perform in the show ring; others are strictly for conditioning purposes. It's a good idea to

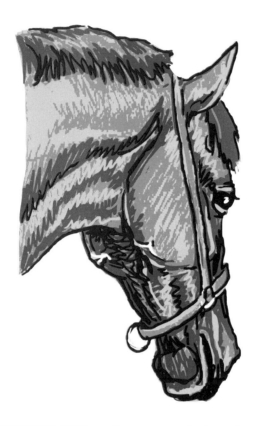

FIGURE 5. Taking pulse—artery under lower jaw.

"cross-train" or vary exercise methods in order to condition the horse in different ways, exercise other muscles, and keep him interested and happy in her work.

Riding is the most common method of exercise, as the rider can train his horse, practice his own riding, and enjoy himself at the same time. Trail riding is excellent for conditioning because changes in terrain and footing condition the horse more than work in a level arena, and new sights and places keep the horse (and rider) from becoming bored. Working uphill at a walk and trot is good for developing muscle and wind, but downhill grades should be taken slowly, as they increase concussion on bones and joints. Working in deep sand or riding on a beach is also good for strengthening muscles, but it is easy to overdo with an unfit horse. A quiet hack or trail ride is an excellent letdown after concentrated training or when a horse needs an easy day's work.

Driving is frequently used by trainers of saddle horses for training as well as exercise. Young horses can be driven before they are mature enough to carry a rider, and it is a good developer of the back and hindquarter muscles. *Long-lining* or *ground driving* is working the horse in long reins from the ground; this is often used for training as well as good exercise.

Ponying, or leading one horse while riding another, can be used to condition two horses at once or to exercise a horse that is not ready to be ridden. It requires an experienced handler with a reliable pony horse, and should be done in an enclosed field. The handler may pass the lead rope around the saddle horn for leverage, but *never* tie one horse to the saddle of another. Ponying is usually done at the walk and trot.

Longeing is a good way to warm up a horse or settle down a fresh horse before riding or showing. Longeing should be done by an experienced person, using a line at least thirty-feet long. When done correctly, it can be used to train and condition a horse, developing his top line muscles, flexion, carriage, and acceptance of the bit. However, working on a continuous circle puts extra stress on legs and joints, and overdoing it or too much speed on too small a circle can lead to lack of balance and injuries. The horse's legs should be protected with boots or bandages, and she must maintain rhythmic, well-balanced gaits and change directions periodically to prevent one side from being overworked. Very young horses should not be longed, as they are more vulnerable to injuries from too much speed on too small a circle.

Roundpenning: Free schooling or working at liberty in a round pen fifty to sixty feet in diameter is an alternative to longeing. Because there is no sideways pull as on a longe line, there is less chance that a horse will interfere (strike a foot against the other leg); this is a better method for very young horses than too much longeing. Skillful roundpenning can be good training for respect, attention, confidence, and manners.

As in longeing, the trainer should work the horse in rhythmic gaits, with changes of gait and direction and rest breaks often enough to prevent overstressing the horse. If the schooling ring is surfaced with deep sand, roundpenning will develop the muscles through harder work, but it is important to build up slowly and not overdo it. Horses should wear protective boots or polo bandages during roundpenning.

FIGURE 6. *Horse moving hollow; horse moving round.*

Cavaletti is a grid of poles spaced for walking or trotting. The object of cavaletti work is to encourage the horse to regulate his stride while rounding his back and reaching out and down with his neck. This develops his "circle of muscles" (hindquarters, back, loin, neck, and abdominal muscles), while the raised poles make him flex the joints of his legs at each step. Walking over cavaletti can help limber up a horse's muscles during a warm-up. The rider should take a half-seat position that frees the horse's back to stretch and round up.

Cavaletti must be set at the right distance for the horse. For an average sixteen-hand horse, trot poles should be placed 4'3" to 4'6" apart; approximately 3'6" for walking. These distances should be modified for the size and stride of the horse; he should be able to step in the middle of the spaces without tripping or reaching.

Galloping, jumping, reining: These and other performance skills are required in some competitions, so they must be practiced during training. A horse should not be asked for hard work until he is fit. It is easy to injure an unfit horse by overdoing fast, strenuous, and for many riders the most enjoyable, work. Horses must be warmed up before fast work, and it must not be prolonged to the point of fatigue.

MECHANICAL EXERCISERS

Some trainers, especially those preparing halter horses, use treadmills, mechanical exercisers, or automatic walkers or to exercise horses. This requires a good understanding of the working of the machine, its safety precautions and proper use, and skilled supervision whenever a horse is being worked. Automatic walkers work horses in a relatively small circle, which has the same disadvantages as too much longeing. They are a labor-saving device because several horses can be exercised at once, but if used too mechanically without adapting the exercise to the needs of the individual horse, they can produce a sour, stiff, or even lame horse. Treadmill work is primarily for muscle development. Some treadmills can be set on a slope to simulate hill work and develop the hindquarters or incorporate working in water as a conditioning factor.

Some high-tech training centers offer an equine swimming pool as a conditioning or therapeutic option. The horse is led down a ramp into the water and then guided around a dock or a round pool, swimming laps until he is led out again. Swimming exercise works the heart, lungs, and muscles without weight on the back or the effects of concussion. It was first used for conditioning racehorses suffering from foot and leg ailments and is now used for other types of horses to improve cardiovascular fitness. It requires a trained attendant and, of course, special pool facilities. Most horses seem to enjoy swimming.

Basic Conditioning Program

A soft, unfit horse needs a basic conditioning program to bring him into shape for ordinary work. Horses that are more fit can handle more exercise and take less time to condition. Adjust the daily work and overall program to the individual horse's progress and soundness. As the horse becomes able to do more active work, training may be substituted for conditioning rides. Here is a basic program for bringing an unfit horse into condition:

> *Week 1:* Exercise twenty to thirty minutes at a walk daily, with one or two brief periods of slow trot.
>
> *Week 2:* Increase exercise thirty to forty minutes daily; gradually adding trotting periods of one to two minutes, followed by five minutes of walk.
>
> *Week 3:* Exercise forty-five minutes daily; increase number of two- to three-minute trot periods (followed by five minutes of walk). Add one or two brief periods of canter. Add walking up and down gentle hills twice a week.
>
> *Week 4:* Work forty-five minutes to one hour daily; increase trot periods to five minutes (followed by three to five minutes of walk). Increase canter periods to one to two minutes. Walk up and down gentle hills twice a week.
>
> *Week 5:* Work forty-five minutes to one hour daily, doing "sets" of trotting five minutes, walking five minutes, cantering one to three minutes. Walk up and down gentle hills twice a week; add slow trotting up hills.
>
> *Week 6:* Work one hour daily, doing "sets" of trotting five minutes, walking five minutes, cantering three minutes. Continue hill work twice a week.

After six weeks of conditioning, most horses should have reached ordinary riding fitness, ready for lessons, training, and more athletic work. If you plan to enter many classes on each show day or if you are competing in demanding events like jumping or speed events, you may need to condition further.

Always walk the first fifteen minutes and the last fifteen minutes of every ride; proper warm-up and cooldown will do more to prevent injuries than anything else. Be aware of your horse's breathing; if he begins to huff and puff, he is feeling the strain and needs to walk. Keep weather and footing conditions in mind—hot, humid weather takes a lot out of a horse, and hard footing can pound his legs into unsoundness.

Foot and Leg Care

In order to show and win, a horse must get to the show ring on four good legs. Considering the strain of carrying a rider and the hazards of work, showing, and just being a horse; this isn't always as simple as it sounds. The feet and legs are the parts of the horse most vulnerable to injury, and like the rest of the horse, they must be properly conditioned to carry him through training and into the show ring.

Getting Evaluated

Before starting conditioning, a horse's feet and legs should be evaluated with your veterinarian and farrier. Is the conformation and structure of his feet and legs basically sound and correct, or does he have functional defects that might affect his way of moving or old injuries that need watching? Are his feet in good condition, too hard or soft, brittle, cracked, or contracted?

Horses whose feet have not been kept trimmed often grow long toes and low heels, which puts stress on the tendons and can cause tripping, stumbling, or injuries. Their feet must be trimmed to give the bones of the foot the proper angle before they can begin serious work. If his feet are cracked, worn down excessively, or tender, a horse will need shoeing; and if his soles are thin or bruised, he may need protective pads. If a horse must undergo major changes to the angle of his feet or the weight of his shoes, this should be done gradually so as not to strain joints and ligaments with too great a change at once.

At one time it was common for farriers to perform "corrective" trimming in an effort to force horses with crooked legs to travel straight and stand correct and square. While this had some cosmetic effects, it often caused strain and lameness by forcing bones and joints out of their natural, although crooked, alignment. Most farriers today feel that any corrective trimming to straighten crooked legs must be done while the leg bones are still growing, preferably during the horse's first year. For

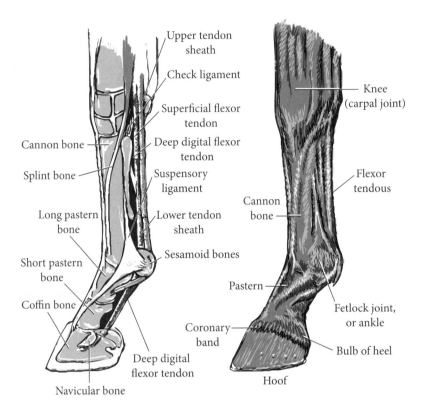

FIGURE 7. Structure of lower leg.

mature horses, whether straight or crooked, the foot should be trimmed or shod to allow it to travel and land in its best natural balance. Much can be done to help a horse with less than perfect legs, but overcorrection can cause more trouble than the original problem.

Most horses need their feet trimmed or their shoes reset every six weeks; those that need their feet "fine-tuned" may require attention every four weeks. If your horse wears special shoes, it is prudent to have your regular farrier make and fit an extra set or shoes, which can be taken along to shows. Should the horse lose a shoe, a local horseshoer can replace it with a shoe that has already been custom fitted, with only minor alterations.

DAILY HOOF CARE

Daily hoof care includes picking out the feet and brushing the sole clean to inspect the ground surface of the foot. Too-dry feet may be packed

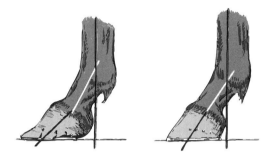

FIGURE 8. Overgrown hoof with long toe, low heel, and broken angle; hoof aligned with pastern.

overnight with prepared clay such as White Rock. Hoof dressings applied to the outer wall of the foot may soften the coronary band and may have a cosmetic effect, but they do not actually moisturize the hoof. Moisture is absorbed through the ground surface of the foot and the coronary band and supplied to the inner structures of the foot through the circulation, which is stimulated by exercise. Sticky hoof dressings collect dirt; they should be applied sparingly around the coronary band and any excess wiped off.

Rasping or sanding the outer wall of the foot is a common show practice to make hooves look clean and smooth. However, this removes the periople (the shiny outer coating of the hoof), which is like sandpapering the surface of your fingernails—it can cause the hoof to dry out. Those who insist on this practice should apply a hoof sealant to the outer surface of the hoof. A less invasive way to clean the hoof wall is to scrub it with a nail brush or vegetable brush.

CHECKING LEGS

Make a habit of examining your horse's legs each day when you first take him out, during grooming, and after exercise. If you look closely at each leg and feel it with your hand, you will come to know your horse's legs and feet so well that you will notice any little bump, heat, or swelling before the problem has a chance to escalate. A normal leg is clean, tight, and hard, without puffiness, swellings, or hot spots. The tendons should be tight and cool and should stand out clearly under the skin, and the horse should not show tenderness at any spot when the leg is palpated. "Filling" refers to swelling that fills in the normal spaces around the tendons, ligaments, and joints; this can be an early sign of inflammation. Some horses may have old injuries such as an old bowed tendon or an enlarged ankle; these areas should be watched for any signs of flaring up with inflammation.

Leg Problems

"Stocking up" is a generalized cool swelling of both hind legs or all four legs caused by poor circulation. It is common in older horses and horses that stand in the stable with insufficient exercise and rarely occurs in horses kept in pasture. Horses that do not lie down to rest are more likely to stock up; standing on hard surfaces with insufficient bedding aggravates the problem. Stocking up does not cause lameness and usually subsides with exercise. Horses that stock up may be stiff when they begin exercise and benefit from being walked to loosen them up before being ridden. The use of standing bandages can help prevent stocking up.

Windpuffs are soft, bunchy swellings on or near the fetlock joint, caused by excess secretion of synovial fluid. They are considered a blemish rather than an unsoundness. Windpuffs are cool and painless; a hot, tender swelling suggests a fresh injury that should be treated immediately. Standing bandages and preparations such as leg sweats and leg tighteners will cosmetically reduce windpuffs, but they will soon reappear.

Windpuffs and stocking up must not be confused with heat and "filling" in a leg, which points to inflammation and possible injury. When an injury occurs, inflammation results in "cellulitis"—the area becomes engorged with fluid, making it hot, tender, and swollen. Although this is part of the body's healing process, the sooner it is reduced, the better for the injury.

When checking legs, compare one leg with the other. If one leg is puffy, warmer, or thicker; shows filling around the tendons or joints; or the horse flinches when it is palpated, it should be investigated further. Never pass off seemingly minor heat or swelling; if treated promptly, it may be minor and temporary, but if it is missed and the horse continues to work, it might develop into serious inflammation that can sideline him from training or competition. Whenever a "hot" leg is discovered, it should be treated immediately—don't wait a day or two to see if it will get worse!

Cold-hosing, or running a continuous stream of cool water over a leg, is good first aid for heat, swelling, or minor leg strains and bruises. The

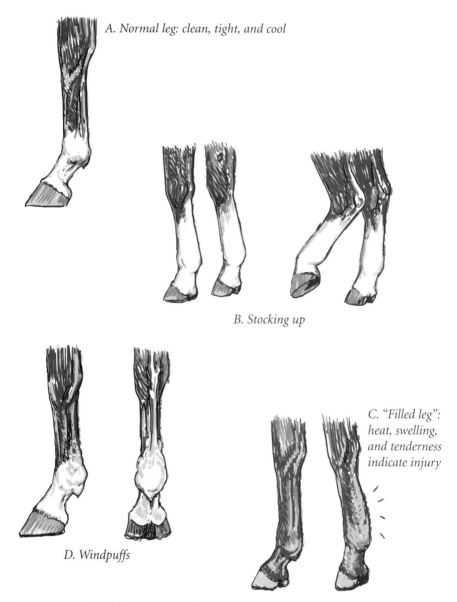

A. Normal leg: clean, tight, and cool

B. Stocking up

C. "Filled leg": heat, swelling, and tenderness indicate injury

D. Windpuffs

FIGURE 9. Normal leg and leg problems.

area should be hosed for twenty minutes, dried, and left for twenty minutes, and the hosing repeated several times a day. Applying a cooling wrap, poultice, or support bandage (standing or treatment bandage) can also help to reduce heat and swelling and minimize any damage.

Leg Protection

Unfit horses tire easily and are more likely to injure themselves by interfering (striking a leg with the opposite hoof) or overreaching (grabbing the back of the heel with the toe of a hind foot). Horses that wear certain types of shoes (especially egg bar shoes) may tend to overreach or pull their shoes off during turnout, schooling, jumping, or when ridden in mud. They should wear bell boots for protection during exercise and turnout.

Various types of splint boots, galloping boots, tendon boots, and polo wraps may be used to protect horses' legs during work or turnout, especially for longeing, lateral movements, fast turns, or jumping. Some trainers routinely brace and wrap legs after every workout, but horses may become dependent upon the support of the bandages if they are used constantly. Bandages must be applied correctly, or they may cause injury to the tendons or come loose, tripping the horse.

Boots must be kept clean and free of dirt and dried sweat to prevent them from rubbing sores on the legs. Some horses are allergic to certain types of rubber, neoprene, or plastic boot linings—these horses may need a thin sheet of cotton next to their skin under the boots. (For more about boots and bandages, see chapter 6.)

Conditioning the Skin and Hair Coat

A good daily grooming is an important step in conditioning. This clears the extra scurf, dirt, and loose hair from the skin and hair coat; sheds out old loose hair; stimulates healthy skin; and prevents sores and galls. If a horse is very dirty, it may help to start with a bath (see page 105), but bathing is no substitute for the massage, friction, and rubbing of good grooming. This is also a good time to begin dressing and conditioning the mane and tail and to do basic trimming of the head, bridle path, and legs. Horses with a heavy coat may benefit from being body clipped, but this depends on their work, lifestyle, and the time of year.

If a horse has a long winter coat, body clipping may allow him to work in comfort, makes cooling out and grooming much easier, and improves her appearance. However, body clipping requires blanketing and extra care, so it should only be done if it is necessary.

PREVENTING SORES AND GALLS

A soft horse has tender skin and easily develops girth galls and saddle sores. Hot weather, dirt, sweat, and stiff, dirty tack increase the problems of heat, sweating, friction, and the likelihood of sores. It is easier to prevent sores and galls than to treat them, which usually requires the horse to be laid up while he heals.

The skin and coat should be brushed clean before every ride, especially under the tack. Tack and harness must be kept clean and supple, and saddle pads laundered frequently. Some horses may need protective equipment such as a girth cover, string girth, neoprene girth, or fleece padding. All tack, especially saddles, must be properly fitted, without rubbing or creating pressure points.

The skin of the back and girth area should be inspected after every ride and rinsed with plain water or body wash. When the saddle is removed, small dry patches in the wet saddle mark indicate pressure points, which will eventually lead to tissue damage and a deep sore. (If the dry spots are swollen, hot, and tender, tissue damage is already occurring.) Pain from saddle or girth sores can make a horse bite or kick when being saddled and act up when ridden.

Minor rubs may be treated with strong tea—the tannic acid in the tea toughens the skin. If the skin is raw, it must be treated as an open wound and protected from any further contact until it is healed. The penalty for inflicting a girth sore on your horse is to ride bareback until it has healed! Padding up a sore to keep working is risky, as the padding may slip and grind dirt and sweat into the sore, making it many times worse. No padding can make pressure on a raw sore tolerable.

FIGURE 10. Saddle mark with dry pressure point.

Mental Attitude

A horse's mental attitude must be considered along with his physical conditioning. Horses are not machines that can be worked when it is convenient and switched off when the trainer goes home. Concentrated work and confinement are not natural to horses, and they may develop unpleasant dispositions or neurotic habits if they are treated without sympathy and understanding for their nature. A happy horse is healthier, more resistant to stress and disease, and performs better, too.

Horses are herd animals who need companionship, especially with other horses. Stalls with bars or windows that allow horses to see other horses are more in keeping with the nature of the horse than solitary confinement in a solid-walled box. If a horse must be kept stabled, he should have a large window or Dutch door that permits him to see other horses and activities going on around him. Some horses are happier if they can be stabled or turned out with a companion horse or if they have the companionship of a "pet" such as a dog, cat, or goat. There are some exuberant clowns who delight in playing with a rubber ball, a plastic bottle, or other horse toys in their stall or paddock.

Horses feel most secure when a steady routine is followed, so try to keep to a regular daily schedule for feeding, grooming, exercise, and turnout, etc. Break up long periods of idleness by spacing out feedings, breaking exercise into two shorter periods instead of one long one, and allowing as much turnout time as possible. Feeding several small meals throughout the day is better for horses' digestion and gives them something to do. If you feed a pelleted complete feed ration, a horse may eat up his pellets and then chew wood if he has nothing else to do. Providing some hay to nibble on may help. Horses may also be kept busy by slow feeders, including a device that dispenses a few feed pellets at a time as the horse rolls it around with her nose. Placing the hay in two hay nets (one over the other), makes it take longer to eat his hay, which is more like natural grazing.

With nothing to do, a stalled horse may find herself a "hobby" such as chewing wood, digging holes, stall-walking, weaving, or cribbing. Stable vices may be nervous habits, though they are more often caused by boredom, and may indicate that a horse is being confined too much for his mental and physical good. Cribbing is an addictive habit that causes the horse to release endorphins, the brain's "feel-good" chemicals, so a horse that cribs may continue this habit even under the best of management. In this case, the only solution is to keep a cribbing strap on him to prevent the habit.

A good trainer tries to keep his horses in a pleasant and confident state of mind. He should be aware of each horse's interest in his work—or lack of it—and be alert to any change in attitude that might signify fatigue, sourness, illness, or stress. The treatment a horse receives in his daily care is just as important to his performance in the show ring as his training under saddle—a horse that is confused, hurt, frightened, or frustrated in the stable will carry these attitudes into her performance. Gradually introducing such things as noisy environments, crowds, trailer loading, and new places with a quiet, confident handler and a minimum of fuss helps horses learn to handle the experience of showing better. There are special tapes that can be played at home to accustom horses to show noises.

As horses reach peak condition they will be—and should be—full of high spirits and playfulness. A show horse that feels full of himself is consequently more difficult to handle than a placid pleasure horse. It takes a firm but sympathetic handler with her mind on the job to keep such a bundle of equine energy safely under control. Don't let yourself become distracted or inattentive and never let your temper get the better of you. Anticipate a keen horse's playfulness and energy, insist on good manners and obedience, but don't punish him for feeling good; that's what you have been working so hard to achieve!

Chapter 2

Skin and Hair Care

The skin is the largest organ of the horse's body; it encloses the body, protects against injury and harmful organisms, and serves as a sense organ. The skin also helps regulate the horse's temperature. The hair coat protects and insulates the skin, keeps the body warm, and is one of the horse's chief beauties.

The Skin

The skin consists of an outer layer, the epidermis, from which the hairs grow, and a thicker inner layer, the dermis, which contains the support system for the skin and hair: hair follicles, sweat glands, sebaceous glands, and blood vessels. The skin's health depends on good nutrition and exercise, which produce good circulation and deliver the necessary proteins, oils, vitamins, and other nutrients to grow a healthy, functioning skin and a shiny hair coat.

MAINTAINING A GLOSSY COAT

Skin oil or *sebum* is secreted by the sebaceous glands in the skin. Sebum is a source of moisture for the skin and hair follicles and keeps them smooth and pliable. When distributed over the hair shafts, it waterproofs the coat and makes it glossy. Stimulating the skin to produce sebum and distributing it over the hairs are important for a healthy and shiny coat. Exercise and skin movement stimulate the sebaceous glands, and sweat rinses the coat and helps distribute sebum over the hairs. Grooming also helps this process.

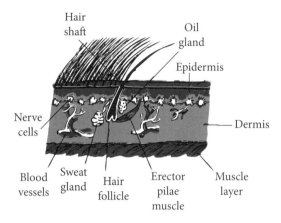

FIGURE 11. Skin structures—healthy skin.

KEEPING WARM

When a horse is cold, the skin helps him warm up by shivering and by increasing the loft of the coat. Each hair follicle is attached to a tiny muscle that can make the hair stand up straight. This traps air within the coat, insulating the horse and protecting him from loss of body heat. On a cold day, a horse's coat looks extra fluffy as the hairs stand out. Horses that are sick with chills and fever may have a "staring" coat because the hairs stand up in an effort to conserve body heat, making the coat appear dull and rumpled.

SWEATING—STAYING COOL

The sweating mechanism plays a vital role in regulating the horse's temperature. When the blood and inner body temperature rise, the part of the brain called the hypothalamus triggers sweating. The sweat glands release sweat, which wets the skin and hair. As the watery sweat evaporates, it cools the skin and the network of blood vessels within it, and the cooled blood is pumped back into the body, lowering the horse's temperature in much the same way that a car's radiator cools the engine. However, the horse's "radiator" is all over his body.

Sweat contains salt and other minerals, but it is mostly water. A fit, well-groomed horse sweats a thin, watery sweat that evaporates quickly, cooling him efficiently. An unfit horse's sweat is thicker, containing more salts and waste products; it mixes with skin oils, dandruff, and scurf to form a thick, scummy lather that evaporates slowly. This makes the skin less efficient at cooling the body, and the unfit horse gets hotter, is stressed more, and cools more slowly, with a greater risk of heat exhaustion. In cold weather, sweat may soak through the hair coat, removing its insulating qualities—the long wet coat dries slowly, and the horse is susceptible to chills.

Scurf is the greyish greasy substance that collects on brushes, tack, and your hands when grooming, a mixture of sebum, dandruff, dust, and dead skin cells. One important reason for grooming is to clear away the excess scurf from the coat so that the skin can function better to sweat, dry, and cool the horse.

The Hair

Each hair is made up of an outer shaft (cuticle) and an inner core (cortex). A healthy, shiny hair coat has many smooth, uniform, straight hairs that taper toward their tips. These hairs lie flat except in cold weather. Thin, broken, and irregular hairs, fewer in number, with many uneven, bent hairs and a rough surface on the hair shafts produce a dull, uneven, and unhealthy coat. Crusty, scaling skin, excessive dandruff, poor circulation and inactive sweat glands and sebaceous glands all result in poor skin and coat condition. Itching, rubbing, sunburn, and harsh chemicals can also damage the skin and hair coat.

Cleaning the Skin and Hair Coat

To condition the skin and hair coat, the skin must be cleared of dirt, dried sweat, waste products, and excessive scurf. This is best done by good daily

FIGURE 12. Smooth hair shaft, and rough, damamged shaft.

grooming, massaging the skin with a rubber curry comb, and brushing the skin and hair coat to remove debris and loose hair. The friction of grooming stimulates the production of skin oils and distributes them evenly over the surface of the hairs, producing a glossy coat. Grooming is most effective when done after exercise, when the skin is warm and the pores are open, but horses should be brushed clean before being ridden in order to prevent sores and galls.

Bathing, especially with detergents, removes some of the skin's natural oils and may temporarily decrease the shine of the coat. That is one reason why bathing is no substitute for good daily grooming. Excessive bathing can cause dry skin and a coat that is less shiny than a healthy natural hair coat. However, rinsing a horse off after exercise with clean water and a small amount of body wash doesn't hurt the hair coat and makes it easier to keep the skin clean and comfortable. Leaving the coat full of dried sweat will make a horse itch and rub himself, and may bleach the coat in strong sunlight. In the sections that follow, I give you some guidelines on how to keep the skin and hair coat healthy, clean, and in competition condition.

STAINS: PREVENTION AND TREATMENT

It's natural for horses to roll and get dirty, but long-term exposure to manure and urine can cause deep stains that penetrate the hair shafts and may be difficult to remove, especially on white or light colored coats and tails. Stains should be prevented as much as possible by keeping the stall clean, using enough bedding to keep the horse from lying in wet spots, and sometimes by protecting the hair coat and tail hair with sheets, blankets, or tail bags. It is much easier to keep white markings or a white coat clean if you remove any stains during daily grooming and protect the horse's favorite "dirty spots" by applying a coat conditioner that repels stains.

PROTECTING THE HAIR COAT

A show coat may be protected from sun, stains, and insect bites by using a scrim fly sheet during the day and a light sheet at night. This makes the hair lie flat, leaving the coat smooth and shiny. Coat dressings or conditioners, applied to clean hair, bond to the cuticle or outer surface of the hairs, keeping them smooth, slippery, and supple so that they are less likely to break off or absorb stains. Silicone or polymer dressings give the coat a high gloss and make hairs slippery, which enables detangling of the mane and tail and helps the hair coat resist stains for several days. However, some products are cosmetic, not therapeutic—they improve the appearance but not the quality of the hair, and overuse of certain detanglers or coat polishes can make hair brittle.

Topical products are those applied directly on the coat for therapeutic purposes. Some of these smooth and coat the hair shafts, bonding with the keratin of the cuticle and making the hair smoother and more flexible and restoring moisture. Some excellent ingredients are aloe vera, lanolin, and protein. If a horse's skin is dry, flaky, itchy or produces too much dandruff, bathing him with a medicated shampoo may help. If shampooing does not help the problem, the veterinarian should be consulted, as the trouble may be dermatitis, an allergy, a vitamin deficiency, or a symptom of a systemic problem.

Good nutrition is essential for growth and quality of the hair coat and mane and tail hair. A deficiency of vitamin A, or an excess of vitamin A, zinc, or sulfur in the diet may cause dull or dry, scaly skin. Unsaturated fats (corn oil, soybean oil, or canola oil), biotin, or lysine may improve coat quality and hair growth. Some feed supplements are especially formulated to develop a shiny coat—these usually contain oil or oil meal and a vitamin supplement.

WINTER COAT

Horses are actually subarctic animals, and, left to nature, most grow a full winter coat with a thick, dense undercoat and longer "guard hairs" to let water run off. Extra skin oils and scurf make the hair coat water-resistant, and the mane, tail, and long hair on lower legs, face, and ears protect against loss of body heat. When it's cold, tiny muscles in the skin cause the hairs to stand out, giving the coat extra loft and insulating the horse by trapping air close to the skin, like a down comforter. A long-coated horse may have ice on his whiskers and snow on his back, but his skin may still be warm and dry.

While a natural winter coat can keep a horse warm even in harsh climates, wind and wetness can defeat its insulating qualities. A cold wind can blow through the hair and chill the skin, and the coat cannot keep the horse warm if it is soaked through with rain or sweat.

FIGURE 13. Winter coat.

Horses shed their winter coats beginning in midwinter as the weather warms, and usually finish shedding out late in the spring. The winter coat begins growing in late summer and becomes longer and thicker during the fall. The rate of hair growth is influenced by temperature—a few nippy nights will cause the winter coat to grow in faster. In the spring, the shedding-out process is triggered by lengthening daylight as well as warmer temperatures. Older horses or those with Cushing's syndrome, sometimes shed their winter coat slowly or incompletely, or may retain a long coat all year.

Horses can be induced to shed out early by keeping lights on in their stalls through the winter to provide extra hours of "daylight." This also brings mares into their spring reproductive cycle earlier.

THE MANE AND TAIL

The mane, tail, and forelock protect the horse against flies and also keep him warm. The dock has approximately twenty vertebrae and many muscles to move the tail in any direction; it can lash like a whip! The mane and tail are used for expression, such as shaking the head and mane in a threatening gesture or switching the tail in irritation. The dock is an extension of the spine; its carriage indicates how well the horse is using his back, which is noted by dressage judges. The tail is also an indicator of the horse's mental state; an excited horse "flags" his tail, a fearful horse tucks his tail tightly into his hindquarters, and switching or wringing the tail indicates discomfort or irritation.

Mane and tail hair is not shed, but grows at a steady rate of eighteen to twenty-five millimeters (about two-thirds of an inch) per month. At that rate, it can take years to grow a shoulder-length mane or a tail that sweeps the ground.

The growth of mane and tail hair is stimulated mostly by good health and good nutrition, not by lotions or potions applied to the hair or skin. However, long mane and tail hairs are constantly broken off or pulled out by being caught on burrs, fences, splinters, stall fittings, or other projections, or by rubbing, careless combing, or being chewed on by other horses. Protecting long hair from such damage can result in a noticeably longer and fuller mane or tail, not because the hair grows faster, but because it is not being lost to everyday wear and tear. For detailed directions on mane and tail care and protection, I've dedicated an entire chapter to it—chapter 5, "Mane and Tail Care."

Chapter 3

Grooming and Daily Care

Benefits of Grooming

Good horse care and show conditioning include a thorough daily grooming. Any horse that is kept stabled and in work should be groomed every day, whether he is ridden or not. Grooming is important for health and comfort as well as appearance. It cleans and massages the skin, promoting good circulation and healthy skin and hair, and prevents sores and galls. Grooming also involves a daily hands-on examination of the whole horse so scrapes, bumps or swellings, a loose shoe, or other problems will be noticed before they become serious.

Outdoor horses need less grooming than stabled horses; they use rolling and dust baths to keep themselves comfortable. The extra scurf and skin oils in the coat of an outdoor horse should not be removed by excessive grooming or bathing, as they help him stay warm and dry in all weather. He also needs the protection of her natural hair, including the whiskers, mane and tail, fetlocks, and hair inside the ears. However, outdoor horses should be checked daily for condition, minor injuries, skin problems, and ticks, and should be brushed clean and have their feet picked out before they are ridden.

Grooming is a good way to establish trust and respect, and can be excellent training for obedience and stable manners. Horses use mutual grooming (scratching, nibbling, and brushing flies off each other) as a gesture of trust and friendship. When you groom your horse and make him feel good, he'll relax and enjoy it. However, don't let him return the favor by nibbling on you; he must treat people with more respect than one of his herd buddies or he could hurt someone.

Making Your Horse Feel Good

Grooming should be pleasant for the horse and should develop confidence, cooperation, and trust between you and your horse. Among horses, mutual grooming is a sign of trust and friendship as well as a way to make each other feel good. Studies have shown that horses' heart rates drop (a sign of relaxation) when they are groomed, massaged, or even stroked pleasantly, especially on the neck and withers.

The aim of grooming is not just to produce a shiny horse, but to warm and relax tight muscles and improve circulation through the whole body. Bracing, tensing, or becoming upset while being groomed causes a horse to develop a defensive, incorrect posture, with his head high, back tense and hollow, tail clamped, and a raised heart rate—the opposite of what you want to achieve under saddle. Sympathetic grooming can produce a horse that is more relaxed, more focused and ready and willing to work.

To groom a horse well, you must look, feel, and "tune in" to his body and behavior. Horses vary in their sensitivity to grooming, but all have tender or ticklish areas—usually the flanks, belly, face, or between the legs. Some horses dislike being groomed with certain tools or on certain parts of their bodies; their expressions of discomfort and protest range from pawing, making faces, or grinding teeth to snapping, kicking, or defensive behavior.

The underlying reason for all such behavior is discomfort and anticipation of pain. If grooming makes a horse feel good, he will enjoy it and cooperate instead of fighting. Many horses are so sensitive that ordinary grooming tools and techniques irritate them beyond their tolerance level. While you must protect yourself from getting hurt, threats and punishments only temporarily suppress the behavior and make the problem worse. Provoking a horse by grooming him painfully and then punishing him for saying "Ouch!" is abusive, and getting angry only makes it worse.

It's mostly a matter of adjusting your touch to the horse's sensitivity. While some horses like being curried hard, others need a softer touch and softer tools. Try using a rubber grooming mitt, a soft body brush, a sheepskin mitt, or a soft rag, or a hot, damp towel, which will feel good if he has sore muscles. Slow down your motions and use long, slow, gentle strokes until you find a level he can tolerate. Supersensitive horses usually have fine coats that don't need hard grooming to get them clean.

To desensitize a horse to normal grooming, start by brushing with only the amount of pressure he can accept in areas that he doesn't mind. Little by little, push the boundaries; if he flinches, temporarily retreat to a "safe" body area, then try again. Work slowly, stay relaxed, and use a soothing voice. Don't try to do everything in one session, and don't let it become a test of wills.

If you are smooth and gentle in your grooming and your grooming tools would feel comfortable to your own skin, the problem may be soreness or mental and physical tension. Painful conditions such as Lyme disease, gastric ulcers, or chronic tension and muscle soreness can make a horse as touchy as a person with a tension headache; in fact, cranky behavior and especially touchiness around the girth are common symptoms. Hot towels, massage therapy, or bodywork can help relieve muscle tension and soreness, which is as important for the horse's ability to perform as for her grooming behavior. Such horses should be checked by a veterinarian, and may benefit from massage therapy.

High-strung horses that are "wound up tight" sometimes fire off excess energy by fidgeting, pawing, or kicking at nothing. Sometimes it works best to place them in a situation where they cannot hurt themselves or you, and groom as quietly and efficiently as possible, ignoring occasional fussing. You must be calm and nonconfrontational, but alert and careful to protect yourself from accidental injury. Such horses should not be picked at or fussed over—if possible, they should be groomed after they have been turned out or worked and then left alone to relax.

Grooming Safety

You should groom in a safe, convenient area, with your horse safely restrained. A horse may be tied in a stable yard or in his stall, cross-tied or even ground-tied in the aisle while you work. The ideal workspace is a grooming stall with cross-ties, good lighting, safe footing, hot and cold water, and shelves or cupboards for grooming tools and supplies. Trying to groom a horse that's loose in a stall is foolish and unsafe; if he should nip, kick, or move around, you are helpless to control him.

When grooming someone else's horse or one you do not know, always ask if the horse is safe to tie or cross-tie. Some horses pull back and panic if they are tied or cross-tied.

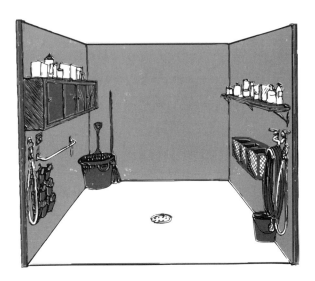

FIGURE 14. Grooming stall and wash rack.

SAFELY TYING HORSES

Basic Tying

A horse should be tied with a halter and tie rope, using a quick-release knot. Tie only to a solid object that a horse cannot move or break off (never to a fence board or a door), and be sure there is nothing nearby that he could injure himself on or catch a foot in. He should be tied at wither height or slightly higher; if tied too low, he could injure his neck if he pulls back. The tie rope should allow him to turn his head but not quite reach the ground with his nose; with too much slack, he could get a leg over the rope or catch the rope over her poll and scare or injure himself. Never tie a horse with the bridle reins or snap cross-ties to the bit; this could severely injure his mouth.

Cross-tying

Cross-ties restrain horses best for most grooming. The halter should have rings on each side of the noseband for cross-ties, and it is convenient if the throatlatch unsnaps for grooming of the head. When grooming an aggressive horse or one that does not pay attention to you, you can run a chain end lead shank over his nose. Never jerk on a chain shank—a light tug is sufficient to get a horse's attention and remind him of his manners.

FIGURE 15. How to put a chain over the nose.

Never tie a horse with a chain over her nose or under her chin—he could injure himself severely. This also applies to letting the end of a shank hang on the ground where he could step on it.

Cross-ties aren't without their own hazards. They prevent a horse from turning his head to see what's going on, which makes some horses anxious, and if a horse pulls back hard on cross-ties, he can lose his footing and hang from the cross-ties or even flip over backwards. It is risky to cross-tie a horse in a busy barn aisle, with people, wheelbarrows, and other horses passing by. Certain horses, especially those that pull back, should not be cross-tied or may only be cross-tied safely in a stall.

Here are some cross-tie safety precautions:

- Cross-ties should be placed at wither height, on nonslip footing.

- Cross-ties should be equipped with a safety *breakaway link,* in case a horse pulls back. (A breakaway link can be made by fastening the cross-tie to the wall ring with a piece of breakable baling twine.) A breakaway link may also be placed on the halter rings.

- If possible, a horse should be cross-tied with a solid wall behind him. If he pulls back, the wall will stop him before he gets into trouble. It is safer to cross-tie inside a box stall than in a stable aisle.

- If someone wants to pass by a cross-tied horse, unsnap the cross-ties and move the horse over. Don't duck underneath cross-ties, especially when leading another horse!

- Unsnap the cross-ties during bridling, clipping, or any procedure that might cause a horse to pull back.

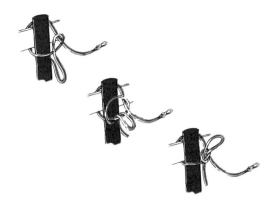

FIGURE 16. *How to tie a quick-release knot.*

- Be aware of anything going on nearby that could spook a cross-tied horse.

- Never leave a horse unattended on cross-ties.

Handling a Horse

Basic Precautions

Be aware of your body position whenever you work around a horse. Horses do not look where they put their feet, especially if they are distracted or dancing around, and they can step on you without knowing it. If a horse steps on your foot, push against him—this will get him off quicker and with less injury to you than if you try to pull your foot away.

Horses have three blind spots:

- Directly behind the tail

- Underneath the head

- Directly in front of their nose

When working around a horse, be careful not to duck into and out of a blind spot, which can startle him into spooking, kicking, or pulling back. When a horse is tied, don't duck under his neck to get to the other side; by doing so, you pass into the blind spot beneath his head. If anything makes him jump forward, you are in trouble!

Speaking to a horse before touching him, talking quietly to him, and keeping a hand on him as you work can help prevent unpleasant surprises, such as a reflexive kick.

Keep your head out of the danger zone around a horse's head—his skull can weigh as much as fifty pounds and can really hurt if she throws his head up and your face is in the way. Pay attention to the legs—horses instinctively kick or strike at flies under their belly or head, and they can hurt you by accident if you are in the way. Never sit down or kneel when working around a horse; bend your knees to get lower, but be ready to move in case he should move suddenly or kick.

When grooming the belly, flanks, or legs, keep your free hand on the horse's back; you will feel him tense up if he's about to move or kick. If you must pass behind a horse, stay close and keep a hand on his tail or rump; this lets him know where you are, and a warning word may discourage kicking. If a horse should kick and you are close to his legs, you will not get the full force of the blow as you might if you were several feet away. Of course, with a kicky horse it is safer to walk around the front or safely out of range.

When leading a horse, even for a short distance, *always* use a lead rope or shank—never lead with just a hand on the halter. If anything should make him act up or bolt, you may be dragged or have to let go, which can teach him a bad habit. Wear shoes or boots that offer some protection in case a horse steps on your foot, but not metal-toed work boots—these can bend under the weight of a horse and injure your toes more than the horse himself.

A neat barn is a safer place for horses and people. Pick up trash and put away tools; clear the aisle before you bring a horse through, and

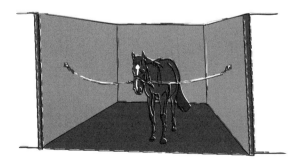

FIGURE 17. Safe cross-ties with breakaway links.

notice hazards such as a protruding nail or an open gate latch that could injure a horse or a person. Always open stall doors fully when leading a horse through so the door cannot catch on his hip. Keep lead ropes, reins, and lunge lines neatly coiled and off the ground, and be sure that a tied dog cannot wrap his rope around a passing horse's legs. Anything unfamiliar may spook a horse, especially if it moves or blows around, so pick up papers or any such other items.

Handling a Difficult Horse

If you must groom a horse that nips, fidgets, or pulls back when cross-tied, a handheld cross-tie can make the job safer and easier. This method also can be used to teach a horse to stand while cross-tied.

Run a lead shank over the horse's nose from the left side, as previously described. Attach a long line to the right halter ring, pass it through a tie ring or around a post, then run it back through the chin ring of the halter, holding the end in your hand along with the lead shank. You can use this to gently teach a horse to stand where he is asked without swinging around, or to keep his head turned slightly away from you if he is nippy. *Never* jerk on the shank or try to hold the horse forcibly in place; use it tactfully so that he is not held too tightly and scared. To handle the horse on the other side, reverse the shank and handheld cross-tie.

When grooming a horse that nips or bites, hold the cheek-piece of the halter, keeping your arm firm enough to prevent him from turning his head. If he nips at you when you are not holding the halter, let his cheek bump into your ready elbow while you keep a casual attitude and continue to groom. Slapping, jerking, or making a fuss can make a nipper

FIGURE 18. Handheld cross-tie.

into a sneaky biter who bites and then jerks away. Letting him punish himself while appearing to ignore her behavior works better.

Some horses act difficult because of previous bad handling, inherent temperament, or because they are supersensitive and associate grooming with discomfort. Some horses may be a handful when highly conditioned and "on the muscle." A horse afflicted with ulcers or Lyme disease may be especially touchy and cranky; in fact, unusual irritability, especially around the girth, is often a sign of those problems. A good horseman won't allow a horse to act dangerously or become spoiled, but will try to discover the reason behind the behavior, and stay aware, safe, and in control, but avoid picking a fight.

Grooming Your Horse

BASIC GROOMING PROCEDURE

You should groom systematically, starting at the same place with each tool and working over the body in the same order. Besides being more efficient, your horse will learn the routine, feel more secure, and cooperate. Currying, brushing, and rubbing are forms of massage and should be done vigorously for the best effect. If you get tired before finishing one operation, pick out the feet or do the mane or tail; this gives you a rest so you can go back to grooming with energy. Of course, you must moderate your grooming efforts according to the sensitivity of the horse. Pay attention to the kind of touch he likes best, go easy on his ticklish spots and never groom so hard that you make him upset or sore. Grooming should make a horse feel good!

To begin grooming a horse:

1. *Remove the blanket and stable bandages if these are used.* (Always unfasten the back surcingles or leg straps first and the chest fastenings last.) Blankets should be brushed clean, folded, and hung up; bandages may be rerolled for reuse or put aside to launder.

2. *The first tool to use is the currycomb, which breaks up caked dirt; loosens scurf, dead hair, and dandruff; and massages the skin and muscles.* Use a soft, flexible currycomb that can flex

with your hand (rubber works best for removing loose hairs, as it is slightly "tacky") so that you can bear down and massage the skin well. If a currycomb is too stiff, you cannot use it firmly enough to do any good, or it will drive your horse to rebellion at the intense discomfort. Scrub in a circular or side-to-side motion, using more pressure on heavily muscled areas and gently rubbing sensitive spots. Knock the scurf out of the currycomb from time to time. A currycomb is primarily a massage tool for use on the neck and body; never run it harshly over bony or sensitive places.

If a horse has a long winter coat, a metal currycomb or a fine-toothed scotch comb (curling comb) may be used gently to break up heavily caked mud on the less sensitive parts of the body, and to help shed out thick winter hair. Metal teeth can scratch the skin, so use it carefully, and never on fine-coated or sensitive horses.

Some horses are too sensitive to tolerate a currycomb or stiff dandy brush. For these horses, start with a soft long-bristled whisk brush to sweep the coat clean, then follow up with a soft body brush. Such horses usually have fine coats that can be cleaned and brought to a shine with only a towel and the softest of brushes.

3. *Next, use the dandy or stiff brush to sweep the skin free of larger particles of dirt and loose hair.* With the brush at arm's length, use short, firm strokes to get between the hairs and down to the skin. Don't "pet" the coat with a dandy brush; use short, firm, flicking strokes to penetrate the hair and lift the dirt out; you should see a little cloud of dust fly out at every stroke. Brush in the direction of the hair growth all over the body, including the legs, head, and belly, and not neglecting the elbows, pasterns, and the roots of the mane. Since the bristles are coarse and stiff, be careful when brushing sensitive areas like the face and legs. Clean the brush frequently by brushing the bristles against a currycomb or stall screen.

4. ***Use the body brush to rub the horse firmly in the direction of hair growth, all over the head, neck, body, and legs.*** When you have finished with the dandy brush, the skin should be clean, but the hair will still be full of dust and the whitish, greasy debris called *scurf*. The body brush is used to clean dust, dandruff, and scurf from the skin and hair, and its rubbing action stimulates the skin and distributes skin oils over the coat, making it shine. When you apply enough pressure at each stroke, the short, close-set bristles penetrate the coat, and the dust and scurf cling to the bristles of the brush instead of the hair. The heat and friction generated by vigorous body brushing distributes the skin oils over the hair and brings up the shine of the coat. As a body brush picks up dust and scurf, it becomes dirty and less effective, so it should be cleaned every few strokes by scraping the bristles across the teeth of a metal currycomb. This way, the dirt goes into the brush and then out into the air, not back onto the horse. (This is the *only* correct use of a metal currycomb on fine-skinned horses!) A body brush is a good tool for removing dust from hard-to-clean areas like the head, the top of the croup, and the roots of the mane.

5. ***Finally, to remove the last of the dust and polish the coat, rub the horse all over with a soft rag, a piece of silk wrapped around a body brush, or with your bare hand.*** Fold the rag and rub it firmly in the direction of the hair to straighten the coat. The longer and harder you rub, the more you stimulate the production of skin oils and bring up the shine of the coat. Rubbing the coat for up to thirty minutes a day helps achieve the "bloom" so desirable on a show horse.

6. ***Using a large sponge or a damp towel, go over the face, ears, and lower legs, including the skin at the back of the pasterns.*** Gently clean the lips, nostrils, and corners of the eyes (disposable baby wipes are more sanitary than sponges), using a separate sponge or baby wipe to clean the underside of the dock, beneath the tail, and the sheath or udder. If you see a dry yellow or gray discharge from the anus, this is a sign of pinworms, which can cause tail rubbing; the horse should be dewormed.

A. Using a curry brush

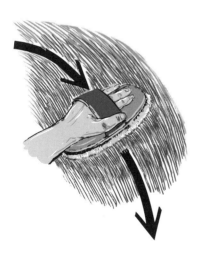

B. Using a dandy brush

C. Flicking upward

D. Cleaning brush with curry comb

E. Using a body brush

FIGURE 19. Grooming technique.

7. **Pick out each foot, brushing the sole clean, and check the feet, shoes, and nails before and after work.** For more details, see "Care of the Feet," pages 55–59.

8. ***The mane and tail should be carefully picked or brushed out.***
For details, please see "Mane and Tail Care" in chapter 5. Work
from the bottom of the tail upward toward the roots, carefully separating a few hairs at a time and taking care not to
pull out hairs. In some areas, you must check for ticks, which
crawl up the long tail hairs and fasten themselves to the end
of the dock. As a final touch, "lay" the mane over to the
proper side by brushing it with a wet brush. The top hairs of
the tail may be treated similarly, and for formal occasions,
sport horses may have a tail bandage applied to the dock for
an hour or two to shape the tail hair and leave it looking neat
and trim.

Stain Removal

If your horse is light colored or has white markings, he may have
manure, mud, or grass stains that do not come out with normal
grooming. Most stains will come out with vigorous rubbing with a
damp towel or cactus cloth. Dampen a towel slightly with hot, soapy
water and rub the stain until the part of the towel around your hand
becomes darkened; then shift to a clean portion of the towel. Large or
stubborn stains may be spot-cleaned with stain remover, waterless
cleaner, or whitening shampoo, or make a paste with Bon Ami cleanser
and water and rub it into the stained area. After it dries, brush the
powder out of the coat, and the stain will come out with it. Once the
hair is clean, a little silicone coat dressing sprayed on that spot will
help repel future stains.

Minor Injuries

If you discover any scrapes, wounds, or irritations as you groom, they
should be taken care of. An open cut or scrape should be cleaned with
plain water and may be treated with a dab of nitrafurazone salve, or it
may be left clean but unmedicated. Never apply petroleum jelly or harsh
antiseptics on an open cut—this can contaminate and irritate the
wound and retard healing, and may result in *proud flesh* (excess granu-
lation tissue).

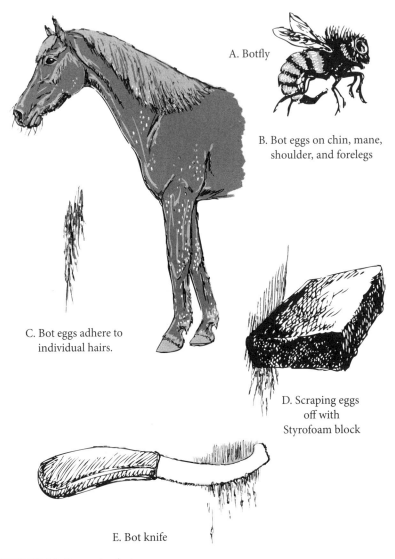

A. Botfly

B. Bot eggs on chin, mane,
shoulder, and forelegs

C. Bot eggs adhere to
individual hairs.

D. Scraping eggs
off with
Styrofoam block

E. Bot knife

FIGURE 20. *Removing bot eggs.*

BOT EGGS

Any bot eggs that you notice should be removed, as each one is a parasite waiting to invade your horse. The bot fly, which looks like a large bee but does not sting, lays small yellow eggs on the hair of the legs and forequarters. When the horse rubs his face on these areas, larvae find their way into his mouth and eventually his stomach, where they mature into "bots," internal parasites that live on the lining of the stomach. Bot eggs may be scraped off the hair with a styrofoam block, a "bot knife" or a piece of fine sandpaper. You can scrape the parasites off easier if you lubricate the hair with a dab of shampoo or baby oil first.

In fly season, horses should be protected with fly spray. Some horses may have skin reactions to certain brands of fly repellent, so when trying a new product, test it on a small patch of hair before applying it all over. Avon Skin-So-Soft bath oil will keep flies off the ears, face, and muzzle and is gentle to the skin.

Care of the Feet

CLEANING THE FEET

A horse's feet should be picked out before and after work and checked daily, even if he is not ridden.

When cleaning a foot, use the hoof pick from back to front in order to avoid accidentally digging it into the frog. Pick quickly so that the horse doesn't have to hold his foot up too long. If you dig the point of the pick under a packed-in mass of dirt and lever it out, this cleans the foot more efficiently than scraping away a little at a time. Be sure to clean all the way to the bottom of the commissures (the depressions on each side of the frog) and pick out the cleft (the crease in the center of the frog) carefully but thoroughly. Use a stiff brush to brush the ground surface of the foot clean, so you can inspect it.

Check the shoes, nails, and clinches, especially before work and after turnout. A loose nail or a sprung shoe can lead to loss of a shoe or cause a stumble or injury. Risen clinches that stick up from the outer surface of the hoof wall show that a shoe is becoming loose. If the feet become excessively dry and brittle or too soft and chalky, they may crack, and the horse may lose shoes easily.

PICKING UP FEET SAFELY

To get a horse to lift a front foot, you need to stand facing backward and press against his shoulder until he shifts her weight to the opposite leg. Slide your hand down to the flexor tendons below the knee and squeeze briefly, giving a voice command to pick up the foot. If he ignores your request, you can tap on the coronary band or gently squeeze the skin around the chestnut, which will usually make him lift her leg. As the leg

FIGURE 21. Picking up a front leg.

comes up, cradle the hoof with the hand closest to the horse. Hold the hoof, not the pastern—it is more secure.

To lift a hind leg, stand next to the hindquarters facing backward and press against the hip, asking him to shift his weight over. Slide your hand down the outside of the leg to the flexor tendons below the hock, and squeeze briefly, pulling forward against the tendon. Keep your hand on the outside of the hind leg so you can deflect a kick if a horse should try one. Do not run your arm around the inside of the hind leg—if he should snatch up his leg suddenly, he could trap your arm as he flexes his hock. As the leg comes up, your other hand can take the cannon bone and bring the leg backward, a bit behind the horse's hindquarter. Bend your knees and assume a half-squatting position, with your thigh behind and supporting the hind leg. If a horse should try to take his leg away, he cannot kick you but can only stretch it out behind him. Never pull the leg too high or out to the side—this causes pain in the hip and can make a horse kick or struggle.

Insist on good manners when you are working with your horse's feet. Give him time to balance on three legs, but don't allow him to lean on you. If he leans or tries to take his foot away, use a toe hold: place the palm of your hand over the sole of his foot, with your spread fingers holding the toe. In this position, a resisting horse will simply flex his own ankle more, and you can move with him if necessary; if you must let go, you can easily get out of the way. Never snatch up a foot without warning,

FIGURE 22. *Picking up a hind leg.*

pull it uncomfortably high or out to the side, or drop it suddenly. If a horse puts her foot down before you are finished, make him pick it right up again. If you are patient and consistent, horses will learn to pick up their feet easily and stand politely without leaning. Be clear, calm, and patient, and reward with praise and a pat when she cooperates.

THRUSH

Thrush is a fungus infection that attacks the soft parts of the foot, especially the cleft of the frog and commissures. The characteristic signs of thrush are a watery discharge and a particularly foul odor. The surfaces within the pockets of thrush become raw and tender and filled with blackish debris containing dead cells and contaminants such as manure and bedding. Thrush needs a moist, dirty, and airless environment; it is often found in horses kept in wet, dirty conditions, but can occur in any horse, especially if the frog is deep or ragged.

To treat thrush, wrap the end of a hoof pick in a clean gauze pad and gently wipe out the area, discarding each used piece of gauze and replacing it until the discharge and debris are cleaned away. The veterinarian or farrier may have to pare away the diseased parts of the frog and open the area to light and air, and the foot may have to be soaked or treated with antibiotics.

HOOF DRESSINGS

Hoof dressings are used to improve the texture and condition of the feet and for their cosmetic effect. Lanolin, animal fats, and pine tar are common ingredients in hoof dressings.

Horses' feet reflect the conditions they live in, becoming hard and dry in dry conditions and softening when exposed to moisture. The foot is moisturized primarily by its internal blood supply, which is stimulated by exercise and inhibited when the horse stands without working for long periods. The hoof wall is made up of tiny hollow tubules, which run from the coronary band to the ground surface and can absorb moisture from the ground; the coronary band can also absorb moisture. The periople, a shiny, varnish-like outer layer, prevents moisture from escaping from the hoof wall.

The best place to apply hoof dressing is around the coronary band and across the heels, wiping off any excess. When applied to the hoof wall, hoof dressing does not do much to moisturize the foot but is mainly cosmetic. Thick, sticky dressings tend to build up on the hoof wall and pick up dirt.

The outer wall of the foot should be clean for show purposes, especially on horses with light-colored feet. In some breeds it is a common practice to sand the outer wall of the hoof with sandpaper, steel wool, or an electric sander until it appears smooth and clean. This removes the natural protective covering of the hoof (the periople), which can lead to drying and cracking, If you insist on sanding down the feet, you must apply a special hoof sealant afterward for protection. A less extreme method is scrubbing the hoof wall clean with a nail brush or a vegetable brush.

PACKING OR STOPPING THE FEET

When the feet are clean, they may be packed or stopped with a prepared clay such as White Rock. This exposes the sole of the foot to moisture for twenty-four hours and can soften feet that are excessively hard and dry, so they are less apt to sting on impact with hard ground. Hoof packing should not be overdone—packing too often or packing feet that do not need it can leave the hoof too soft and even make it difficult to keep shoes on. Packing the feet may help when a horse suffers a stone bruise; the moist clay acts like a poultice and draws out the soreness.

To pack the feet, the mud must first be prepared—it must soak overnight. It should be the consistency of stiff clay, not runny or jelly-like Using a wooden spoon or a spatula, place a large ball of clay in the sole of the newly cleaned foot. Use the spatula to press the clay down into the commissures and fill the bottom of the foot so that the packing mounds up slightly above the level of the shoe. Place a piece of paper over the packing and let the horse set his foot down. His weight will compress the packing into the foot, and the paper will fall off as the surface dries. When you pick out his feet the next day, the mud should come out in a single mass molded to the shape of the foot, and the foot will be damp, cool, and flexible.

Chapter 4

Grooming Tools and Supplies

The saying, "A workman is only as good as his tools" is never more true than in show grooming. While it is possible to do an adequate job with only fair equipment, it is easier and more efficient to have the right tools for the job and to keep them in good working order.

Basic grooming tools include anything from currycombs, stiff brushes or dandy brushes, to soft brushes or body brushes, scrapers, sponges, hoof picks, combs, and rub rags. You can even use a variety of other specialty items that make specific chores easier.

You will need a grooming kit to keep your tools together. To prevent the spread of skin infections and contagious diseases, it's best for each horse to have his own set of grooming tools and not to use the same brushes on other horses. You can paint each horse's tools in a distinctive color so it's obvious whose tools they are. Grooming tools should be cleaned and disinfected periodically. In this chapter, I cover the tools you need as well as how to use them and keep them in good, clean, working condition.

Grooming Tools

CURRYCOMBS

Currycombs come in several shapes and types. Rubber currycombs are usually soft and their slightly tacky surface makes them good for removing loose hair. A grooming mitt, shaped like a rubber mitten covered with

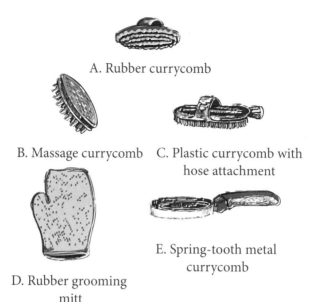

A. Rubber currycomb

B. Massage currycomb   C. Plastic currycomb with hose attachment

D. Rubber grooming mitt

E. Spring-tooth metal currycomb

FIGURE 23. Currycombs.

small raised dots, works well on clipped horses or those with sensitive skin. A massage curry with flexible rubber "fingers" massages the skin and underlying muscle and does a good job shedding out winter hair as well. Plastic currycombs are stiffer; many horses find them uncomfortable if they are used for massage, but they do shed out long hair well. They should not be used to brush tails, as they break off and pull out tail hair. Metal currycombs are too sharp to be used on the horse's skin; they should be used to clean the body brush while working, or they may be used with care to break up heavily caked mud and to shed out horses with thick coats.

BRUSHES

When buying brushes, especially body brushes, it is often more economical to buy good quality tools and then take good care of them than to make do with cheap brushes that do not work as well or last as long. This doesn't apply to all tools, of course—a fifty-cent hoof pick will do just as good a job as a ten-dollar one!

Types of Brush Materials

Brushes come in a variety of types, shapes, bristle materials, and models for different purposes. Bristles may be natural fibers (animal hair or plant fibers) or synthetic. Synthetic brushes are less expensive, hold up under hard use and are easier to disinfect, but brushes made from natural fibers do a better job of buffing and shining a fine coat.

Types of bristle fibers include:

Synthetic—polystyrene or polypropylene (coarse to medium) or nylon (soft) bristles. Waterproof, easy to disinfect, tough, and long lasting.

Horsehair—soft to slightly stiff texture; springy and durable, but not resistant to acids or alkalis. Mane hair is softer than tail hair. The best body brushes are usually made from horsehair.

Goat hair—very fine hair bristles, less elastic than horsehair, used for short hair body brushes.

Bassine fiber (Palmyra)—brown plant fiber; stiff and coarse, used for dandy, mud, and scrub brushes.

Tampico—softer, off-white plant fibers; absorbs water, and works wet or dry. Stiffer than horsehair; used for medium to soft dandy and body brushes.

Union fiber—mixture of tampico and palmyra fibers; medium stiff texture, used for dandy brushes.

Rice root—crinkly yellow fibers, used for water brushes.

Brass bristles—sometimes used in combination with synthetic fibers in special body brushes, for removing mud from dense coats.

Some brushes are wire drawn—the bristles are drawn through one half of the back and fastened with wire, and the top half is then attached. On a wire-drawn brush you will see four screws holding the two halves of the brush together; leather-backed brushes are glued or stitched together. Cheaper brushes are machine drilled—the bristles are stuck into the holes by machine and held in place by glue.

Types of brushes

Body brushes are the most important tool in grooming the coat and producing a deep bloom, so a quality body brush is worth the fairly high initial cost. A good body brush with short, close-set horsehair bristles will remove dust and scurf, bring up the shine of the coat, and can get a horse really clean. You may want a soft horsehair body brush for fine-coated horses, and a body brush with stiffer bristles for working on thicker coats. A good body brush will last for years if it is not abused.

Dandy brushes have longer bristles for various purposes. A dandy brush will not remove dirt particles much smaller than the size of the bristle. Brushes with stiff, heavy fibers are used to break up mud and brush thick winter hair; medium fibers are used for initial cleaning of the body, head, and legs. Some dandy brushes have mixed fibers; these make a good general-purpose brush.

Sweep brushes are made with longer, resilient bristles to sweep the coat clean.

Finishing brushes have long, soft bristles. They're used to remove dust from the head, legs, and surface of the coat, but will not penetrate the hair or spread the skin oil to produce a shine as well as a body brush. A *face brush* is a small, soft finishing brush for the head and ears.

Water brushes are used for bathing, scrubbing out stains, to lay the mane and tail down, and for making quarter marks. An open-backed brush allows the water to drain through; rice-root or crimped synthetic bristles retain water better. The *English water brush* has close-set natural bristles like a body brush and is tapered to a point at each end. A *sponge brush*, which has a sponge in the center surrounded by a rim of synthetic bristles, does a good job of removing sweat marks and stains or applying quarter marks. Inexpensive plastic scrub brushes or vegetable brushes are useful for washing feet.

Hoof picks come in plastic or metal, in all colors. One model has a small brush attached, which can be used to brush the sole of the foot clean. Some grooms like to snap a hoof pick to their belt to keep it handy.

Cactus cloths are loosely woven grooming cloths made from the fibers of the maguey plant; they contain a little natural oil, which helps to shine

A. Dandy (stiff) brush

E. Sweep brush

B. Bassine fiber mud brush

F. Shaped dandy brush

C. Tampico fiber finishing brush

G. Water brush with crimped bristles

D. Union fiber (mixed) brush

FIGURE 24. Brushes.

the coat. The rough surface makes it easy to scrub away sweat marks and dried mud; it can also be rubbed briskly over a stain to remove it.

Rub rags dry wet coats and are used for stain removal and for cleaning with waterless cleaner or the hot towel method. Towels work well as rub rags. Get them in a light color so you will notice when they are dirty so you can launder them.

A. Leather backed body brush

B. Stiff body brush
with brass bristles

C. Soft body brush

D. Soft face brush

E. English water brush

FIGURE 25. *Body brushes and water brushes.*

Moisture magnets, a soft cloth like an artificial chamois, are useful items. They can be used to dry the face, head, and belly or for getting stains out of the coat.

Body sponges are needed for washing your horse—you'll need a large one for the horse and a couple of smaller sponges to clean his face and dock. Most grooms use synthetic sponges, which are much less expensive than natural sea sponges. Sponges should be stored in an open-mesh bag or basket so they can dry.

Wash mitts or scrubbing mitts are useful for bathing, as is a plastic currycomb with a hose attachment, which allows you to massage the horse's skin as you rinse him.

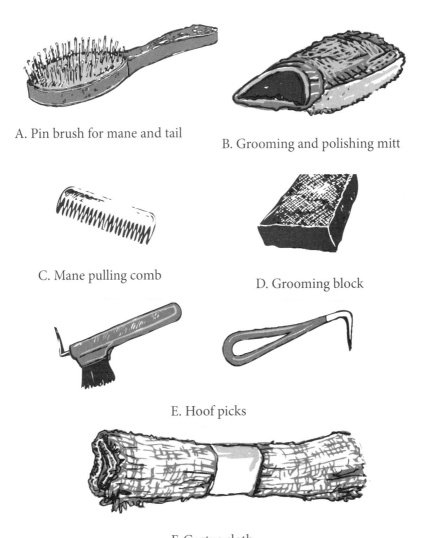

A. Pin brush for mane and tail

B. Grooming and polishing mitt

C. Mane pulling comb

D. Grooming block

E. Hoof picks

F. Cactus cloth

FIGURE 26. *Grooming tools: assorted grooming aids.*

Sweat scrapers are needed for washing and cooling out; either a simple "sweat stick" or the squeegee type with a strip of rubber to squeeze water out of the hair.

Shedding blades are used to shed out long winter hair. A shedding blade has a flexible blade with a serrated edge for shedding and the smooth edge can be used as a sweat scraper.

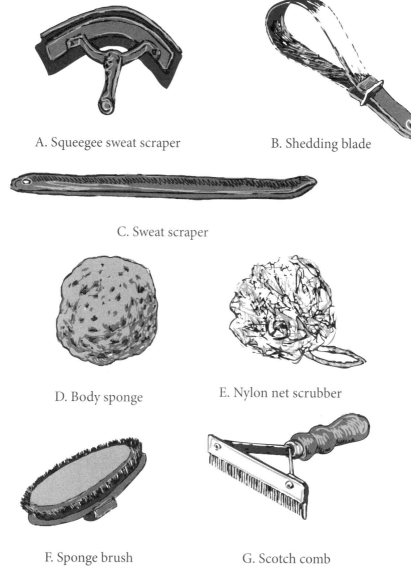

A. Squeegee sweat scraper

B. Shedding blade

C. Sweat scraper

D. Body sponge

E. Nylon net scrubber

F. Sponge brush

G. Scotch comb

FIGURE 27. Bath and shedding tools.

Scotch combs (fine-toothed) or curling combs (used on show cattle) can be used to break up and remove caked mud, and to remove loose or shedding hair.

Styrofoam grooming blocks (small ones) can be used to remove bot eggs, stains, caked-on dirt, and loose hair. The edge of the block works well when shedding out hard-to-reach places around the head.

Synthetic fleece applicator mitts are useful for applying fly repellent, particularly to the head, where most horses will not tolerate fly spray. You can also use a fleece mitt for rubbing the coat. For real luxury, use a sheepskin mitt; the lanolin in the natural fleece helps to shine the coat, and sensitive horses enjoy the softness of the fleece.

Hard wisping (also called banging or strapping) is a traditional English form of massage, using a massage pad, a folded towel, or a *wisp* made of plaited hay. This should be done only on heavily muscled areas of the body, and not on horses that are disturbed by it. The massage pad or wisp is brought down on the muscle with a firm, sliding blow; it causes the muscles to contract and relax in a rhythmic cycle, like doing isometric exercises. The groom starts with ten "bangs" on each muscled area and works up to thirty or more repetitions.

Tools for the Mane and Tail

For the mane and tail, you may want a *tail brush* or a *mane comb*. A plastic human hairbrush works well on manes and tails and pulls out less hair than a metal comb or currycomb. Another good brush is a *pet slicker brush*, which has a rubber backing with metal pins set into it. Metal mane and tail combs are not recommended for grooming mane and tail hair, as they break off and pull out too many hairs and can leave the mane and tail short and bushy. If you must use a comb, it should be plastic and the teeth should be very smooth. Small metal *pulling combs* are used to pull, thin, and shorten the mane. A patented *mane trimming comb* may be used to thin and shorten the mane without pulling.

CARING FOR YOUR GROOMING TOOLS

Whatever grooming tools you have deserve proper use and good care. A dirty brush will not make a horse clean; it will waste your time. Clean your brushes frequently as you work by scraping the bristles against the teeth of a currycomb or across a stall screen; this way, the dust goes into the brush and out into the air, not back onto the horse. Tools should be put away cleaned of hair and dirt. Try not to get good brushes wet—save a water brush or scrub brush for removing stains and washing feet. Never rub wet, dirty surfaces with an expensive body brush—it should be saved for rubbing and polishing the coat.

Currycombs, plastic brushes, and other waterproof items can be washed with pine oil soap, a diluted solution of bleach, or a similar disinfectant. Leather-backed body brushes or those with natural bristles should not be immersed in water but can be cleaned by working through the bristles with a damp soapy towel. When a brush is wet, stand it on the bristles to dry so that water will not run down into the back and damage the bristles. Towels and rub rags should be laundered frequently, and sponges should be rinsed out and wrung out clean before putting them away.

VACUUM CLEANERS

A vacuum cleaner can be a great help in getting horses clean, especially when horses are turned out and get muddy but need to be gotten "show ring clean" afterward. A full-power livestock vacuum cleaner does the best job, particularly for a large stable, but a smaller canister model or a shop vacuum will also do the job. Most horse vacuums also have a blow-dryer function, which can be used to dry a wet coat with warm air.

A vacuum cleaner removes loose dirt, dust, and hair from the coat and saves time and work in getting a dirt-caked horse clean. However, it doesn't rub or distribute skin oils over the coat as currying and brushing do, so it is no substitute for regular grooming. It is best to vacuum away loose dirt and then finish grooming by hand. For grooms who are allergic to horse dander, a vacuum cleaner with a filter can cut down on the amount of dust, hair, and scurf one is exposed to.

It works best to curry the horse first, or you can use the currycomb attachment to break up and vacuum away caked-on mud and dirt. Press the tool well down into the skin and work it back and forth across the hair, so the suction gets all the loose dirt. You can use a vacuum on the neck and body, and carefully on the larger muscles of the legs, but do not use it on the head, mane, tail, or ticklish areas. After vacuuming, the coat should be brushed out.

Most horses get used to a vacuum cleaner quite easily, as most find the suction feels pleasant even if they dislike the noise. Have someone hold the horse when you introduce him to the vacuum cleaner, and start on a less sensitive area of the body. Let him investigate the machine and rub him with the hose and the brush attachment before turning the motor on, and try feeding him a few treats during his first experience with the vacuum.

Vacuum cleaners, blowdryers, and grooming machines should always be used on a dry surface and should have a grounded plug. Don't leave them plugged in within reach of a horse; an experimental nibble on the cord can give him a jolt of electricity.

GROOMING PRODUCTS

While there are so many grooming products that they could fill a catalog and more are being developed all the time, there are some standard products that are used in most show stables. It's a good idea to try out different brands and new products to decide which works best for your purposes. Some commonly used grooming products include:

SHAMPOOS

Used for bathing, washing manes and tails, and removing stains, dirt, scurf and other contaminants from the coat, shampoo, when lathered with water, is a surfactant (oil remover), which can remove natural skin oils (sebum). You can use human hair care products on horses, but because the pH (acidity) of equine skin is different than human skin, too frequent use of human hair care products may dry the skin and hair.

Shampoos may be soap-based or detergent-based. Detergent-based shampoos tend to remove more of the natural skin oils and may cause a dry coat. Soap-based shampoos are gentler to the coat but do not always work as well in hard water. Shampoos and cleaners using enzymes that dissolve dirt may be less likely to dry the skin and hair coat. There are various types of shampoos, including:

- *Color-enhancing or whitening shampoos:* Some shampoos contain a whitening agent to remove stains and prevent white hair from yellowing, or a mild colorant which enhances chestnut, brown, or black coats.

- *Orvus shampoo:* Orvus is a commercial name for sodium lauryl sulfate, a concentrated shampoo and detergent in paste form, effective for removing stains.

- *Medicated shampoos:* Iodine-based anti-bacterial and anti-fungal shampoos are used to treat dermatitis and fungus infections of the skin.

WATERLESS CLEANERS

Waterless cleaners clean and condition the coat without bathing or rinsing. They are applied by spraying on a towel, which is rubbed through the coat to remove dirt and sweat. Most waterless cleaners contain citrus oil, which is effective at removing dirt, scurf, and stains.

STAIN REMOVERS

Used to remove stains while grooming or as a last-minute touch-up at shows, many brands and products are available; some are especially formulated to remove grass and manure stains:

- *Home-made stain remover:* Combine ten ounces of rubbing alcohol, ten ounces of water, and a capful of purple shampoo in a spray bottle. Spray on the stain and rub out with a towel.

- *Bon Ami cleanser:* To remove stains, make a paste of Bon Ami cleanser and water and rub into the stain; when it is dry, brush the powder out of the hair. Bon Ami does not burn the skin; do not substitute other cleansers, which may contain bleach.

- *Wisk laundry detergent:* Good for stain removal and to get white markings sparkling white. Should not be used on the whole horse as it is too drying.

- *Ivory or other mild soaps:* For spot-washing, cleaning the sheath, and other chores.

CONDITIONERS AND OTHER HAIR PRODUCTS

- *Mane and tail conditioners, creme rinses, and moisturizers:* Applied after shampooing to condition and moisturize the hair. Most contain humectants (water-attracting substances), which help to keep the hair moisturized and supple.

- *Detanglers:* Conditioners that leave hair smooth, slippery, and straight, releasing and preventing tangles. Using a conditioner or detangler after shampooing makes long hair easier to comb out without damage to the hair. However, overuse may make the hair brittle.

- *Coat polishes:* High-gloss coat sprays used to enhance shine and texture of the hair coat, mane, and tail. Those that do not contain silicone leave the hair shiny but softer and less slippery than silicone-containing products.

- *Silicone coat polish and detangler:* Used to produce a high gloss on the coat, detangle manes and tails, repel dirt, and protect against stains. Silicone bonds to the hair shafts, leaving them slick and shiny, and protecting against stains for several days. However, it makes the hair coat so slippery that tack may slip, and too frequent use may make the hair brittle.

- *Hot oil treatments:* Used to condition the coat after clipping and to condition dry, brittle manes and tails.

- *Setting gel:* Used to lay down mane hairs or to make quarter marks.

- *Braiding spray:* Used to make clean mane and tail hair slightly tacky, so it is easier to braid and braids stay in better.

COSMETIC PRODUCTS

- *Highlighters:* Gels applied to the skin of the face to enhance highlights and draw attention to the eyes, ears, and contours of the face.

- *Whiteners, cover-ups, or French chalk:* White or colored creams, chalks, or sprays used to enhance white markings or cover scars. Baby powder and cornstarch are also used to whiten white markings.

- *Glitter or high shine products:* Creams, gels, and sprays intended to enhance shine of the coat, especially under lights.

- *Neck sweats:* Used under a sweat wrap to temporarily reduce a heavy neck.

Hoof Products

- *Hoof dressings:* Used to condition the feet, especially on the coronary band and heels. Dark oil hoof dressing is used to darken and shine the hooves of some types of show horses.

- *Hoof packing:* Prepared clays (White Rock, Denver mud) packed into the sole to moisturize and condition the feet.

- *Hoof polish:* Used to enhance the shine of the hoof for showing; comes in clear, black, or brown. Use *hoof polish remover* to take it off after showing.

Other Products

- *Body wash:* A mild astringent and cleanser added to rinse water when washing horses down after exercise; helps remove salt and sweat and keep the skin from itching. Some liniments can be diluted to use as a body wash.

- *Sheath cleaners:* Cleaners designed to dissolve smegma without irritating the tissues of the sheath. Mild soap such as Ivory soap may also be used.

- *Liniments or rubbing alcohol:* Used for rubbing, bracing, and wrapping legs. Alcohol can also serve as a quick stain remover.

- *Poultices:* Prepared medicated clays or under bandages to draw heat and soreness out of the legs.

- *Fly repellents:* In spray or wipe-on form, may contain natural pyrethrins or synthetic repellents. May be oil-based or water-based; some contain sunscreen. Some horses may have a skin reaction to certain ingredients, so test on a small area before use. Roll-on repellents, gels, and creams are available to keep flies off the face.

- *Homemade fly repellent:* Combine three ounces of Skin-So-Soft, one ounce of oil of citronella, twelve ounces of white vinegar, and twelve ounces of water in a spray bottle.

- *Sunscreens:* Used to prevent sunburn on light-colored horses, especially on face. Some human sunscreen products can create problems for horses if they contain para-aminobenzoic acid (PABA), which in horses can cause a skin reaction to UV light rays.

Chapter 5

Mane and Tail Care

The mane and tail are two of the horse's chief beauties, and they also serve a practical purpose. The tail is an effective fly swatter (tail hairs can sting like a whip if they're lashed across your face!), and the mane and forelock shade the eyes and keep flies off. In cold climates, the mane prevents loss of body heat from the neck, and the tail protects the thin-skinned groin area as the horse habitually turns his rump to the wind and snow. Horses use their tails for expression and communication—a frightened horse tucks its tail tightly against its rump; an irritated horse angrily switches its tail, preparing to kick, and an animated, excited horse "flags" the tail, carrying it in a high arch. The dock is an extension of the spine; a rhythmically swinging tail denotes a relaxed, efficiently working back, while a crooked, stiff or wringing tail points to mental or physical distress.

Basic mane and tail care includes detangling, keeping the skin clean and healthy, occasional shampooing, and protection against hair loss and damage. Manes may be kept long, pulled, or shortened, depending on the type of horse, but most horses are shown with the tail as long and full as it will grow. The only way to induce hair to grow is good nutrition; hair growth is stimulated from within, not by lotions or potions. However, good mane and tail care can reduce the problems of damage and hair loss, and the texture and condition of the hair can be improved with certain treatments.

Mane and Tail Grooming

Routine mane and tail care starts with careful detangling. It's important to avoid pulling out or breaking off hairs, as it can take years to regrow hair lost to careless grooming. Each hair left in a comb, brush, or on the barn floor after grooming diminishes the length and fullness of the tail or mane. Many grooms do not brush the tail every day; instead, they remove bedding and debris daily and pick it out once a week.. Thick manes and tails can take more brushing, but it's not a good idea to brush long hair too often, as each brushing pulls out some hairs.

If neglected, long hair can become twisted into "ropes" or full of burrs, which are difficult to untangle without breaking or pulling out hair. If the tail is tangled and full of bedding or debris, spray it lightly with conditioner or a detangler. As the hair dries it becomes slippery and tangles, burrs, and debris slide out more easily. But don't brush the hair while it's wet, as it will stretch and break.

When detangling long mane or tail hair, start at the end of the hair and work carefully up toward the roots. Separate a small section of hair and gently work it free from bottom to top, carefully loosening any tangled hairs, gradually working through the whole tail or mane until all the hairs hang straight and free.

It is best to pick out all tangles by hand, as any tool will pull out or break off some hairs each time it is used. Many show stables forbid the use of anything but the hand alone on the precious mane and tail hair. Combs will break off hairs unless used with great care; plastic combs are smoother and less damaging than metal combs, which should only be used for pulling manes. If your horse has a long, thick mane or tail and you are not concerned about pulling out some hairs, you can brush it carefully with a hairbrush or a wire pet brush (the type with wire bristles set into a rubber backing. *Never* rip through a mane or tail with a comb or brush!

The skin and roots of the mane and tail should be kept clean and healthy. You can use a short-bristled body brush on the roots of the mane along the crest and on the dock, parting the hairs in small sections to get down to the skin. The skin can also be cleaned with a damp sponge and a towel.

How to Hand Pick a Mane or Tail

1. Start at the edge of the mane or tail, holding the hair loosely in one hand. (If working on the tail, stand to one side.)

2. With the other hand, separate a few hairs and carefully work them free from the rest of the hair for their full length. Let these hairs fall to one side as you work.

3. Continue through the mane or tail until all the hairs have been separated and hang straight and free of tangles, bedding, or debris.

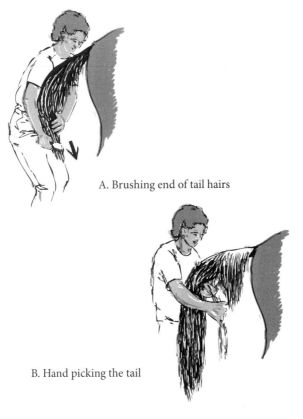

A. Brushing end of tail hairs

B. Hand picking the tail

FIGURE 28. *How to hand pick the tail.*

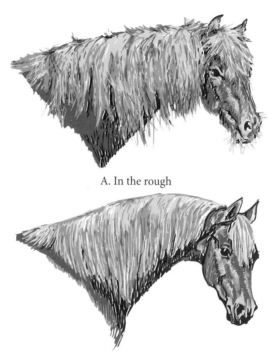

A. In the rough

B. Basic trim with long mane

FIGURE 29. Basic trim for long manes.

Mane Care and Trimming

A long mane should not be all one length, which looks unnatural, but should gradually grow longer toward the middle of the shoulder; from that point it should gradually taper toward the withers. Natural manes usually vary in thickness, with the hair being thickest at the upper end of the neck, where the crest and mane is widest, and thinnest near the withers. Sometimes this results in an unattractive bushy look at the front that does not blend well with the finer, thinner mane back near the shoulders. Cutting a bridle path eliminates some of the thickest hair, but a little judicious thinning near the front can improve the overall appearance of the mane. Any thinning and shortening should be done by hand pulling, not by cutting the mane with scissors.

Protecting a Long Mane

Long, heavy manes are sometimes kept in protective braids that keep mane off the horse's neck, making the horse cooler and protecting the mane from sweat and getting tangled during work. It also helps to preserve the mane hair and keep it from getting broken off or pulled out or otherwise damaged. Sometimes the forelock is braided to keep it out of the way of the bridle, especially for driving.

The simplest way to braid a long mane is to part it into three- to four-inch sections, braiding each section into a long pigtail, and fastening each braid with a non-pulling elastic band. These braids may be left in as long as a week at a time; they should be unbraided, carefully picked out, and

A. Long, heavy mane

B. Working braids

C. Running braid

FIGURE 30. Working braids for long manes.

A. Mane in braids

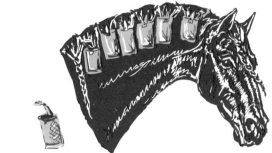

C. Mane cover   B. Braids inserted into
mane covers

FIGURE 31. Protecting long manes.

rebraided weekly. This will also help train the mane to lie over on the correct side of the neck.

A long mane may also be put up in a French braid or running braid (for directions, please see page 229) for a work session, but this braid will stretch and buckle as the horse moves her head and neck, and cannot be left in the mane for more than a few hours.

For some breeds (Andalusians, Friesians, Gypsy Cobs, Palominos, and others), an extremely long, full mane is desirable. These horses' manes are often kept in braids with each braid protected in individual mane bags, similar to tail pouches.

Another method of dealing with a very long, thick mane is parting the mane down the center and dividing it into two-inch sections contained by rubber bands. This method is used on the long, thick manes of Icelandic horses and Haflingers, to prevent the mane hair from becoming tangled and breaking off or pulling the crest to one side.

Mane Pulling

Hunters, sport horses, western horses, and some driving horses usually wear their manes pulled, shortened, and thinned to an even length for braiding, neatness, or show ring conventions. The cardinal rule is that a mane should never be cut with scissors or clippers unless it is roached or hogged (clipped off entirely). Cutting a mane shortens without thinning and results in an unnatural, squared-off "Dutch boy" look that is unacceptable for showing and makes neat braiding impossible. A pulled mane should be short and even—but it must look like it grew that way. This appearance can best be achieved by pulling and thinning the mane by hand.

Before pulling a mane, it should be brushed out free of tangles. A pair of thin gloves and a small metal pulling comb are helpful, although pulling can be done entirely by hand.

Begin pulling at the longest spot in the mane. You should first make the mane even, then work along the whole length of the mane, shortening it only a half inch or so at a time along its entire length. This keeps you from pulling the mane too short in one spot and then having to pull the rest of the mane to match it!

How to Pull a Mane

1. Grasp a few of the longest hairs at the underside of the mane firmly between the fingers and thumb of one hand.

2. With a pulling comb, tease the other hairs up toward the neck. You will be left with a few hairs—half a dozen or so—which should fan out to a section of neck about an inch wide.

3. Wind the long hairs around the pulling comb.

4. Pull the hairs out with a swift jerk. (Pull with the side of the comb, not against the edge—you want to pull the hairs out, not cut them off with the edge of the comb.)

5. Comb down through the teased hair before picking up the next few hairs.

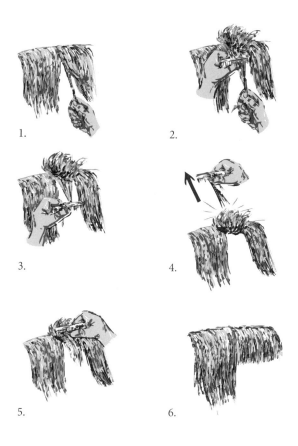

1.

2.

3.

4.

5.

6.

FIGURE 32. Pulling a mane.

As you work, feel for the thickest part of the mane and always pull the hairs from the underside. This allows the top hairs to turn over and lie down, and thins the mane to a uniform thickness. Some parts of the mane (especially near the head) have thicker hair and require more pulling, while other parts are finer and thinner, such as the hair back near the withers.

When pulling a mane, it takes some judgment to arrive at the right length. The shorter the mane is pulled, the more it tends to stand up and fly around. You can always shorten it a bit more, but if you pull it too short, you'll have to wait until it grows out. If a horse is usually shown braided, his mane should be pulled to the best braiding length, regardless of how it looks when unbraided; this might be as short as four inches on some horses. But if you rarely braid and everyday appearance matters more, pull the mane to a length that lies neatly on one side and flatters the horse's neck—perhaps slightly longer than ideal braiding length. A massive horse with a long neck needs a longer mane in proportion to his body than a smaller, finer horse or a pony.

Pulling a mane is not as painful as it appears, because horses have fewer nerve endings in their hairs than humans do. Nevertheless, it can be uncomfortable or downright painful for some horses. Work below your horse's pain threshold—start by pulling so few hairs that he doesn't notice, perhaps only two or three hairs at a time, and gradually increase until you find the level at which he begins to object. Once you know his limit, pull fewer hairs at a time so that he doesn't mind. The hair comes out more easily if the skin of the mane is warmed from exercise or with a hot towel, and a swift jerk straight up is less painful than pulling slowly downward (try it on your own hair!). If you pull only a few hairs from different places along the neck every day, staying under your horse's pain threshold, you can gradually thin and shorten the mane without taxing his toleration.

One exception might be an extremely sensitive horse or one that has been manhandled and forced to endure painful mane-pulling sessions. Such horses may have to be sedated in order to pull their manes; the tranquilizer raises their pain threshold as well as calming them, or the mane may be "dressed" with a patent mane-trimming comb instead of pulling it. This is safer and more humane than fighting with a horse or trying to force her to hold still while you do something that hurts her. His tension and anticipation of pain may eventually diminish after several pain-free experiences.

Dressing a Mane: Thinning and Shortening Without Pulling

A mane that has been perfectly pulled by hand always looks best, but sometimes it is necessary to find alternatives to hand pulling. These methods can produce a mane with a neat, even, and tapered appearance when unbraided. However, because the hairs are cut off instead of pulled out, it may result in a thicker mane or one with many short, bristly ends that do not look as nice when braided. It's important that the final result is a mane that tapers to an even length; the hairs on top should be the longest, and those on the under side of the mane are shorter.

DRESSING THE MANE WITH SCISSORS

If you have the skills of a good hairdresser, you may be able to use scissors to thin and shorten a mane, simulating a pulled mane. You will need a very sharp pair of scissors. Instead of cutting straight across the mane, angle the tips of the scissors upward into the hair and take tiny snips straight up. Some grooms back-comb or tease the long hairs first, then snip upward into the underside of the teased portion, combing it out and checking the results as they go. This method can be used to shorten a long, thick mane to a couple of inches longer than the final length; it can then be finished by hand pulling until it is the correct length and thickness.

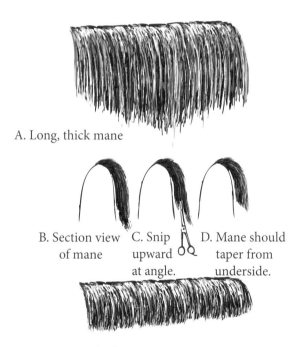

A. Long, thick mane

B. Section view of mane   C. Snip upward at angle.   D. Mane should taper from underside.

E. Finished mane should look as if pulled.

FIGURE 33. *Dressing a mane with scissors.*

MANE-TRIMMER COMB

A mane-trimmer comb is a patent device for shortening and thinning a mane without pulling. It has a section of teeth with a moveable blade, which is activated by squeezing a trigger.

The mane-trimmer comb should be used on the long hair on the under side of the mane, not snipped across all the hairs, which will produce unattractive squared-off sections. To use a mane-trimmer comb, untangle the mane hair first. Then grasp the longest hairs at the bottom of the mane, holding the comb underneath the mane with the teeth pointing outward, so that a section of hair lies in the teeth of the comb. Press the trigger to clip, but keep moving the comb downward, so the hairs are clipped at intervals instead of all in one place. This should result in a thinned mane that tapers on the underside to the desired length.

RAZOR TRIMMER

If a horse's mane is so fine and thin that you don't want to thin it but need to shorten it, you could try carefully trimming the hairs with a "thinner"—a wire-wrapped razor trimmer used in dog grooming. Be careful to use the razor trimmer from the underside to produce a tapered cut—if you pull the hair straight across the blade it will make an obvious flat-edged cut, just what you are trying to avoid. It is best to practice with the razor trimmer on some part of the mane that you will be pulling out anyway, until you can use it skillfully enough to produce the tapered, natural effect you want.

Mane Taming: Help for Problem Manes

While manes may be short, medium, or long, depending on the conventions of the breed and type of horse, we always want a neat, smooth mane that falls on one side of the neck. Certain disciplines have conventions regarding which side of the neck the mane falls on; western horses are traditionally shown with a left mane and most English horses have the mane on the right. This is not mandatory, and sometimes the trouble involved in training a mane to fall on the opposite side is not worth the effect. But if a mane wants to stand straight up or fall to both sides, you may have to train it to lie on one side.

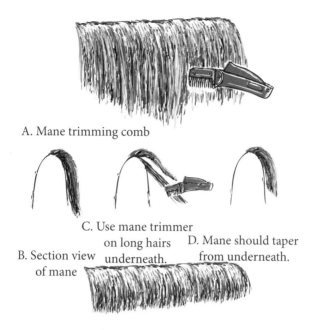

A. Mane trimming comb

C. Use mane trimmer
on long hairs   D. Mane should taper
B. Section view   underneath.   from underneath.
of mane

E. Finished mane should look as if pulled.

FIGURE 34. Mane-trimming tools.

Often problem manes are especially thick and wiry, or the hairs may be stiff and brittle. The shorter the mane, the more difficult it is to train it to lie down, so you should train the mane over to the correct side before pulling or shortening the hairs. Leaving a problem mane an inch or two longer, and carefully pulling and thinning will also help it lie down.

TRAINING A MANE OVER TO ONE SIDE

To train a mane to lie over to one side, wet the hair and braid it into small, tight "pigtails" no more than two inches wide at the top. Pull the hairs across the crest of the neck and start the braid on the side, not on top. The pigtails may be fastened at the ends with rubber bands or turned under and tied off as in hunter braids. Once fastened, the braids may be saturated with setting gel. (If you put setting gel on the hair before braiding it will be too slippery.) Leave the braids in for several days, applying more setting gel daily. When you undo the braids, dampen the hair and brush it over to the correct side of the neck.

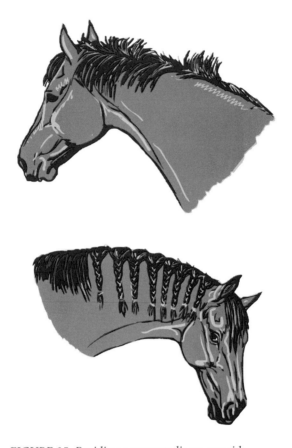

FIGURE 35. Braiding a mane to lie on one side.

A full hood, lined with silk or nylon, can be used to help train a long mane to stay on the correct side of the neck. The mane must be carefully brushed, dampened, and laid down before the hood is applied. Watch the mane carefully for signs that the hood is rubbing the hair out, however.

A mane-tamer is a kind of equine hairnet, applied for an hour or two before a class to lay the mane flat on the correct side of the neck. The mane should be dampened and combed through with setting gel, and the mane-tamer fastened firmly down over it. This method is usually temporary, with the effect lasting just long enough for a show class.

A mane that has been roached and is being grown out is a special problem. Roaching or clipping closely shortens all the hairs to the same length, so as they grow out, all the hairs stick straight up. You must wait until the hair is long enough to be put into tiny braids, pulled off to the desired side, and saturated with setting gel. As soon as the mane begins to lie over to the desired side, the hairs on the underside should be pulled as short as possible. You can use pliers to grasp and pull out a few short hairs along the crest, taking only a tiny bit of hair from the underside edge of the mane. This allows room for the remaining mane to turn toward the desired side and lie down. The mane will not lie smoothly until the hairs from the far side grow long enough to cross over and lie flat on top, and the middle and underneath hairs are thinned until they are shorter than the top hairs. It can take six months to a year for a mane to grow out, so keep this in mind if you cut a bridle path or roach a mane!

Some long manes have a tendency to mat and tangle or to become ropy. These can be protected by being kept in long, loose braids much like the skirt of a tail. The mane is divided into sections of three to five inches in width, and a piece of cotton sheeting can be braided into the braid as in tying up the tail. These braids are not turned under or tied up, but keeping the mane braided prevents it from becoming tangled. The braids should not be too tight at the top or they may cause the hairs to break off, creating an unsightly fringe. The condition of the hair, especially the hair at the top of the mane, must be watched carefully, and the mane should be unbraided and gently picked out once a week. If the hair seems dry or brittle, it should be treated with a conditioner or a hot oil treatment.

Rubbed or ragged manes usually result from a horse's habit of rubbing his mane under a fence board or against the edge of a window. Sometimes a horse may lose a section of mane if it gets caught on a nail, gets full of burrs, or another horse chews on her mane. You will need to camouflage the damage for show purposes while the short area grows out. If the horse has a pulled mane, pulling the rest of the mane fairly short will help the whole mane even up sooner. If a long mane is mandatory, mane and forelock extensions are available in colors to match the mane; these can be clipped or braided into the existing hair. In one case of a hunter that had reduced his mane to bald spots with a few short wisps, artificial mane braids were made out of tail hair and sewn on to the remaining hair. The horse looked presentable, but his rider had to be warned not to grab the mane over fences, lest she come out of the ring with her horse's braids in her hand!

Tail Care and Grooming

Left to nature, horses' tails tend to become thick and bushy at the top, while the skirt becomes thin and straggly at the bottom. This is the opposite of the desired look for the show ring, where we would prefer the top of the tail to be slim, to show off the hindquarters, and the skirt should be full, long, and flowing. Producing a beautiful show tail requires care, maintenance, and sometimes some cosmetic help.

PROTECTING THE TAIL SKIRT

For horses shown with long, full tails, the skirt of the tail is usually protected by being kept in a braid or a tail cover, except when the horse is being groomed or shown. This keeps the precious tail hairs from being pulled out or broken off by being caught on burrs, splinters, and other "tail catchers" in the horse's environment, or even chewed off by other animals. Because tail hairs grow only half an inch or less per month, it can take years for a single new hair to grow from the dock to the bottom of the skirt. While you cannot make the hairs grow faster, keeping the tail protected leaves it much fuller and longer than it would otherwise be.

BRAIDING THE SKIRT

One way to protect the tail skirt is to keep it in a single braid, fastened at the end with an elastic fastener. This prevents individual hairs from getting caught and broken off, yet the horse can use the long, soft braid as a fly swatter. The braid can be left in during turnout and exercise, and is only unbraided once a week for grooming or when showing. This method is most suitable for horses that are stabled and are not exposed to burrs, thistles, or severe fly problems.

Braiding the Skirt

1. Before braiding, the tail should be picked out, clean, and conditioner or moisturizer should be applied.

2. Starting at the end of the dock, divide the tail into three sections and braid it to the end, not too tightly.

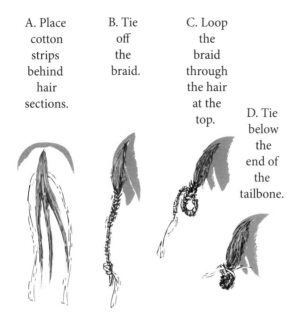

A. Place cotton strips behind hair sections.

B. Tie off the braid.

C. Loop the braid through the hair at the top.

D. Tie below the end of the tailbone.

FIGURE 36. Using braiding strips.

3. Secure the end of the braid with (wrapped) elastic, about three to six inches from the end of the tail.

4. The braided skirt may be left uncovered or protected with a tail bag or tail pouch.

The tail may be braided with cotton braiding strips, especially if the skirt is long and fine or the tail is kept tied up in a tail pouch. You will need a piece of cotton cloth three inches wide and about six feet long, torn from an old bed sheet.

Using Braiding Strips

1. Divide the tail into three sections. Place the center of the cotton strip behind the skirt, creating two long strips. Add the strips to the two outer hair sections and begin to braid. At each braid, twist the cotton strip so that it encloses and protects the hairs.

2. When you reach the end of the tail, wrap one of the cotton strips around the braid and pull it through, forming a slip knot around the braid to secure it.

3. The braid may be looped up to the end of the dock and covered with a tail pouch, or wrapped with Vetrap.

TAIL COVERS

Various types of tail covers are used to protect a braided skirt. They include:

Tail bag: A rectangular bag made of nylon, with ties or a Velcro fastener at the top and fringe at the bottom for a fly swatter. The braided skirt is put into the tail bag, and the ties or fastener are passed through the center of the braid just below the end of the dock, and fastened. Tail bags keep the skirt clean, but the weight of the bag may pull out hair, and the bag may slap against the horse when he swishes his tail at flies.

Tail sock: A long pouch of nylon, Lycra, or other soft, stretchy material, applied in the same way as a tail bag. Because the material is lighter and softer it is less likely to pull out hairs or irritate the horse when he switches his tail.

Tail tubes: A tail pouch made of nylon, Lycra, or stretch fleece divided into three long tubes. The unbraided skirt is divided into three sections and each section is pulled through a tube before the skirt is braided. This protects each section and is the most popular tail protector.

Tail pouch: The braided skirt is looped, doubled, and tied just below the end of the dock, and a stretchy cotton tail pouch is pulled over the looped up tail and tied through the tail. This is most often used on horses that do not have a full, thick skirt.

VetRap: The looped and braided skirt may be wrapped with VetRap or a similar crepe bandage.

A horse should not be turned out in bad fly conditions with his tail tied up, as he will hit himself with his tail bags and may become upset or even damage the tail. For some owners it is more practical to keep the tail tied up only during the months when flies are not a problem. If the tail is tied up during fly season, the horse must be protected with a fly sheet, fly repellent, and other fly-control measures.

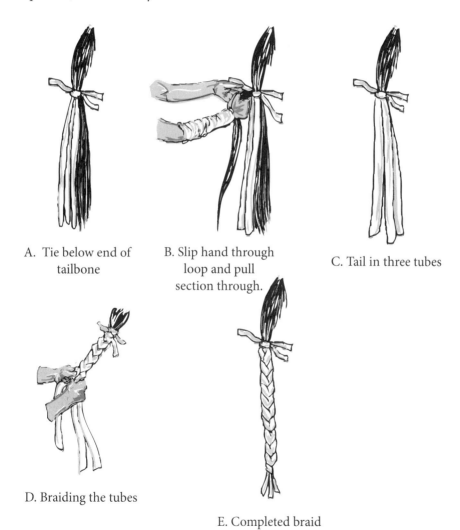

A. Tie below end of tailbone

B. Slip hand through loop and pull section through.

C. Tail in three tubes

D. Braiding the tubes

E. Completed braid

FIGURE 37. Applying a three-tube tail braid.

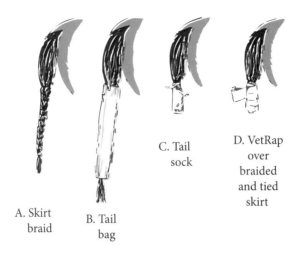

C. Tail
sock

D. VetRap
over
braided
and tied
skirt

A. Skirt
braid

B. Tail
bag

FIGURE 38. *Protecting the braided skirt.*

Washing the Tail

Horses do not need their hair shampooed as often as people do, but their tails can get soiled, stained, and soaked with mud, and sometimes the skin of the tail becomes dirty, greasy, or full of dandruff. Shampooing and conditioning the tail hair improves its appearance for a show, but it must not be overdone. Too frequent tail washing, especially with detergents, can remove the natural skin oils and result in dry skin and hair, so it should not be done more often than necessary.

Tails may be washed with an equine shampoo or a mild human shampoo, but harsh detergents should be avoided. There are a wide variety of products for various colors, purposes, and conditions: stain removers, color-enhancing and detangling shampoos, medicated shampoos, creme rinses, conditioners, and hot oil and other cosmetic treatments.

White Tails

Keeping a white tail white is a challenge because white hair shows dirt and easily becomes stained and yellow. (Some manes and tails are flaxen or blonde, with a naturally yellow cast to the hair.) If white hair is badly stained or damaged by harsh chemicals such as peroxide, the hair shafts become roughened and porous and may absorb the staining agent. Dirt and stains can be removed from the surface of the hair, but once a stain has penetrated the hair shaft it is permanent. It is best to stay ahead of this problem by keeping the tail hair clean, and sealing and protecting the hair against stains.

Some shampoos (usually purple in color) contain an anti-yellowing ingredient that leaves the hair silver white, similar to rinses used by gray-haired ladies. To remove stains and discoloration, the tail should be wet and thoroughly lathered with the product, which can be left on the wet hair for up to three or four minutes and then thoroughly rinsed. Purple shampoos are effective stain removers, but don't leave them on the hair too long, or they may turn it purple! Wisk laundry detergent or Orvus shampoo may be used on the skirt of the tail, but don't use it on the skin too often as it can dry the skin. The skirt of the tail may need to be washed several times to remove deep-seated dirt and get it as white as possible.

When the hair is as clean and white as possible, it should be sealed and protected against stains. Silicone coat spray smooths, seals, and bonds to the hair shafts, resulting in slippery hair that reflects light, repels stains, and allows dirt and debris to slide off. If you wash a light-colored tail and spray it with silicone, it will resist staining for several days. Keeping the tail hair clean, conditioned, sealed against stains, and protected in a tail cover is the best way to produce a dazzling white tail. However, overuse of silicone products or detanglers can make the hair brittle.

CONDITIONERS

Conditioners and creme rinses may be applied after shampooing the tail; they replace some of the oils that are lost by shampooing, and leave the tail hairs smooth and slippery. Some conditioners are applied to the hair and left in, especially before the tail is placed in a tail cover. If the tail or mane hair is long and thick and tends to become "ropy," a detangling shampoo or conditioner will help keep it free. Horses' skin naturally has more skin debris, scurf, and dandruff than human hair, and the pH (acidity level) of horse's skin is different from that of humans, so don't use human hair care products too often as they can dry the skin too much. But if a horse has excessive dandruff, a human dandruff shampoo such as Head & Shoulders may be used for a one-time treatment. If a horse has dry skin or his tail or mane hair is dry, brittle, or sun-bleached, she may benefit from a conditioner containing lanolin, oil, or protein, or from a hot oil treatment. Don't shampoo or use a creme rinse or conditioner right before braiding a mane or tail, as it will make the hair too slippery and the braids may come out.

How to Shampoo the Tail

You can wash a tail when it would be too cold to bathe the whole horse, if you only get the skirt wet. You will need a hose with warm water or two large buckets of warm water, a large body sponge, shampoo and conditioner, creme rinse, or silicone coat spray, and a towel.

1. Wet down the tail, including the dock, with a hose or sponge, or lift up the bucket and dunk the skirt to wet it. Be careful—when a horse feels the water on his dock, he may squat down and might want to kick.

2. Apply shampoo to the skirt and rub it into the whole tail, working up a lather. Use the sponge to wash the skin of the dock.

3. Rinse out the sponge and use the hose or sponge to rinse the tail from the top down, making sure the hairs are rinsed until they "squeak." Dunk the skirt and swirl it around in the bucket until no more soap comes out.

4. Wring the skirt out gently and blot with a towel. Creme rinse or conditioner may be applied (follow product directions) or silicone coat spray sprayed on the damp tail hairs. Don't brush or comb the hair while it is wet, as it will stretch and break easily.

Tail Bandages

The dock of the tail is sometimes bandaged for protection during shipping, or to shape the hairs at the top of the dock before showing. A braided tail should be protected with a bandage when not showing.

A traveling tail bandage must be very secure so that it will not slip off. It prevents the horse from rubbing hair off his tail by leaning against the back of a trailer stall; neoprene tail guards are sometimes used for the same purpose. Tail bandages should not be used when shipping horses for long distances or by commercial carrier. If the bandage slips or begins to cut off circulation, as may happen when it is left on for many hours, the shippers may not notice the problem until serious circulatory damage has been done to the tail. This can cause the horse to lose the hair of his tail or, in severe cases, to develop gangrene, requiring amputation of the tail!

How to Apply a Travel Tail Bandage

Use a cotton stockinette bandage, not an Ace or elastic bandage. Do not dampen the bandage or the tail, and never pull tape or other fasteners tightly enough to make an indentation in the bandage.

1. Anchor the bandage by taking one and a half wraps around the dock, two thirds of the way down the dock. Wrap snugly but never tightly enough to cut off circulation.

2. Pull a section of hair (about two inches wide) from below the wraps and fold it upward. Take a turn or two of the bandage over the turned-up hair.

3. Turn the end of the hair section downward and continue wrapping over it and on up to the top of the dock. Keep the wraps snug and uniform, overlapping each time.

4. Wrap downward, back over the bandaged area. Finish the wrap by securing with Velcro or with two safety pins. The fastening can be reinforced with elastic adhesive tape.

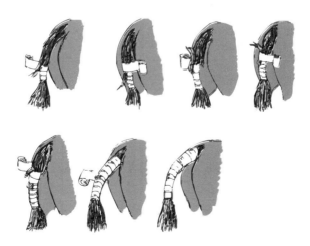

FIGURE 39. *Applying a shipping bandage for the tail.*

A shaping or finishing bandage is applied over the dampened hairs of the dock to smooth and flatten the upper hairs of the tail or protect a tail braid. It is only applied for an hour or two, though bandages over braids are sometimes left on longer. Be sure to remove the tail bandage before the horse enters the ring—to forget this it spoils the effect and is cause for elimination in dressage competitions!

How to Apply a Finishing Bandage to the Tail

1. Slightly dampen the hairs of the dock (don't wet the bandage or it may shrink).

2. Start the tail bandage about eight inches down from the top of the dock. Pull the end of the bandage up into a three-inch tab, then wrap one and a half times over it.

3. Pull the end of the tab down over the wraps, and continue to wrap over the tab, the previous wraps, and on up to the top of the dock. The wraps should be firm and snug but not uncomfortably tight; each wrap should overlap the one below it by half the width of the wrap.

4. At the top of the dock, wrap downward over the wrapped portion down to the end of the dock.

5. Finish off the wrap by fastening it with Velcro, two safety pins or elastic adhesive tape. Never pull the fasteners tighter than the bandage.

6. To remove a tail bandage, hook two fingers into the top wrap and pull downward, sliding the bandage off the tail.

A tail bandage over a braided tail is applied similarly, except that some grooms use an elastic wrap. An elastic bandage must never be pulled to full stretch, as it could cut off circulation and injure the tail. When the bandage has been run down to the bottom of the dock, lift the next-to-last wrap and tuck the remaining roll of bandage beneath it. This bandage must be unwound, not pulled off like a finishing bandage.

Mane and Tail Problems: Rubbing and Parasites

During grooming, the mane and tail should be carefully checked for signs of ticks, lice, or rubbing. Horses will rub their manes, tails, and hair coat if the skin is dry or itchy; it's important to determine the cause of the problem.

To protect the mane, tail, and hair coat from damage caused by rubbing, first inspect your horse's environment. Wherever you see hair caught on a splinter, door latch, or the handle of a bucket, is a spot where your horse's hair is being damaged. A dirty spot along the edge of a stall door may point to a place where a horse likes to rub his mane or tail. Any thistles or burdocks in your horse's paddock should be cut down and removed, and a favorite rubbing spot on a fence may need to be protected with a strand of electric fence wire.

Check the skin condition; dry, flaky skin may cause itching. This can be due to too frequent or too harsh shampooing, or to a very dry environment.

Treating the skin with lanolin or aloe vera may help. Some grooms smear a large blob of Vaseline on the rubbed area, which often stops the rubbing.

Broken or irritated skin may indicate a bacterial or fungus infection, which are more common in wet or humid weather. The area should be bathed with a mild medicated shampoo, preferably one that is fungicidal as well as antibacterial. The skin may be treated afterward with vitamin A and D ointment or antiseptic cream. If the skin irritation is severe or does not respond to simple treatment, the veterinarian may need to do a skin biopsy to determine the cause. Cortisone or other prescription drugs may be necessary to bring the condition under control.

Tail rubbing is often caused by pinworms; these thread-sized parasites live in the rectum and leave a telltale grayish or yellowish powdery discharge near the anus. Deworming with ivermectin will eliminate these tiny pests.

CULICOIDES GNATS AND FILARIAL PARASITES

One cause of severe, persistent itching can be hypersensitivity to the bites of Culicoides gnats ("no-see-ums") and blackflies. This condition is called Recurrent Summer Dermatitis or Sweet Itch; it is an allergic reaction in certain horses which tends to worsen over time; affected horses are chronically sensitive to gnat bites. These insects are active at dawn and dusk; so affected horses should be protected with fly repellent and by keeping them inside when gnats are active, in a stall with small mesh screening and a fan to keep the air moving. They may need extra protection such as closely-woven fly sheets, neck covers, and tail covers.

Microfilaria, the tiny larvae of Onchocerca parasites, are carried by Culicoides gnats; they migrate through the horse's skin, causing extreme itching, especially along the midline of the belly. Dewormers containing ivermectin and moxidectin are effective against Onchocerca.

TICKS

Ticks are common in warm climates, especially in spring and summer. They crawl up the long tail hairs and fasten themselves to the end of the dock, where they suck blood. Crusts of amber fluid show where a tick has been, or you may find one still attached. To remove a tick, wear gloves and use tweezers or a tick remover. Make sure you remove the entire tick, not just the body—if the head is left embedded it can cause an infection. The tick should be dropped into a can of alcohol and the spot where it was attached should be disinfected. Because ticks can carry human diseases, wash your hands after checking for ticks or removing one. Tick infestation can be serious—if neglected, ticks can cause a nasty infection. Deer ticks, which are smaller than the common wood tick, carry Lyme disease, which can infect both horses and humans.

LICE

Lice are a less common problem where horses are well cared for; they are usually found on thin, run-down animals with long winter coats, where horses are kept without much individual attention. Individual lice are difficult to see; the nits or eggs are more obvious, resembling tiny, pale-colored sesame seeds attached to the hair. Lice may be treated with Captan; the treatment must be repeated in ten days to kill those that hatch out later. In the meantime, the horse should be isolated from other horses, and its blankets, brushes, and tack disinfected.

Tail Extensions

Even with good nutrition, care and grooming, some horses have naturally thin or short tails, or a tail may be damaged in some way. At the same time, show ring fashions have come to demand especially long, full tails. For many breeds and divisions, tail extensions have become a popular way of adding length and fullness to the tail for the show ring.

Before purchasing a tail extension, check the rules for your breed, division, and show association. Some breeds prohibit the use of tail extensions or have specific rules on the type of extensions and fastenings that are permissible. American Quarter Horse Association, Paint, and Appaloosa rules state that "tails may be lengthened by hair to hair attachment only, with no attachments of any kind to the tailbone." It's important to select a tail extension that is legal for your breed and division.

There are other types of hair extensions, including mane and forelock extensions and special tail appliances made for horses whose tails have been amputated or otherwise damaged. Some mane products attach with metal clips and some are glued to existing hair. Most mane and therapeutic tail appliances are custom made.

SELECTING A TAIL EXTENSION

Tail extensions come in different sizes and models and in every hair color. You should select a tail extension that matches and blends with the hair color of your horse's tail. Methods of attachment include a simple loop, tie-in, loop-on, slide-on, and multi-layer attachments. Some tail extensions are made of natural hide, which wraps around the base of the dock. The way in which a horse carries his tail also influences the type of extension that will work best on him; wrap-around or multiple attachment points work better on horses that tend to carry their tails higher or are active with their tails. A simple loop fastening may be adequate for a tail that is to be hunter braided, as the braiding reinforces the security of the tail extension.

Most tail extensions are squared off at the bottom, which is the common fashion in breeds that use tail extensions, though tail extensions are available as a natural "switch" tail.

Tips on Applying Tail Extensions

There are many types of tail extensions, and each has its own special method of application. It's important to read, follow, and save the directions that come with the model you select.

Tail extensions should usually be applied to the upper side of the dock, just above the tip of the tailbone. The exact spot depends on the length of the dock and the length of the tail extension; the tail extension should fall to the fetlock joint. If a tail extension is attached incorrectly or at the wrong spot, it may swing from side to side or fail to blend and move with the horse's natural tail hair, which makes it appear unattractive and obviously fake. It may help to make several small braids to anchor the tail extension to the dock at several points, which makes it less likely to swing when the horse switches his tail.

When applying a tail extension, check the height by backing the horse for a few steps. If the tail extension drops to the ground when backing, it is attached too low; the horse may step on the hairs and pull it out, damaging the extension and his tail. The extension should be placed higher.

How to Apply a Natural Loop-Type Tail Extension

1. Measure three to four inches up from the end of the dock. (The extension should fall to the fetlock joint.)

2. Part the tail hair, lift up the upper tail hair, and secure it up out of the way in a large clip or rubber band.

3. Pick up three small strands of hair (about one fourth inch thick) from the center of the tailbone, at the attachment point.

4. Put the center strand through the loop of the extension, with the extension lying right against the tailbone.

5. Braid all three strands together tightly for two to three inches and secure the end with a rubber band.

6. Release the tail hair and gently brush it over the extension hairs.

CARING FOR TAIL EXTENSIONS

Tail extensions are made of natural horsehair, and must be used, cleaned, and stored properly so they don't lose their hair. They can be damaged if the horse steps on the tail extension when backing up. A long tail extension should be kept in a loose braid that can be looped up when the horse is not showing. A tail extension should only be left in place for the show day; it should be removed for the night or before shipping.

Tail extensions can be hand-washed (off the horse) with shampoo and conditioner, and should be fluffed and blow-dried. They should be picked out and straightened carefully by hand. A tail extension should be stored in a tail carrier hanging up.

Chapter 6

Bathing, Bandaging, and Other Procedures

Besides daily grooming, there are some important procedures that are important in caring for a show horse. These include cooling out, bathing, massage and rubbing legs, bandaging, and other procedures.

Cooling Out

Thermoregulation is the body's temperature control process, by which a horse maintains his body heat during cold weather, and cools himself in hot weather and after exercise. During exercise, a small increase in temperature helps the muscles work at their best, which is why warming up is important. Strenuous work produces a great deal of extra heat, which the body must get rid of. Cooling out is the process by which a horse's body temperature and systems return to normal after work.

Horses can cool down by radiation (body heat escapes into the cooler air), by evaporation (as sweat or water evaporates, it lowers the skin temperature), by direct transfer of heat (by pouring cool water over a hot horse, or by a current of air passing over the skin (from a breeze or a fan).

Cooling out is important, but how you do it depends on how hard the horse has worked, his coat, and the temperature and weather conditions. In hot, humid conditions, a horse can easily become overheated, which can lead to heat exhaustion and muscle cramps. In cold weather, a hot, wet horse may cool down too quickly and must be protected against chills until he is dry.

ORDINARY COOLING OUT

After exercise, a horse that is moderately warm, sweaty, or breathing slightly hard should be walked for about fifteen minutes, until his breathing returns to normal and his nostrils and small blood vessels are no longer distended. This allows his heart rate and breathing and the circulation in his feet and legs to return to normal. It is more comfortable for the horse if you loosen his girth and noseband, but make sure his tack is still secure.

Back at the stable, the tack should be removed, and depending on the weather, he may be rinsed and scraped or rubbed dry. In hot weather he should be washed with cool (not icy) water with a little body wash added, and the excess water scraped away. Use lots of water to float away the salt, sweat, and dirt, and rub out any caked-on mud and sweat with the body sponge. The horse should not be left wet any longer than necessary, so scrape each part as you go and get him finished as quickly as possible. A little body wash added to the rinse water acts as an astringent and helps clean the coat. Use a big sponge, wrung out as dry as you can, to pick up any excess water from the head, legs, belly, and parts that are hard to scrape dry. His head, flanks, and chest should be rubbed with a towel, and he should be walked until he is dry.

If it is too cool to wash a horse down, he may be rubbed dry and all sweat marks removed with a towel, a cactus cloth, or a handful of straw. He may need to be covered until his coat is completely dry.

While a horse is cooling out, he should be offered water (cool, but not icy) and allowed to drink as much as he wants. It was once believed that allowing a hot horse to drink or pouring cool water on a hot horse could cause cramps or colic, but research has shown that this is not true. A hot horse needs to rehydrate himself and return his body temperature to normal as soon as possible; drinking plenty of water, especially if he is kept walking afterward, is the best way to do that.

A horse is completely cooled out and back to normal when his breathing and circulation have returned to normal, his coat is dry, and he is no longer sweating. A horse should be cool and dry before he is put away, and he should be completely cooled out for an hour before being fed grain or shipped in a trailer.

COOLING OUT IN HOT, HUMID WEATHER

In very hot or humid weather, cooling out may become more critical; it is more difficult for horses to cool down, and special measures may be necessary. A very hot horse needs to cool down rapidly, returning his core temperature to a normal range and replacing the water and electrolytes he has lost through heavy sweating. Rapid cooling does not cause muscle cramps, colic or tying up, but remaining overheated can be dangerous.

The best way to cool down an extremely hot horse is to hose or sponge him all over with cool water, continuing to hose, sponge, and scrape until the water scraped off his skin is no longer hot. Cold water can be applied with a sponge along the jugular groove, on the head, between the hind legs, and to the large blood vessels close to the surface on the legs. This helps the body to cool down faster when it is overheated. Extreme measures such as applying ice to the large blood vessels, should be done under a veterinarian's supervision.

Hot horses should be offered cool but not icy water to drink, and electrolytes may be administered, preferably by oral paste.

Under these conditions, don't cover the horse with a cooler or anti-sweat sheet; this holds the heat in and prevents him from cooling as quickly as he needs to. Keep the horse in the shade and take advantage of any breeze, which will hasten evaporation and cooling; set up a fan if necessary. Special misting fans that blow a cool, damp mist are especially helpful in extremely hot, humid conditions.

COOLING OUT IN COLD WEATHER

In cold weather, a horse needs to cool down gradually, but avoid chilling. If the weather is cool but not windy, he may cool down and dry off while walking, and can then be rubbed clean and dry. If it's cold or windy, he should be covered with a cooler or an anti-sweat sheet.

If a horse has a long coat, it may be wet with sweat and may remain damp long after the horse has cooled off, exposing him to chills. He should be protected with a warm but "breathable" cover such as a wool or fleece cooler or an open-weave anti-sweat sheet while he walks and cools down, and must be protected from chills and drafts until his coat is completely dry. Materials that "wick" moisture away from the coat are useful for cold-weather cooling out.

An old method of drying a wet coat in cool weather is *thatching,* or stuffing a thick layer of straw next to the horse under a sheet or breathable cover. This creates air spaces that insulate the coat and keep the horse warm while he dries, and the straw absorbs moisture. When the horse is dry, the straw is brushed away and his coat may be brushed out to restore its loft and insulating qualities.

Some horses appear to cool out normally and then break out in a sweat later. This may be due to stress and fatigue, incomplete cooling out, or hot, humid weather. Check your horse later if he has been very hot or stressed, and if you find he has "broken out" and is sweaty again, he should be towel dried, covered with an anti-sweat sheet, and walked until he is back to normal. If humidity is the problem, getting him out of the close confines of the stall will often help.

COOLERS, COVERS, AND ANTI-SWEAT SHEETS

Coolers, walking covers, and anti-sweat sheets can be an aid in cooling out. In cool, windy, or freezing weather, a hot and sweaty horse must be protected from chilling. He should be covered promptly with a cooler made of a breathable material (wool or synthetic fleece) that wicks moisture away from the surface of the body and conserves body heat while allowing sweat to evaporate. If the day is windy, a cooler clamp is snapped onto the underside of the cooler beneath his belly, creating a warm "envelope" and preventing the cooler from blowing off and spooking him.

Thermal anti-sweat sheets have a loose weave that traps air next to the horse, stabilizing his temperature and allowing him to cool and dry slowly. In warm weather an anti-sweat sheet can be used alone; when it is cold or windy, it should be used under a cooler or sheet. Anti-sweat sheets are useful for safely drying horses with long hair, or as a precaution against sweating up while shipping. They should not be left on a horse that is free to roll, as they can be torn easily.

Bathing

When a horse must be extra clean for a show, or if he has gotten stained or especially dirty, you may want to give him a bath. When starting to condition a horse whose coat is dirty and full of scurf, bathing can be a good first step in getting the coat into manageable condition. However, bathing is no substitute for regular grooming, and too frequent use of detergents can strip too much oil from the skin and hair, leaving dry skin and a dull coat. (Rinsing a horse off after exercise with plain water or body wash does no harm and helps remove sweat, salts, and impurities from the coat.) When bathing a horse before a show, it's better to do this a day or two beforehand so his coat has time to regain its maximum shine by show day. But the lighter colored the horse, the more he seems to enjoy rolling in the mud, and a bath is sometimes the best way to get him clean.

A horse should not be bathed when the weather is cold, any more than you would go swimming when it is chilly. If you have access to a heated wash stall and a draft-free area where he can dry, you can bathe a horse even in the winter, but if it is too cold, it's better to do a thorough grooming, vacuum him, and give him a hot towel bath instead. (Hot toweling is described on page 108.) If the weather is cool, you will need a fleece or wool cooler to protect him while he dries.

To bathe a horse, you'll need several buckets of warm water, a large body sponge, a rubber currycomb, a sweat scraper, towels, and a cooler. A wash stall is the ideal place to work, with cross-ties, a hose, and grooming supplies handy. If you can get warm water from a hose, this makes washing and rinsing much easier; most horses will accept a hose if you keep the water a comfortable temperature, use a slow stream, and do not spray their head or ears. Use a halter that will not be hurt by being wet and that will not stain when wet (beware of red or yellow latigo leather!). Choose a shampoo made for horses; there are some that will whiten grey coats or enhance bay, chestnut, or black coats. It's a good idea to use a coat conditioner after bathing, and perhaps a creme rinse or conditioner on the mane and tail.

First, wet the horse all over down to the skin, using the hose or a body sponge. Horses accept this better if you start with a trickle of water and work up from the hoofs, wetting the legs and then the body gradually. Wet down the mane and tail down, too.

Make up a bucket of soapy water by squirting shampoo into a bucket of water, and sponge this liberally over the horse, working from the neck back and down. As each section is soaped, use the currycomb to massage the skin and work up a lather. Keep the soapy parts wet, and rinse as you work by running the hose or squeezing out large spongefuls of clean water above the part where you are scrubbing, until the water runs clean.

The hair and skin should feel "squeaky clean" and free of soap before you move on. Any soap that dries on the coat will leave a sticky scum and a dull coat. A hose attachment that resembles a perforated currycomb lets you massage as you rinse and makes the job easier.

The face and head should be washed with as much water as the horse will tolerate and as little soap as you can use and still get them clean. Often hot toweling or waterless cleaners work better on the head, especially on horses that dislike water used on their heads. Be careful and gentle when working on the head; don't let water run into the ears or soap get into the eyes. Most horses hate water on their heads, and a bad experience can make your horse difficult the next time.

The mane and tail should also be washed and thoroughly rinsed, with special attention given to the skin and roots of the hair. The skirt of the tail can be doubled up and dunked into a bucket to rinse it. If you want the mane and tail especially full and flowing, apply a creme rinse or mane and tail conditioner. Never use creme rinse on a mane or tail you intend to braid—it will make the hairs too slippery to braid.

If your horse is a grey or has white markings, these can be whitened by applying a whitening shampoo (purple shampoo) full strength and leaving it on the hair for up to five minutes. It should be kept wet, and occasionally scrubbed into a lather to prevent it from drying into the coat. When rinsed out, it removes stains and yellowing and gives the coat a silvery cast. White markings and tails may also be scrubbed with Orvus paste shampoo or Wisk laundry detergent. A capful of laundry bluing added to a large bucket of rinse water can make a white coat sparkling white, but don't overdo it—too much can turn your horse green!

The wet coat should be scraped, starting high on the neck and working down and backward, in the direction the hair grows. Use a body sponge wrung out nearly dry to pick up water from the head, legs, flanks, and other areas that are hard to scrape. The tail hair should be gently wrung out to remove excess water.

A coat dressing or conditioner can be sprayed over the damp coat. Silicone dressings coat the hairs with a slick, shiny surface that repels stains and reflects light, making the coat glossy. It repel stains for several days, and makes them easier to remove, but excessive use of silicone products can dry the hair coat. Because it makes the hair slippery, silicone should not be used on the area beneath the saddle.

FIGURE 40. Bathing a horse.

After bathing the horse should be covered with a cooler (according to the weather) and kept out of drafts until he is dry. Don't leave him where he can lie down—newly bathed horses love to roll in the mud!

HOT TOWEL BATH

Hot toweling can be used to get a horse clean when it is too cold or impractical to give the horse a bath. It is a good way to get the coat clean and remove dust and scurf from the head, the croup, and the roots of the mane. Hot toweling can help on days when the air and the horse's coat seem electrically charged and dust sticks to the hairs as if magnetized. Hot toweling feels good to the horse, and is a good way to get a sensitive horse clean.

To hot-towel a horse, you will need a large, light-colored towel or two, a pail of very hot water, rubber gloves, and a small amount of detergent or shampoo. The small amount of soap (less than a capful in a large bucket) causes the dirt and scurf to release their hold on the skin and hair and be picked up by the towel.

Wearing rubber gloves, dunk the towel in the bucket and wring it out until it is almost dry—it should be too hot to handle comfortably without rubber gloves, though it will lose heat quickly. Place one hand behind the towel and rub it quickly through the hair coat. The hair should not be soaked, but dirt and scurf will quickly blacken the towel; shift your hand to a clean place on the towel and continue. When the towel begins to lose its heat, dunk it in the hot water and wring it out again; continue until the area is clean. If the coat is becoming too damp, rub it with a second, dry towel immediately after the hot towel.

This procedure produces a clean coat very quickly. It is a good procedure to use before body clipping or when the horse needs to be extra clean for showing. Coat dressing may be applied to the clean hair coat after hot toweling.

CLEANING THE SHEATH OR UDDER

Cleaning the sheath is a distasteful chore to many people, but it is necessary for the horse's comfort. The skin of the sheath secretes a waxy substance called *smegma,* which combines with dirt and skin debris to form lumps and crusts that accumulate inside the sheath and on the surface of the penis. A small lump of smegma, called a bean, may form in the opening of the urethra. If this accumulation is not removed, the area may become inflamed or even infected. The sheath should be cleaned every two to six months, depending on the needs of the individual horse. Streaks of smegma found on the inside of the hind legs, refusal to "let down" for urination, or a strong odor are signs that the sheath needs cleaning.

In mares, smegma and dirt may accumulate between the folds of the udder. This should be checked occasionally but use caution, as many mares are touchy about their udder being handled and some may kick. Baby wipes can be used to wipe the udder or the entrance to the sheath clean during grooming.

To clean the sheath, you will need sheath cleaner gel (or a mild soap such as Ivory), a small sponge, and a warm water hose or two buckets of

FIGURE 41. The sheath.

warm water. Disposable gloves are a good idea for your own hygiene. Most horses will behave for sheath cleaning, but you may need an assistant to restrain the horse by holding up a front foot or applying a twitch. If a horse is really difficult, he may have be tranquilized; this will cause him to let down his penis as well as calming him, so cleaning is much easier.

When cleaning the sheath, stand close to the hindquarters, and keep one hand on the horse's loin, so you can feel if he is about to kick. Lubricate the sponge well with sheath cleaner gel (or lather), sponge the entrance to the sheath, then gently enter the sheath. Carefully loosen the lumps and accumulations of smegma, rinsing frequently with a warm water hose (if possible). Unless the horse drops his penis, which makes sheath cleaning much easier, you must enter the inner chamber and clean the folds of the sheath and the retracted penis. When you have removed all the smegma that will come off with gentle scrubbing, rinse thoroughly. Check the blind pouch at the opening of the urethra for the "bean," and remove it.

If a horse's sheath is very dirty, clean him gently and apply a little KY jelly to the area, then clean the sheath again in a few days. This will soften the lumps and make it easier to remove them without irritating the skin. Do not apply oily products such as Vaseline or baby oil; they tend to attract more dirt. Too frequent cleaning or application of inappropriate products can irritate the sheath and may actually result in excess smegma production.

Neck Sweating

Neck sweating is a form of "spot reduction" practiced by trainers of Quarter horses and other breeds that are sometimes thicker in the neck and jowl than is desirable. The thickness is partly due to the individual horse's body type and conformation, and partly because these horses are usually overweight. The extra fat they carry gives them a fashionably rounded outline and a showy "bloom," but also shows up in the form of fat deposits in the neck, crest, jowl area, and forequarters. While neck sweating has a cosmetic effect of slimming the neck and throat, this is temporary because it achieves its effects by causing water loss in those areas. (Overweight humans have found that plastic exercise suits, body wraps and the like have a similarly short-lived effect!) Unfortunately, for horse or human, fat cells are not eliminated by sweating, only temporarily reduced.

The area most often targeted is the throat and jowl area. Thick throated horses have difficulty flexing at the poll and do not present a refined, clean-cut neck in halter classes. Some trainers sweat the whole neck or the neck and shoulder area. Sweating of larger areas, such as the whole body, is less advisable and can result in dehydration if overdone

To sweat the neck or throat, you will need a sweat wrap, and glycerine; Listerine antiseptic or a commercial neck sweat preparation is applied to the skin. Some trainers augment the sweat wrap with plastic food wrap applied next to the skin; then a rubber or vinyl sweat wrap is applied over it. After applying a sweat wrap, the horse is tied and left to stand for an hour before being exercised with the wrap in place. After exercise, the wrap is removed and the neck is washed clean.

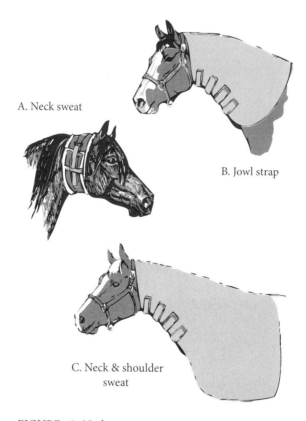

A. Neck sweat

B. Jowl strap

C. Neck & shoulder sweat

FIGURE 42. Neck sweat.

In cool weather, plastic or even a second sweat wrap may be needed to achieve enough sweat to be effective. Keep a close eye on the horse when using a sweat wrap—it is easy to cause too much water loss and the horse may become severely dehydrated, especially in hot weather. Test for dehydration by pinching up a fold of skin on the neck—the skin should snap back into place immediately when you release it. If the skin remains tented for three seconds or longer, the horse is dehydrated and needs water, electrolytes, and relief from exercise and sweating.

Some stallions or thick-necked horses may need to be sweated every day in order to maintain a clean-looking neck. If much sweating is required, two shorter sessions per day are often more effective than one long one, and less stressful for the horse.

A jowl strap or jowl hood is a fleece- or felt-lined strap or hood may be worn in the stable to keep the throttle slimmed down. It supports the muscles of the throat and helps to maintain the slim appearance achieved by sweating. It should be adjusted snugly but not so tightly that the horse cannot eat, drink, and move comfortably. Sweat lotions should not be applied under a jowl strap, as the lining may absorb the active ingredient and cause the skin to blister or hair to come out.

Massage and Rubbing Legs

Massage and stretching can be very beneficial in relieving aches and pains, alleviating stiffness and helping a horse recover after injury or hard work. It may also be used to release tension in muscles, to help a stiff horse loosen up before work. Hand rubbing legs stimulates the circulation and helps the lymphatic system carry away excess fluids that cause "filled" legs, joints, and tendons. Some forms of massage help tone up certain muscles, as isometric exercises do for human athletes. Therapeutic deep massage, using muscle "trigger points," can be beneficial for some horses, but this requires expert knowledge and hands-on experience. Rubbing, "strapping," and hand massage stimulate the skin and distribute skin oils over the hair coat, improving the shine of the coat. Never massage areas that are inflamed, infected, tender, or have open wounds, as this may do more harm than good. The best way to learn massage is hands-on instruction from an equine massage practitioner, who can show you specific techniques that are especially beneficial for your horse.

STRAPPING (BANGING OR HARD WISPING)

Strapping (also called *banging* or *hard wisping*) is a form of massage traditionally practiced by English grooms. It tones up specific muscles by causing rhythmic contraction and relaxation, and stimulates the skin, making the coat shine. Use a massage pad, folded towel, or a woven hay wisp.

To *strap* a horse, start by swinging your arm slowly and striking the massage pad against a heavily muscled area, such as the muscles of the hindquarters. Strike the muscle slowly and gently at first, sliding the wisp down and off the body with a long, firm sweep. As the horse gets used to the steady bang-and-sweep, he will learn to contract his muscles and then relax them after each stroke. As he gets used to it, you can build up to harder strokes—about ten on each muscle area at first. Add a few strokes each day until you are banging each muscle area thirty times or more, putting all your weight into each bang and stroke.

Strapping should be practiced only over large muscle masses, never over bony or thinly muscled areas, the sensitive loin area or any place that is tender or sore. Some horses obviously enjoy it and lean into the stroke; others may be too sensitive or nervous to tolerate it. If you start slowly and gently, your horse may learn to like it; if not, it is better to omit this procedure than to hurt or upset a sensitive horse. Strapping only helps if done faithfully and vigorously every day. It will certainly develop muscles in the groom!

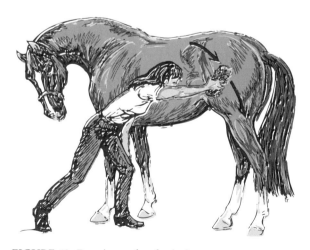

FIGURE 43. Banging or hard wisping.

Soft wisping is a milder form of rubbing, used to rub the skin and coat. A hay wisp, rub rag or folded towel can be used. The wisp or massage pad is rubbed firmly back and forth across the hair coat to stimulate circulation and work the skin oils throughout the coat. The coat should be rubbed for thirty minutes or more in order to shine up the coat and warm the skin. Some grooms finish off the job by rubbing the horse with the bare palms of the hands. This form of rubbing is so effective that it must be used with moderation on fine-coated horses—you can literally rub the hair off in places!

HAND RUBBING LEGS

Hand rubbing the legs is a good thing to do for your horse, especially when he is tired, stiff, or sore or when he is recovering from an injury. This massage stimulates the circulation and helps the lymph system carry away cellular debris. One of the best reasons to hand-rub legs is that you will become intimately familiar with every part of your horse's legs, and will quickly notice any heat, swelling, or evidence of small changes or injuries. It is always a good idea to hand-rub the legs after work, competition, or before applying standing bandages. Don't massage a bruise or any area that is swollen because of infection, however.

When rubbing legs or joints, it is more comfortable for both horse and groom if the area is lubricated with rubbing alcohol, glycerine, or a mild liniment or leg brace. Be careful when using liniments—some can blister the skin if rubbed in too hard or if used under bandages. Rubbing must be carried out for five to ten minutes to have any benefit; it is the massage, not the liniment, that gets results, so don't just dab on liniment and give it a lick and a promise.

How to Hand Rub a Leg

1. Lubricate your hand and the leg with alcohol or leg brace.

2. Facing toward the rear, bend down and take hold of the tendon with the hand nearest the horse. Your fingers point down, with the thumb on the outside of the leg and fingers on the inside, running along the tendon groove. By grasping the back of the leg, you can apply pressure with your fingers as you move your hand up and down.

FIGURE 44. Hand rubbing a leg.

3. Massage the leg by moving your arm up and down while your hand rubs the flexor tendons, suspensory ligament, fetlock joint, and pastern. Apply most pressure upward, toward the heart.

To rub the shin or knee, face toward the front. The hind leg can be rubbed in the same way as the front. When working on a horse's legs, bend over but never sit or kneel—you might have to get out of his way if he should jump or kick.

Leg Wraps and Bandaging

The feet and legs should be examined carefully each day when the horse is first brought out and later after his workout. Run your hand slowly over the surface of each leg from knee or hock to the hoof to check for heat, swelling, or tenderness, and treat any minor injuries before they have a chance to escalate.

Many race and performance horses' legs are rubbed with a leg brace and wrapped with stable bandages after each workout; this also protects the horse against accidental injuries in the stall. Horses may benefit from

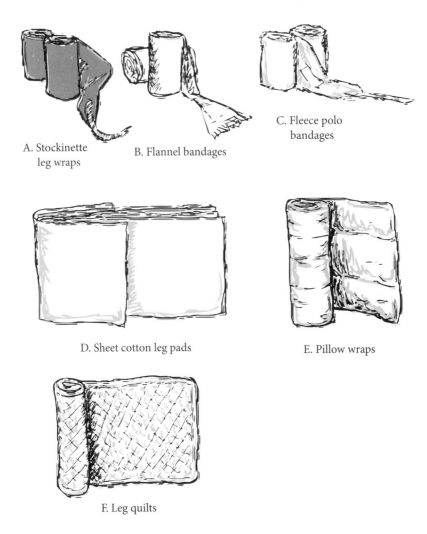

A. Stockinette leg wraps

B. Flannel bandages

C. Fleece polo bandages

D. Sheet cotton leg pads

E. Pillow wraps

F. Leg quilts

FIGURE 45. *Leg wraps.*

support bandages after they have worked hard, if they have an injury, or their legs show signs of filling or stocking up. Some trainers use standing bandages as a precaution when horses are stabled in temporary stalls at shows that are less safe than those at home.

Bandaging materials include bandages or wraps, and pads or cottons, and fasteners Leg wraps are usually made of knitted or semi-elastic material, four to six inches wide and six to seven feet long. Bandages may be fastened with Velcro closures or safety pins; the closure is sometimes reinforced with masking tape or elastic adhesive tape. Except for fleece polo wraps, leg wraps must always be used over sheet cotton, leg quilts, or other padding. It is dangerous to run a bandage directly on a leg without padding or to use uneven or insufficient padding; the pressure may impair circulation and cause inflammation and injury to the tendons. Any padding must be soft enough to compress into the contours of the leg without binding or creating lumps or wrinkles, and should be breathable.

Bandaging can be beneficial, but only if it is done evenly, securely, and with just the right amount of pressure. Loose, uneven, too tight, or incorrectly applied bandages do not protect as they are supposed to do and can cause injury to the legs (known as a *bandage bow* or *cording* a tendon.) When learning to bandage, have an experienced groom or trainer check your work, so you learn exactly how much pressure to use and how to keep it even.

TYPES OF BANDAGE MATERIALS

Knitted stockinette "track" bandages—the most common general-purpose bandage, used for leg wraps (always over a pad) and sometimes for tail wraps.

Flannel bandages—often used by professionals for standing and shipping wraps, over thick cottons. They are not elastic but give good support.

Ace bandages—very stretchy; used for working bandages over leg pads, but need skilled application because they can easily be pulled too tightly and cause damage. Sometimes used for tail wraps over braided tails, but must be put on with care.

Vetrap—elastic crepe bandage that sticks only to itself and conforms to the leg or padding; may be reused once or twice. Useful for wrapping injuries.

Elastic adhesive tape—useful for bandaging wounds or for reinforcing bandage closures.

Polo wraps—elastic bandages of a fleecy material, which incorporates its own padding into the bandage; used without leg pads. Used to protect legs during exercise, they are easily washable and easier to apply than other types of exercise bandages.

Types of Padding Used Under Bandages

Sheet cottons—six doubled sheets are used beneath standing or shipping bandages. They may be covered with cheesecloth to make them last longer. Sheet cotton cannot be washed.

Leg quilts or pads—made of quilted cotton, washable felt, or similar materials, should be sized to fit the horse's legs.

"Pillow" wraps—thick, soft, and washable leg pads of cotton or acrylic batting covered with a cloth outer shell.

Other materials are available, and new wrapping materials are always being developed.

The legs may be "braced" before bandaging, especially after a workout and before stable bandages are applied. A mild liniment or leg brace or rubbing alcohol is massaged into the tendon, suspensory ligament, and fetlock joint until it is absorbed and the leg feels warm. Use a leg brace or liniment that is intended for use under bandages and that will not cause skin irritation or blistering. The massage, along with the astringent and heating effect of the liniment, stimulates local circulation and encourages the absorption of excess fluid. The leg should be rubbed for at least five minutes and then bandaged immediately so as not to lose the effect of the liniment and massage. Do not apply brace, liniment or heat over a bruise or a hot, swollen area. (See page 114 for directions for rubbing legs.)

Stable or Standing Bandages

Stable or standing bandages are used to provide support and pressure for relief of tired legs, to treat strains and sprains, and to take down swelling. They are also used as a precaution against accidental injury in the stall or while being walked in hand, especially when a horse is in a strange stall where he is more likely to get hurt than at home. A standing bandage should have plenty of padding; the wrap is pulled tightly enough to compress the padding into the contours of the leg and provide even pressure against the structures. It must be applied evenly from just below the knee to the pastern, and some padding should extend above and below the edge of the wraps to prevent them from binding against the knee or pastern.

How to Apply a Standing Bandage

1. Place the padding evenly around the leg, starting with the edge in the groove of the tendon, making sure that it lies evenly without lumps or creases. On the left legs, the padding should run counterclockwise (on the right, clockwise).

2. Start the bandage at the top of the ankle by slipping the end of the bandage inside the edge of the padding. Wrap firmly one and a half times over the tucked-in end, then begin to wrap downward, overlapping one third the width of the bandage on each wrap.

3. Wrap over the ankle and down to the pastern, keeping the wraps firm and even. The ankle is not as easily harmed by pressure as the tendons, and this makes a secure base from which to wrap the rest of the leg.

4. Pull the bandage up under the back of the fetlock joint, for support.

5. Wrap back up the leg, keeping the wraps even, firm, and parallel to the ground. Pull the wraps firmly backward against the shin, keeping the tension even as you wrap.

6. Bring the last wrap up to the base of the knee or hock. At least a half inch of padding should extend upward beyond the bandage, to prevent the edge of the bandage from binding.

7. Wrap back down to the middle of the leg. Fasten the bandage on the outside of the leg (not on the tendon, shin, or inside). If a bandage is too long, fold it inward to adjust the length.

8. Fasten with a Velcro closure, or with two safety pins in a horizontal position, pinning through several layers of bandage and into the padding beneath. The pins or Velcro can be covered with elastic adhesive tape for extra protection. If you use bandages with ties, they must lie flat, must not be pulled tight enough to indent the bandage, and should tie on the outside.

Now check the bandage—it should feel firm and even, but not so tight that you cannot insert a finger under the padding at the top and bottom.

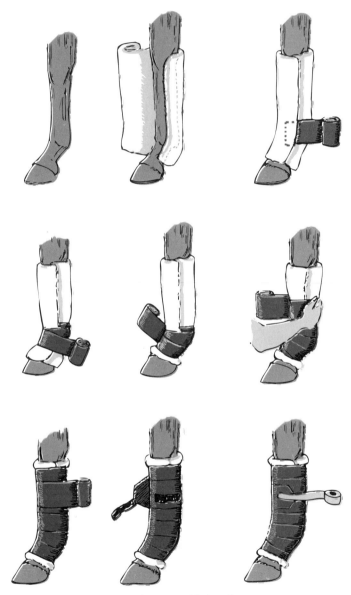

FIGURE 46. How to apply a standing or stable bandage.

SHIPPING BANDAGES

Shipping bandages are used to protect and support the legs while traveling; they are applied like standing bandages but extend down to cover the coronary band, so shipping cottons and leg wraps must be extra long.

Don't put on shipping bandages as "galoshes"—big lumpy bandages around the foot and ankle that end halfway up the tendon; these are clumsy, give no protection to the tendons and may cause uneven pressure on the leg. If you cannot run a neat, firm shipping bandage from the hoof to the knee or hock, it is better to use shipping boots. Another option is to use bell boots to protect the coronary band and apply a regular stable bandage over them. This method offers more protection for horses that tend to scramble or step on their own feet.

How to Apply a Shipping Bandage

1. Place the cotton or pad smoothly over the leg from underneath the heels to the knee or hock. On the left legs, the padding should run counterclockwise; on the right, clockwise. The edge of the padding should start on the outside of the leg, in the groove of the tendon.

2. Anchor the edge of the bandage under the cotton at the top of the ankle.

3. Wrap one and a half times around the anchored end of the bandage, then wrap downward, using firm, even pressure. Overlap each wrap one third the width of the bandage. If the bandage gaps at the front of the pastern, give it a half twist.

4. Run the bottom edge of the bandage underneath the heel (at least one inch). Use a half twist on the front if necessary to keep it tight. The padding should extend below the bandage, and both padding and bandage should extend below the heels and the coronary band.

5. Wrap back up the leg, keeping the pressure firm and even. Check the tension with each wrap, and pull more firmly against the shin, not against the tendon.

6. Wrap up to the base of the knee or hock, leaving at least a half inch of padding above the edge of the bandage to protect the back of the knee. Wrap back down to mid-cannon.

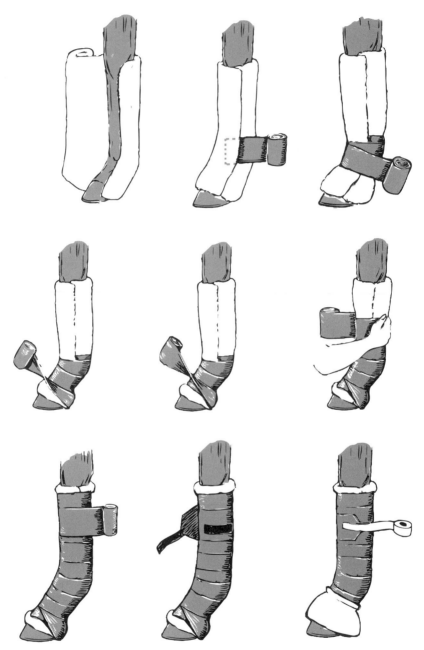

FIGURE 47. *How to apply a shipping bandage.*
Shipping bandage applied over bell boot.

7. Fasten the bandage on the outside of the leg. If necessary, fold the end back underneath to adjust the length.

8. Fasten with Velcro closure or with two safety pins in a horizontal position, on the outside. Reinforce with a strip of elastic adhesive tape over the closure. Do not pull the tape tightly enough to indent the bandage.

EXERCISE BANDAGES AND POLO WRAPS

Exercise bandages and polo wraps are used to protect the legs during work; or for support when a horse is being returned to work after an injury. There are several types of exercise bandages, including tendon bandages, run-down bandages, fetlock supports, and others. Exercise bandages must be applied with just the right amount of pressure, and must not bind or restrict the movement of tendons and joints. They must be fastened especially securely — if a bandage comes loose during work, the horse may step on it and stumble or fall. Exercise bandages should not be used unless they are necessary; if you don't know how to apply them correctly, leave them off!

Polo wraps are the safest kind of exercise bandage. Fleece polo wraps incorporate their own padding into the bandage and are applied over the bare leg, without additional pads. They are washable, and are quick to put on to protect the legs for work, lungeing, or turnout. Polo wraps are not permitted in the show ring except for a few specific classes; they are best saved for schooling. Fleece polo wraps are not suitable for cross-country work, as they pick up burrs and debris and become saturated with water, and stretch and slip when wet.

How to Apply Polo Wraps:

1. Start the bandage at the edge of the tendon on the outside of the leg, wrapping counterclockwise on the left legs (clockwise on the right.)

2. Wrap the bandage one and a half times around to anchor it, then wrap downward, using firm, even pressure. Do not pull as tightly as when wrapping a standing bandage, because there is no padding to compress.

3. Continue wrapping downward, overlapping each wrap half the width of the bandage. Most pressure should be applied backward against the shin, instead of pulling forward against the tendons.

4. At the ankle, keep the front edge of the bandage high, above the base of the joint. Drop the bandage down and under the back of the fetlock joint and then back up in front. This forms an inverted V at the front of the ankle, which allows the joint and pastern to flex.

5. Continue wrapping back up the leg to the bottom of the knee or hock, keeping the wraps parallel to the ground and the tension even and moderately firm.

6. Wrap back down over the previous wraps, using a little less tension. Fasten the Velcro closure on the outside of the leg, never over the tendon or on the inside.

7. For extra security, the closure may be reinforced with a strip of elastic adhesive tape. Do not use non-elastic tape, and never pull the tape tightly enough to indent the bandage.

There are many other types of bandages, including working bandages for support during exercise, run-down bandages, and specialty bandages used to treat injuries. Because they can be complicated to apply, it is best to seek hands-on instruction and have an expert check your work.

Using Boots

Exercise bandages are time-consuming, require skill to apply, and need frequent laundering, so some trainers prefer to use protective boots. Boots are quicker to apply and offer more protection against a blow from a hoof or a jump rail. They come in many styles to protect various parts of the leg, and usually have wide elastic closures that distribute pressure evenly, making them less likely to bind on a tendon or injure a leg than poorly applied exercise bandages. The boot lining must be kept clean and smooth; mud, sand, sweat, or grit that works inside the lining can rub

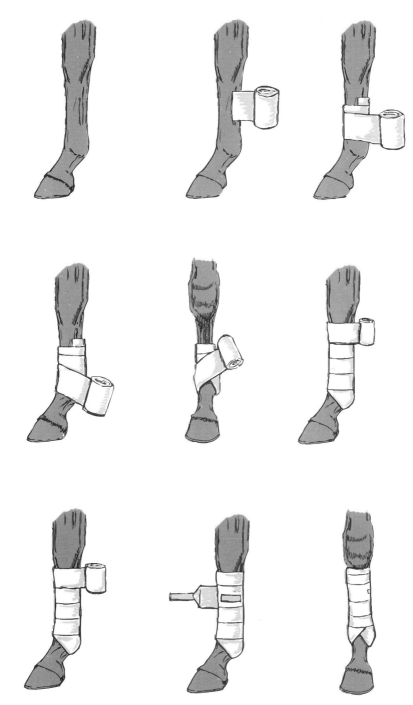

FIGURE 48. How to apply fleece polo bandages.

sores on the horse's legs. Some horses need a thin sheet of cotton worn beneath the boot for comfort. Boots should be cleaned after each use.

Tendon boots, galloping boots, and ankle boots should be applied high on the leg and then pulled down into position before adjusting the fastenings. Recheck the fasteners after the horse has warmed up, as some horses' legs may go down in size as they warm up and the boots may need tightening.

Types of Boots

Tendon boots or galloping boots—protect shins, tendons, splint bones, and fetlock joints from interference injuries, high overreaches, or striking a jump. They are used on jumpers, eventers, and other performance horses.

Open front boots—used on jumpers to protect the tendons and fetlock joints, but let a horse feel a rap if he jumps carelessly.

Splint boots—protect the splint bones and inside of the leg from blows from the opposite foot during turns, lateral work, reining, lungeing, or on horses that interfere because of crooked leg conformation.

Ankle boots—protect against striking the inside of the ankle; usually used on the hind legs.

Sports medicine boots—boots made of neoprene lined fabric, covering the tendons and fetlock joints and incorporating an elastic fetlock support strap. Used for protection during work, turnout, and for performance horses.

Skid boots—protect the underside of the hind fetlock joints on western horses that make sliding stops. Sometimes skid boots are incorporated into boots designed to protect the whole hind leg from the hock down.

Bell boots—protect the heels and coronary band from "grabs" or overreach injuries. They are used on jumpers, reining horses, for turnout and shipping, and on any horse that is likely to injure his heels with the toe of the hind foot.

Quarter boots—protect against injury to the heels and quarters of the foot. They are used on saddle, gaited, and harness horses that work with high action at speed.

Easy-boots—fit over the hoof like a slipper, taking the place of a shoe. They may be used for treatment or to protect the hoof until a lost shoe can be replaced.

Shipping boots—protect the legs from coronary band to the knees and hocks for travel; an alternative to shipping bandages.

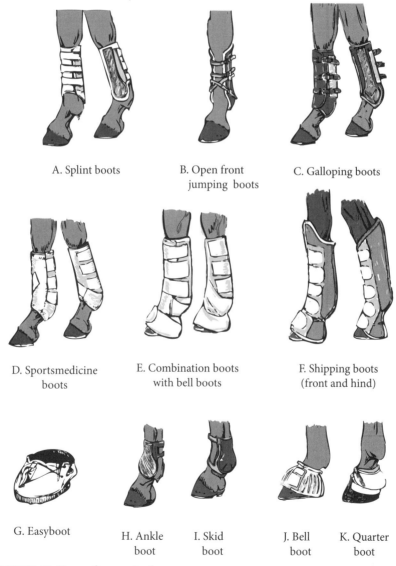

A. Splint boots

B. Open front jumping boots

C. Galloping boots

D. Sportsmedicine boots

E. Combination boots with bell boots

F. Shipping boots (front and hind)

G. Easyboot

H. Ankle boot

I. Skid boot

J. Bell boot

K. Quarter boot

FIGURE 49. *Types of protective boots.*

Chapter 7

Trimming and Clipping

Trimming can make a big improvement in a horse's appearance. A horse in the rough has shaggy fetlocks and long hair that obscures the lines of the lower legs; his ears are hidden in fuzz, and his head may be so hairy that he looks like a billy goat! Long straggly whiskers give his a comic appearance, and his mane and tail may be bushy, tangled, and overgrown. With a little barbering, the country bumpkin can look like a city slicker, with a more refined head, face and muzzle, cleaner throat, sculptured ears, and slimmer, cleaner-looking legs. But before you start up the clippers, consider how much and what kind of trimming your horse really needs.

The Natural Horse

If a horse lives outside or works in rain, mud, or cold weather, all that extra hair serves a practical purpose. The long hair on his legs keeps them warm and dry, and the fetlocks come to a natural point to help water drain away from the sensitive skin at the heels. While you can trim the leg hair enough for neatness, clipping the legs too closely may predispose her to scratches (a chapped condition of the skin of the pasterns).

Some horses grow coarse, heavy hair on their faces, which insulates them in cold weather and helps keep white-faced horses from getting sunburned. Fuzzy ears have a purpose, too; in winter, the extra hair keeps the ears warm and wards off frostbite, and in summer, it keeps gnats and biting flies out of the ears. A horse uses his long whiskers as a cat does, to feel what's near his face in the dark.

Although trimming makes a horse look nicer, it is unkind and not good for a horse to go too far by trimming her inappropriately for her life-style. If he is kept stabled, carefully groomed, and meticulously cared for, and he competes in a specialty that requires the ultimate in trimming, you may do a complete show trim. But if you're cleaning up the old pony for a one-time appearance at the county fair, don't overdo it and deprive her of the important natural protection she'll need as soon as he's turned back out to pasture.

ALL-PURPOSE BASIC TRIM

An all-purpose basic trim makes a horse look neater and easier to groom. (However, there are a few breeds that frown on any trimming at all, so check your breed's standards before removing any hair.) It is easiest to use electric clippers, but simple trimming can be done using hand clippers or scissors and a comb. (For trimming techniques, see p. 137) For a basic trim:

- Trim the fetlocks, and excess hair from the legs, and trim the hair at the coronary band to an even line.

- Trim the long hair from under the chin and jaws. If you decide to remove the whiskers, clip them closely; they may be finished with a plastic shaver.

- Trim the outside edges of the ears, leaving the hair inside the ears but trimming it level with the edges of the ear.

- A short "bridle path" clipped just behind the poll is neater and makes bridling easier. A basic bridle path is an inch or two long; check breed specifications before you clip it too far. *Caution:* if you cut a bridle path too long, it can take six months before the clipped part grows out to match the rest of the mane.

- Long "guard hairs" that stand out from the coat may be clipped away by reversing the clippers and lightly brushing the blades over the ends of the hairs. Avoid pressing the blades into the hair coat, which will create sharp-edged "clipper lines."

The basic trimming job ends with picking out the mane and tail. The mane may be pulled or left long and natural, depending on the type of horse. The tail is usually left as long and full as it will grow, but some

FIGURE 50. *Horse in the rough vs. basic trim.*

horses and ponies with bushy tails look better if the top of the tail is thinned and pulled somewhat to make it more in proportion to the rest of the tail. The mane should be trained to lie smoothly on one side (see Chapter 5 for instructions on pulling and training manes).

COSMETIC EFFECTS

Some cosmetic changes can be made through clever clipping and trimming. A coarse, chunky horse can be made to look finer by clipping the face, head and throat, and trimming the legs closely, or doing a full body clip. If the coat is long, any clipped areas must be blended smoothly or they will stand out in startling contrast from the unclipped areas. Thick legs appear finer when trimmed closely along the contours of the tendons, which gives the legs more definition and appearance of quality. A thick throttle looks more refined when it is clipped closely underneath and the horse is given a slightly longer bridle path. Closely clipping the face, ears, and the skin around the eyes and muzzle can make a plain head appear more sculptured and the eyes look larger. You can minimize a blemish, such as a thickened tendon or enlarged ankle, by clipping a little less closely over the blemish and carefully blending the clipped hair at the knee. White markings look whiter when closely clipped (but not so closely as to leave "clipper stripes" or to appear scalped). A less-than-perfect head may be flattered by judicious shaping and trimming of the mane and forelock—a Roman nose or big ears are minimized by a full forelock, and a thin neck may look more substantial with a little extra mane. Thinning and slimming the top of the tail can make the hindquarters appear wider, and if the hocks or hind legs are less than perfect, leave the tail long and full to camouflage them.

Clippers

To trim a horse, you need electric clippers, hand clippers, or a comb and a pair of sharp fetlock scissors with curved blades. Electric clippers are best by far. Hand clippers are hard to operate and often the blades are not sharp enough to make them worth the trouble. Simple trimming can be done with scissors and comb, though this is not enough for a show trim. When trimming with scissors, a comb is used to lift the hair and it is snipped off over the teeth of the comb; this gives a smoother result and protects the horse from accidental jabs.

Clipping machines have been around since the nineteenth century, when fashionable carriage horses were often body clipped, while working horses were clipped "trace high," or up to the traces on the harness. In those days, clipping a horse was an all-day job requiring expert work with scissors and comb, a singeing lamp, or an old-fashioned hand-cranked clipping machine. Modern electric clippers are safe and easy to use; they cut quickly, evenly, quietly, and without hurting the horse. There are several types of horse clippers and many models, including convenient cordless rechargeable models.

TYPES OF CLIPPERS

Heavy-duty body clippers—used for body clipping, roaching manes, and trimming heavy, coarse hair from the legs. Heavy clippers are air cooled and can be run for longer periods without overheating than smaller and

A. Heavy duty body clippers

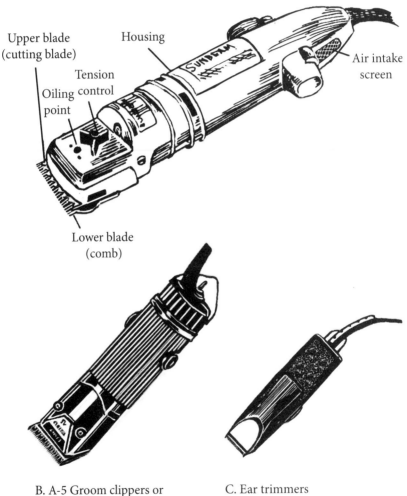

Upper blade (cutting blade)

Housing

Tension control

Oiling point

Air intake screen

Lower blade (comb)

B. A-5 Groom clippers or small animal clippers

C. Ear trimmers

FIGURE 51. *Heavy-duty clippers.*

lighter models, and the motor has the power to cut through coarse and heavy hair. They are too cumbersome for fine trimming, and their loud noise makes them less desirable to use around the horse's head. Clippers with a variable speed control can be turned down to clip at a slow speed, reducing the noise factor.

Small animal clippers or groom clippers—clippers similar to those used by professional dog groomers, perhaps the most versatile and useful model for serious show grooming. This type is more powerful than small ear trimmers, but lighter and easier to maneuver than heavy body clippers. They use interchangeable A-5 clipper blade sets that snap on and off, allowing a wide range of different blades to be used for different types of clipping.

These clippers are powerful enough to trim many horses' heads, legs, bridle paths, etc., in a day, and their smaller size and weight make them easier to use skillfully for a professional-quality trim. They are less satisfactory for body clipping than heavy-duty clippers, especially for heavy-coated horses or if several horses must be clipped. They can body-clip a single horse if the coat is clean and not too coarse, or may be used to finish a body-clipping job by clipping the head, legs, etc.

One groom clipper model combines a powerful motor, which may be wall mounted or attached to the operator's belt, with a flexible cable that transmits power to the clipper head. This type combines the advantages of the small animal clipper with interchangeable A-5 blades, with the power of a much larger clipper.

Small ear trimmers—designed to trim fine hair around the ears and muzzle closely and quietly. They are light, inexpensive, nearly noiseless, and cut more closely than heavy-duty clippers, but are not made to cut thick, heavy hair or to be run for long periods of time. Some models trim fetlocks if the hair is not too thick, but the fine blades tend to leave unattractive "clipper lines" when used on thick hair. One useful type is the battery-powered or cordless rechargeable trimmer, which can be used in a stall or at a show when an electrical outlet is not available.

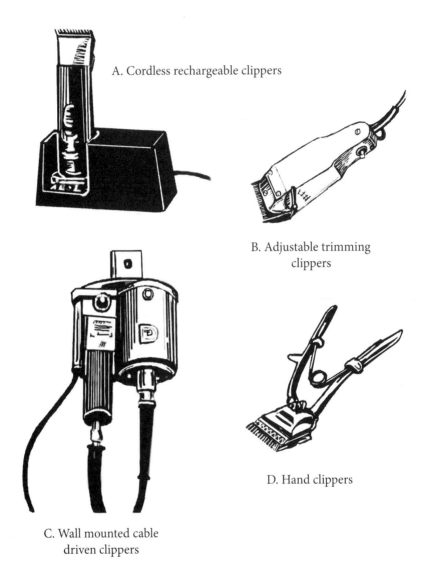

A. Cordless rechargeable clippers

B. Adjustable trimming clippers

C. Wall mounted cable driven clippers

D. Hand clippers

FIGURE 52. Other clippers.

THE MAIN PARTS OF CLIPPERS

Housing—the metal or plastic case that holds the electric motor. This must be free from cracks. The on-off switch is located on the housing.

Clipper head—the part that holds and moves the blades. There are screws or a snap-on arrangement for changing blades, and there may be oiling vents for lubrication.

Blades—Some clipper blades come in a blade set, with upper and lower blades held together by a spring and installed or removed as a unit. A set of clipper blades consists of:

> *Upper blade (cutting blade)*—a zig-zag shaped blade that cuts the hair against the teeth of the comb with a scissors-like action; only the upper blade moves.

> *Lower blade (comb)*—A fine- to coarse-toothed comb that glides over the skin and directs the hair into the cutting blade. The comb keeps the cutting blade from touching the skin. The coarser the comb, the longer it leaves the hair.

Tension adjustment—found on some models, it permits adjustment of the pressure between the upper and lower blades. The tension setting may be increased as the blades wear down, until they become too dull to clip cleanly. Use the lowest tension that will produce a clean cut, as setting the tension too high causes the blades to heat up and wears them out faster.

Lubrication points—may be located on the clipper head, or on some models, only the blades are oiled.

Air intake screen—On air-cooled models, this screen prevents hair and dirt from being sucked into the motor. It should be kept free from hair; if it becomes clogged, the motor will run hot.

Electric motor and cord—most clippers operate on 15 volt AC current; there are also cordless rechargeable and small battery-operated models. For safety, use only UL-approved clippers with a grounded plug. When the clippers are plugged in, the cord is "hot" even if the motor is switched off; if a horse should chew on the cord or step on it, breaking the insulation, he could be shocked. Unplug the clippers whenever you stop for a break, and never operate clippers in a wash stall or on a wet surface.

CLIPPER BLADES

Some clippers use only one type of blade; others accept the popular A-5 small animal clipper blades, which snap on and off and offer a variety of blade types for different purposes A-5 blades are identified by number; the most useful blades for horse clipping are:

- #10 coarse; equivalent to a standard body clipping blade
- #15 medium; for finer body clipping on head, ears, and legs
- #30 fine; for ear trimming, and bridle paths
- #40 surgical clipping; used for very fine trimming
- #10W extra-wide blade for body clipping

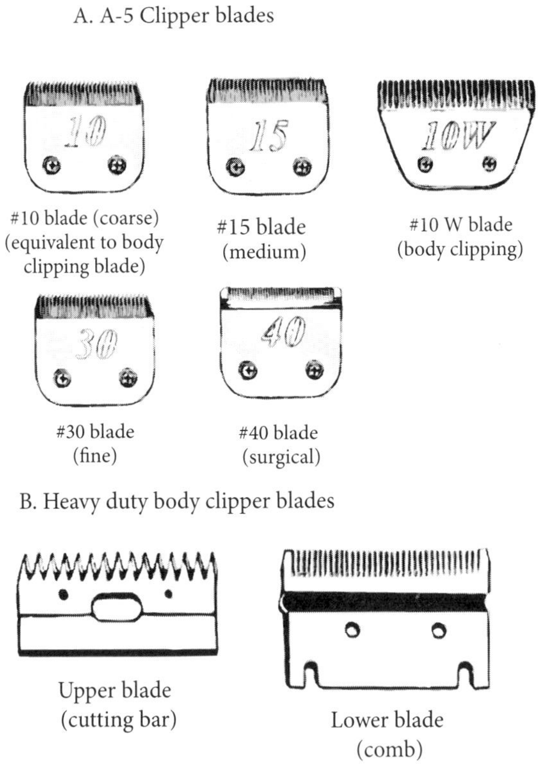

A. A-5 Clipper blades

#10 blade (coarse)
(equivalent to body
clipping blade)

#15 blade
(medium)

#10 W blade
(body clipping)

#30 blade
(fine)

#40 blade
(surgical)

B. Heavy duty body clipper blades

Upper blade
(cutting bar)

Lower blade
(comb)

FIGURE 53. Clipper blades.

Blades must be clean, sharp, and properly lubricated to clip cleanly, especially when used for trimming, brushing, or edging. If the blades become dull, hot, jammed with clipped hair, or are not cleaned, dipped, and lubricated frequently, they will not cut cleanly and will pull the hair, causing discomfort to the horse and a messy trimming job. Dipping the blades frequently in clipper wash keeps hair, scurf, and grease from accumulating between the blades, so they stay cooler, cut cleanly, and don't wear out as quickly. The clipper head should be lubricated with light oil at intervals, according to the manufacturer's directions.

Clipper blades are made of hardened steel ground to a sharp edge; they are brittle, and if dropped a tooth may break off, which will leave a ridge of unclipped hair. Most clipper blades can be resharpened (inexpensive clippers may require replacement of blades instead), but eventually they reach a point where they will not take a sharp edge and further resharpening is impossible. Clipper blades should always be resharpened as a set; replacing only one blade of a set will not work.

One set of clipper blades can do several body clips if the horses are clean and the blades are kept clean and lubricated, but they will wear out on one clip if the horse is dirty, the tension is improperly adjusted, or blade washing is neglected. Clippers should be put away clean and lubricated and kept in a clipper bag or box. Keep the instruction manual handy with the clippers, and read it—it can save a lot of trouble!

Using the Clippers: Clipping and Trimming Techniques

To clip or trim a horse, you need a suitable place to work with good lighting and an electrical outlet. It helps to have an assistant to hold the horse, but some horses are quiet enough to stand tied while being clipped or trimmed. A grooming halter or a halter that unsnaps at the throatlatch is helpful when clipping the head. You will also need clipper blade wash in an open can, clipper oil, and spray lube, plus a brush to clean the blades. The horse must be clean and dry, as wet or dirty hair is impossible to trim neatly and will ruin the blades. The clippers must be clean and lubricated, and the blades must be sharp or they will do a poor job.

CLIPPER TECHNIQUES

There are three basic ways to use the clippers: clipping, trimming, and brushing; a fourth technique is called *edging*.

Clipping—clipping against the direction of hair growth. This shortens the hair to a uniform length, which is determined by the type of blade used. Clipping is used in body clipping, booting up legs, and when a close, uniform cut is desired all over the area clipped.

Trimming—clipping "with" the hair, gliding the blades over the surface of the hair with gentle, even pressure and clipping off only the hairs that stick up into the blades. It removes less hair than clipping, leaves the hair longer and does not change the color.

Brushing—a technique in which the clippers are turned upside down and the edge of the blade is brushed along the tips of the hairs. This is used when blending a clipped or trimmed area into an unclipped area or removing long hairs that stick out from the coat.

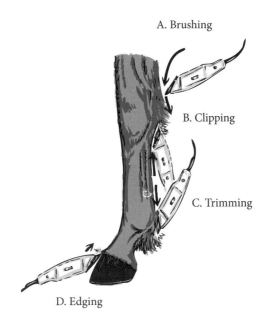

FIGURE 54. Trimming, brushing, clipping, and edging.

A. Clipping cleanly with
overlapping strokes

B. Clip against hair, keeping
blades down against the skin

FIGURE 55. Body clipping.

Edging—used to even up the edge of an area, such as the hairline at the top of the hoof. The clipper blades are brought up to the edge and slowly rocked upward, cutting the hair in a sharp, clean edge.

When clipping, hold the clippers as shown in figure 55. Clip directly against the coat, turning the clippers as required to adjust to the direction of hair growth. The back of the lower blade should glide easily over the skin and through the hair with even pressure. Clip with long, slow strokes, keeping the lower blade evenly against the skin; don't dig the edge of the blade into the skin or it will cause welts. Each stroke should overlap the last by a half inch or so.

When clipping over rounded surfaces, you will have to keep rotating the clippers to keep the blades flat against the skin and cut the hair evenly. On concave surfaces or loose skin, such as the skin of the throat or the flank, you may have to stretch the skin flat with your other hand in order to have a smooth surface to clip.

Clipping exposes the undercoat, which often makes a clipped area appear a lighter color than the surface hair. Chestnut horses appear light palomino when clipped, and bays or brown are sometimes mouse-colored. Greys, roans, and Appaloosas show the least visible difference between the clipped and unclipped coat color, so they are the best to learn on—your mistakes won't show as much!

Show Trimming

Trimming for show purposes is more detailed than the basic trim. It requires a clean horse, electric clippers, a variety of blades (well sharpened), and some skill in handling the clippers and blending the clipped or trimmed areas. The purpose of trimming is to show the refinement and definition of the head neck and legs; a poor trimming job defeats this purpose.

Some hair colors show a distinct color change when closely clipped; it takes skill and care to trim these horses without leaving the area looking "scalped." It is wise to do a major trim a week or so before a show, which gives the trimmed hair time to grow out a little and smooth the appearance.

LEG TRIMMING

For show, a horse's legs should be trimmed to present a clean, smooth, and refined appearance. Often the hair is clipped closely on white markings, to make them easier to clean, make them look whiter, and to prevent the hair from picking up dust.

For leg trimming, the blades must be sharp or they will leave unattractive clipper lines. Start with #10 or #15 blades; sometimes trimming is finished with a #30 blade, but this requires care, as fine blades can easily remove too much hair or leave clipper tracks. Using the wrong blades or uneven pressure can leave an unattractive "scalped" appearance.

To trim a leg, hold the clippers in the "trimming" position, with the blades pointing downward in the direction of the hair growth. Run them down the back of the tendon, over the joint and pastern, and under the back of the fetlock joint, pressing the front edge of the blades down gently and evenly, being careful to lift the blades gradually at the end of each stroke. If you press the blades down or take them off the leg abruptly, it will leave a noticeable line on the leg. By pressing lightly and evenly, you clip only the long outer hairs that stick out beyond the surface. Trimming thins and trims off the excess hair but does not change the color of the trimmed area.

If the horse has long hair or "feather" at the back of the knee or hock, trim this by running the clippers downward, in the direction of hair growth. Blend carefully! Carefully work around the tendon groove and the contours of the leg and pastern. You may have to go over each area several times until it is clean, smooth, and tidy.

Trim the fetlock by picking up the foot and running the clippers around and under the bulge of the fetlock joint. The *ergot* (a small, horny growth at the back of the fetlock, similar to the dew claw of a dog) may have to be snipped off with scissors to allow you to trim the fetlock hair closely. Trim downward and backward, in the direction of the hair growth.

Reverse the clippers and trim the edge of the hair at the coronary band by clipping upward, making an even edge all around the foot.

BOOTING UP

Booting up is closely clipping the lower legs, clipping against the hair growth, from the coronary band up to the base of the knee or hock. This shortens the hair to the length of a short body clip, but may change the color of the hair by exposing the undercoat. It is often done to make white legs appear whiter and easier to keep clean, to show the refinement of the legs and tendons, or to remove coarse, heavy hair that obscures the structure of the legs.

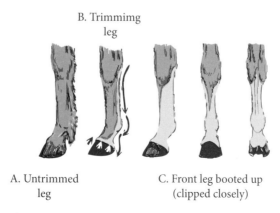

B. Trimmimg
leg

A. Untrimmed
leg

C. Front leg booted up
(clipped closely)

FIGURE 56. Front Leg: trimming and booting up.

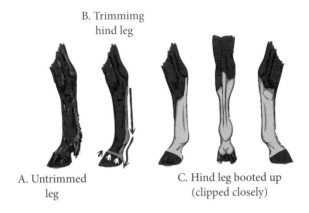

B. Trimmimg
hind leg

A. Untrimmed
leg

C. Hind leg booted up
(clipped closely)

FIGURE 57. Hind Leg: trimming and booting up.

When booting up legs, use #10 or #15 blades; never extremely close-clipping blades such as #40 blades (surgical blades). These cut too closely, leaving obvious lines and clipper tracks, and can leave the legs looking as it they have been shaved for surgery instead of trimmed for a show! If the legs are "scalped" by being clipped too closely, white legs appear pink or inflamed, nicks or blemishes are too obvious, and the legs are left without enough hair for protection.

To boot up a leg, hold the clippers in the "clipping" position and clip upward from the coronary band, working up over the fetlock joint and along the tendons to the bones at the base of the knee or hock. Go over each area until the hair is clipped uniformly short, with no lines, long patches or "clipper tracks." The clipped area must be carefully blended at the top, following the contours of the lower edge of the knee or hock and leaving a V down the front of the cannon bone. If a horse has high white leg markings, sometimes the entire white marking is clipped, blending carefully at the edges.

TRIMMING THE HEAD

You will need #10 blades for general clipping; #15 or #30 blades for finer clipping, and a #40 (surgical blade) if you want super-sharp trimming of the ears.

Closely trimming the long hair between the jawbones and under the throat greatly improves the shape and appearance of the horse's head and neck. With the #10 blades, trim the hair from the sides and underside of

FIGURE 58. Untrimmed and trimmed head.

the lower jaw. Work in the direction of the hair growth, with the blades held in the "trimming" position. You may also hold the blades in the "brushing" position (see diagram) to trim hair around the indentations of the lower face and jaw. Turn the blades around into the "clipping" position and clip closely along the bottom edge and between the bones of the lower jaw. Don't clip the hair of the cheek or jowl unless you plan to clip the entire head.

TRIMMING WHISKERS

For most American show horses, it is customary to trim the whiskers off.

To clip the muzzle hairs, use the #10 blades to trim them off close to the skin. Check the muzzle from all angles to see if you have left any hairs untrimmed. The whiskers can be clipped even closer by switching to #40 blades, or by finishing with a plastic safety razor. Be careful not to clip the fine hair of the muzzle as you clip the whiskers—it will leave noticeable lines and marks if you do. The long whiskers near the eyes may be trimmed in the same way.

If you clip the muzzle whiskers, they should be kept close-trimmed by clipping frequently. The whiskers grow out to short, stiff "nubs," which cause discomfort when they bump into things. *Never* clip the eyelashes or the hairs inside the nostrils—these are essential for the horse's safe functioning and comfort.

EAR TRIMMING

To trim the ears, the #40 blades give the sharpest line. Hold the ear in one hand and clip along the outer edges, clipping downward on the upper part of the ear and upward along the lower curve of the ear. To give the ear a neater appearance without removing the protective hair, the inside hair can be trimmed level with the outer edges. This is sometimes more flattering to horses with large ears, which tend to appear larger if completely clipped out.

Halter horses and high-level show horses usually have their ears clipped clean on the inside; a tiny "diamond" of unclipped hair is left at the tip of the ear, to bring it to a natural point.

FIGURE 59. Trimming the ears.

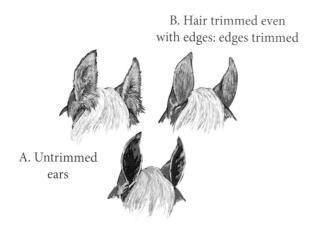

B. Hair trimmed even
with edges: edges trimmed

A. Untrimmed
ears

C. Ears clipped clean inside,
leaving points

FIGURE 60. Trimming and clipping the ears.

Before clipping the inside of the ear, place a large piece of cotton down inside in the ear to deaden the noise of the clippers and to keep hair from falling down inside the ear. Use the #40 blades to clip the hair closely, right down to the skin. You may have to open and gently invert the ear to trim it clean inside. Brush the inside of the ear clean of hair clippings before removing the cotton. Some showmen use human hair remover cream to completely remove the hair from the inside of the ears. If you do this, protect the inner ear with cotton and make sure the cream doesn't run down inside the ear. If the ears are clipped inside, the horse will need a fly mask with ear covers when she is turned out.

Bridle Path

Before trimming a show bridle path, consult your breed standard, as the requirements vary.

Part the mane at the starting point of the bridle path and clip forward to just behind the bump at the poll. Clipping forward helps prevent a bridle path from getting longer each time it is trimmed, as might happen if you clip back toward the mane. Trim the bridle path closely by clipping upward from the hair coat to the center of the crest, but be careful not to clip into the hair coat, which will leave an obvious "scalped" line. The #40 (surgical) clipper blades give the closest, neatest trim.

A. Measuring bridle path by length of ear
(for six-to-eight-inch bridle path)

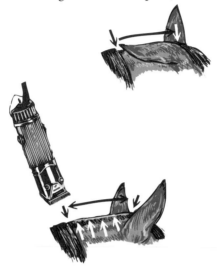

B. Clip forward, backward, and across bridle path.

FIGURE 61. Trimming a bridle path.

Forelock Trimming

If a horse has a large, bushy forelock or long fuzzy hair around the base of the ears, some careful clipping and trimming can make the area appear trimmer. Hold up the forelock and trim a narrow strip from each side of the forelock, and a short section underneath.

The hair between the ears and forelock may be trimmed or closely clipped, but this area is difficult to blend with the longer hair behind the ears and often results in an obvious color change. It is usually best to clip this area only when doing an extended face trim or a full head clip.

Clipping the Face and Head

For high-level halter competition, white markings, the hair around the muzzle and eyes, the face, or the whole head may be clipped closely. However, the hair must be left long enough to protect the skin from sunburn, and the area should not look "scalped." If a horse's face is clipped, he will need extra protection from the sun.

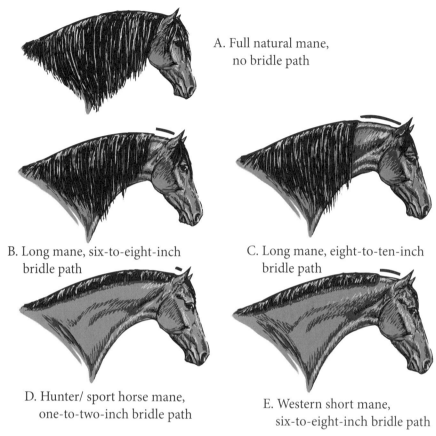

A. Full natural mane,
no bridle path

B. Long mane, six-to-eight-inch
bridle path

C. Long mane, eight-to-ten-inch
bridle path

D. Hunter/ sport horse mane,
one-to-two-inch bridle path

E. Western short mane,
six-to-eight-inch bridle path

FIGURE 62. Bridle path.

FACE CLIP

A face clip involves clipping the sides of the muzzle and lower face up to the edge of the cheekbones. A more extensive facial clip extends up the front of the face to an inverted V formed by the frontal bones and the muscles of the forehead, and over the eyelids. The hair of the eyelids, around the eyes, and above the cheekbones may be closely clipped but should not be shaved bald, and the eyelashes must not be touched. Do not clip the cheek or jowl, or it will change the color of the hair too obviously; they should simply trimmed smooth underneath.

Face clipping must be especially smooth and even or it will look worse than not trimming at all. Use #10 blades; finer blades remove too much hair, giving the face a bald, scalped appearance.

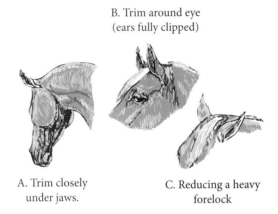

B. Trim around eye
(ears fully clipped)

A. Trim closely
under jaws.

C. Reducing a heavy
forelock

FIGURE 63. Trimming the face.

Holding the clippers in the "clipping" position, clip the sides of the muzzle and lower face up to the edge of the cheekbone. Blend the clipping upward as you approach the edge of the nasal bone. When clipping near the eye, put your thumb over the eye, gently holding it closed. This protects the eye and stretches the skin so it is smoother and easier to clip. A #15 blade can be used to clip the area around the eyes and down to the cheekbones, but the clipping must be very smooth and even. This makes the skin appear darker and the horse's eyes appear larger.

Full Head Clip

A full head clip may be used when it is not feasible to body-clip the whole horse but the head and neck must appear at their finest. It is useful when showing foals or weanlings or when a horse in winter coat needs its head and neck shown off to best advantage.

For a full head clip, the entire face and head are clipped, including the cheeks, jaw, face, forehead, and ears, and back to the end of the bridle path. The clipping is extended a short distance down the front of the neck, making a V by clipping along the jugular groove and up to the back of the jaw.

Apron Clip

An Apron clip is a full head clip that extends the full length of the jugular groove and down to the chest; this shows off the underline of the neck. Sometimes this clip is combined with a strip clip or other modified body clip.

A. Basic show trim : muzzle, jaw, eyes, ears, and bridle path

B. Face clipped to inverted V on forehead; ears, bridle path, and throat trimmed.

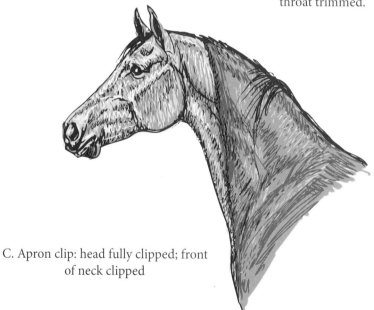

C. Apron clip: head fully clipped; front of neck clipped

FIGURE 64. *Details of trimming the face.*

BODY CLIPPING

Although a horse's winter coat serves him well when he lives a natural outdoor life, it can be a handicap to a hard-working horse and a problem for his groom. A winter coat is designed for warmth and insulation, not cooling; when a horse works hard, the coat becomes soaked with sweat and is heavy, clammy, and uncomfortable. In cold weather a wet coat quickly conducts heat away from the body, exposing the horse to chills, and may take hours to dry. In warmer weather, the sweat mixes with scurf to produce a thick, gummy lather that does not dry rapidly or cool the body efficiently, so the horse tires more quickly and is in danger of over-heating. A heavy winter coat is difficult to groom, as the body brush does not penetrate thick winter hair and the dandy brush only brings more scurf and dandruff to the surface. A horse that sweats excessively in ordinary work and remains wet long after he has cooled out, might be better off with some type of body clip.

Body clipping shortens the coat to a bit below its summer length. It permits quicker evaporation of sweat, more rapid drying and easier grooming, besides making the horse more comfortable while working and improving his appearance. A clipped horse must be blanketed according to the temperature and protected from chills and cold. Body clipping exposes the undercoat, which may temporarily change the coat color.

Some reasons to consider a body clip or partial clip include:

- Horses doing strenuous work (such as foxhunting) in winter

- Horses showing in winter

- Horses ridden daily in indoor arenas

- Horses moving from a cool climate to a hot climate

- Any horse that is frequently overheating or taking too long to cool out and dry off after work

- Horses that retain a long coat, fail to shed out, and suffer from the heat in summer

Body clipping may range from an all-over full clip to partial clips that leave the horse with much of his natural cold-weather protection but shorten the coat over the places that sweat the most. The more extensive the clipping, the more blanketing and care the horse will require; a horse with a minimal clip may be able to be turned out or even live outside in some climates without blanketing.

Types of Body Clips

Full clip—all-over body clip used for show horses; the head, body, and legs are completely clipped.

Hunter clip—used on field hunters and horses that work outdoors across country. The body and head are clipped, and the hair is left on the legs ("stockings"); a "saddle patch" in the shape of the saddle is left to protect the skin of the back.

Trace clip—a partial clip that originated in the days of harness horses; the belly, chest, and sides are clipped to a line at the level of the traces. A trace clip may be extended to include part or all of the head and neck, or along the lower side of the hindquarters.

High trace clip—an extended trace clip with the line of the clip higher along the hindquarters, sides, neck, and shoulders.

Racing clip—more extensive clip, including the neck, shoulders, chest, and sides of the belly and hindquarters, with a "keyhole" following the contour of the flank.

Blanket clip—clipping the neck, chest, belly, and sometimes the legs, leaving a neatly squared-off "blanket" of long hair.

Strip clip—minimal clip including the chest, belly, and a strip on the underside of the neck.

The benefits of partial clips are that the horse has most of his winter coat and may not always need blanketing, but does not get as hot and dries more quickly. The long hair over the loins keeps the back muscles from chills, and the "stockings" (long hair left on the legs) protect against mud, brush, and thorns. Horses with a high trace clip or blanket clip will need blanketing, and those with a hunter clip or a full body clip will need the most blanketing and care.

If you body-clip a horse, he will need at least one warm winter blanket, a cooler, and a turnout rug. A trace-clipped horse can sometimes go without blanketing, but may need a turnout rug if the weather turns cold. A horse with a strip clip usually does not need blanketing.

It is best to wait until the winter coat is well established and the summer coat is fully shed before clipping. If you clip early, you may need to repeat the clip after the coat finishes growing in. In the spring, clipping

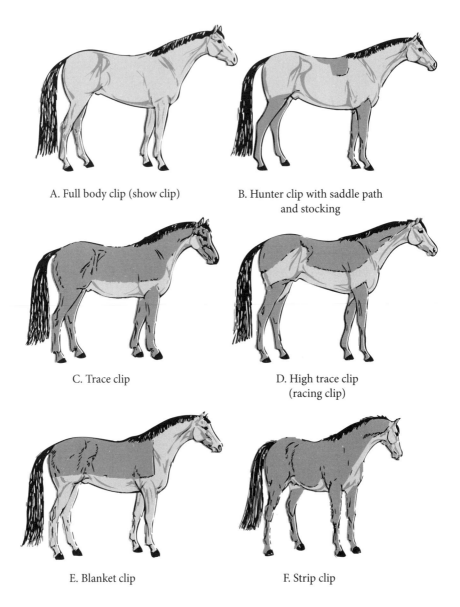

A. Full body clip (show clip)

B. Hunter clip with saddle path
and stocking

C. Trace clip

D. High trace clip
(racing clip)

E. Blanket clip

F. Strip clip

FIGURE 65. Types of clips.

should be done before the horse begins to shed or you will clip the ends of the in-growing summer coat which spoils the looks of the summer coat. A full clip will usually grow out completely in about three months, although this varies from horse to horse and according to the climate.

CLIPPING PREPARATIONS

To body-clip a horse, you will need heavy-duty body clippers with newly sharpened blades, a can of clipper wash, clipper oil for lubrication, and clipper lubricating spray to cool the blades. Work in a well-lighted area with a grounded electrical outlet—not in a wash stall or on a wet surface. A drop light on a long cord is helpful for checking your work. Wear coveralls with a slick surface that will not pick up loose hair and a cap or bandanna to cover your hair.

The horse should be as clean as possible. If possible, he should be bathed or if not, thoroughly groomed, vacuumed, and cleaned all over with a hot towel. Spraying the coat with silicone coat polish makes the hair slick, which helps the clippers cut smoothly and efficiently. Have a blanket or cooler to cover the horse while you work, and do not body clip on an especially cold day.

A novice should learn to clip on a patient, quiet horse that is unconcerned about clippers. (A grey or roan is ideal, as these colors don't show any mistakes as much as bay or chestnut.) If possible, have someone experienced help you the first time you clip.

If you plan to do a hunter clip, trace clip, or a partial clip, the edges of the clipped area must be marked out first. Even if you plan to do a full clip, it is wise to start with a trace clip, extend it to a hunter clip and then finish by clipping off the rest of the legs, etc. This way, if you have to stop before completing the job, you will still be left with an acceptable clip. To mark out an area, you can use a marking pen (washable, not permanent), but masking tape is easier and will not leave marks on the hair. Use strips of masking tape to mark the edges of the stockings or the border of a trace clip or a strip clip.

For a hunter clip, place a saddle on the horse's back and use masking tape to mark around it; this will make sure your saddle patch is properly placed and conforms to the shape of your saddle. When you clip, make the saddle patch two inches smaller than the actual outline of the saddle, so it will not show when the horse is saddled.

Use tape to outline an inverted V at the top of the dock. Before clipping around the hindquarters, the tail should be completely covered with a tail bandage, so it cannot be switched into the path of the clippers and get clipped by accident.

BODY CLIPPING TECHNIQUE

When you start clipping, begin on a less sensitive area like the shoulder. Turn the clippers on and draw the machine backward down the shoulder several times to get the horse used to the vibration; if he's quiet, you can begin to clip. The clippers must always work directly against the direction the hair grows—you will have to turn and maneuver them to follow the swirls and contours of the horse's body. Keep the bottom blade pressed lightly but evenly against the horse's skin and use the same pressure for every stroke, so you don't leave patches of longer hair. Make long, slow smooth strokes, overlapping each stroke by an inch. Don't dig the corner of the blade into the horse's skin—this is uncomfortable and will raise a welt, although the moving blades will not reach his skin. If there is a ridge of unclipped hair or a patch of longer hair, go over that place again until it is clipped evenly.

Stop frequently to dip the blades into a can of clipper wash (*don't* dip the motor!). Run the clippers for a moment to allow the hair and clipper wash to drip away, then turn them off and wipe them dry with a rag. Spraying the blades occasionally with spray lubricant keeps them cooler and running better. A high-pitched, laboring noise indicates that the blades are clogged with hair and need cleaning. Keep the air intake screen free from hair or the motor may begin to run hot. If the clippers stop cutting cleanly, a wad of hair may have become stuck between the blades. Unplug the clippers, clean the blades, and use a screwdriver to remove the

FIGURE 66. Taping and clipping details.

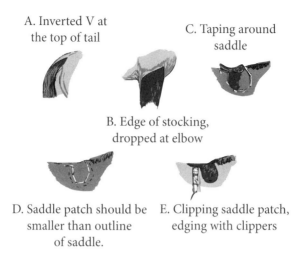

A. Inverted V at the top of tail

C. Taping around saddle

B. Edge of stocking, dropped at elbow

D. Saddle patch should be smaller than outline of saddle.

E. Clipping saddle patch, edging with clippers

FIGURE 67. Body clipping details.

bottom blade. Remove any hair and wipe the blades clean, then replace the bottom blade exactly as it was. Usually this will solve the problem.

If the blades do not cut efficiently, tighten the tension a quarter turn at a time until they produce a clean cut. New blades do not need too much tension, but they will need tightening as they wear down. Overtightening the tension makes the blades heat up and wear out quicker. When the blades will no longer produce a clean cut with the tension fully tightened, they are too dull to clip and need resharpening. Newly sharpened blades should go through about three body clips if the horses are clean, but one dirty horse will wear out a set of blades.

If you notice that the blades are beginning to heat up, stop clipping, clean them and put the machine aside for a while before continuing. Hot blades are uncomfortable for the horse and do not cut efficiently. Besides, both you and the horse may need a rest.

The most efficient way to clip is to work in sections, usually from back to front. Clip each section completely, brush it off with a body brush, and then use a drop light to check your work. If you see "railroad tracks" (ridges of longer hair left by uneven pressure or careless overlapping of strokes) or patches of longer hair, go over them again, carefully clipping against the lay of the hair, until they are as closely and evenly clipped as the rest of the body. By clipping and each part thoroughly, you will take care of any missed spots before you finish the job.

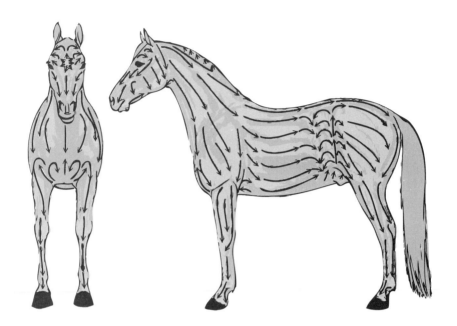

FIGURE 68. Direction of hair growth.

When clipping the head, much patience and care is needed. It is easier to clip the smaller planes of the head and face with small animal (groom) clippers, using #10 blades or a #10W body clipping blade. *Never* use ear trimmers or trimming blades to clip the head and face—they will leave ugly scalped spots, uneven hair and clipper tracks!

Clip upward along the jaw to the edge of the cheekbone and the ridge of bone between the eye and the ear; in some cases, the clipping can end at this spot and still look presentable. Clip up to the base of the ear and the muscles of the top of the neck behind it. For a perfect clip, the face, forehead, temples, and the outside of the ears should also be clipped, but be very careful not to clip into the forelock when clipping the forehead and near the ears.

When clipping along the top of the neck, have a helper place an arm over the mane so it will not fall into the path of the clippers. Be careful about clipping too close to the mane, as any mane hairs you clip will stick straight up as they grow out. When clipping the inverted V at the top of the tail and around the tail area, be careful not to clip any tail hairs.

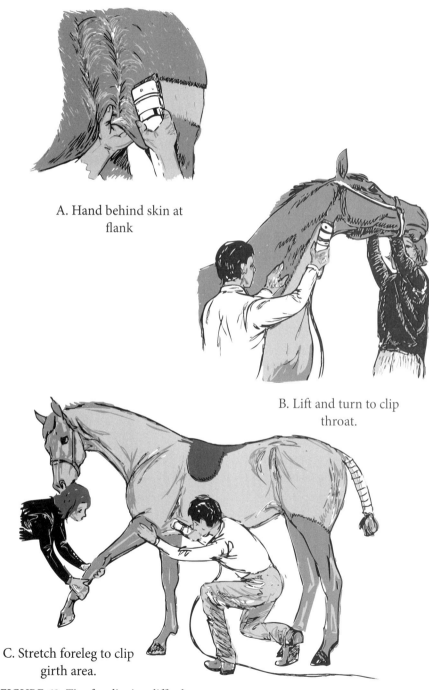

A. Hand behind skin at flank

B. Lift and turn to clip throat.

C. Stretch foreleg to clip girth area.

FIGURE 69. *Tips for clipping difficult areas.*

To clip the throat, have an assistant hold the horse's head as high as she can and turn it away from you. You may also have to stretch the skin with your fingers to give the clippers a taut surface to clip over.

To clip the flank, first clip down the center of the "swirl." Then, move the clippers in an arc toward the center of the clipped area. Hold your hand behind the loose skin at the bottom of the flank and stretch it taut with your fingers.

To clip the girth area and the inside of the foreleg, have a helper hold up the horse's foreleg and stretch it forward. This stretches the skin behind the elbow so you can clip the girth area. While the leg is held up, you can also clip the inside of the opposite forearm.

When clipping stockings, the edge of a trace clip or a saddle patch, you can mark out the edge of the area by clipping in a single slow, smooth stroke. In other areas, you may have to use the technique of "edging." Run the clipper blades run slowly and carefully up to the line, then carefully lift them to cut a sharp, neat edge. When clipping stockings, the top line of the stocking on the hind leg may be slanted, cut straight across or slightly rounded. On the foreleg, the edge of the stocking should follow the contour of the arm muscle.

When clipping, stop frequently to give your horse a rest and a pat and brush the clipped hair away. Check your work and catch any mistakes that need reclipping. Keep the horse covered except for the part you are actually working on; he feels the loss of her winter coat keenly and can easily catch cold.

After clipping, your horse's coat will have a mousy look because the dandruff and scurf is close to the surface and visible. Fine-skinned horses sometimes show temporary "clipper welts" caused by the edge of the machine turning up the hair; these are harmless and quickly disappear. A good grooming and a hot towel treatment will quickly clean the coat right down to the skin, or you can follow up with a bath and a hot oil treatment to restore the shine and softness of the coat.

Introducing a Horse to Clippers

A quiet, patient introduction to clippers can save untold time and trouble. Horses are naturally suspicious of things that buzz, and if they are forced to stand while it is applied to their head and body, it's no wonder if some become terrified. Most horses can learn to accept clippers if they are introduced patiently and quietly, and if they aren't hurt or allowed to escape. However, if a horse comes to associate clippers with pain, fear, or a fight, he will be on the defensive at the first sign of clipping. Good clipper training can make the difference between a horse that's easy to clip and one that is difficult, annoying or even dangerous.

Two helpful training methods are the T.E.A.M. techniques developed by Linda Tellington-Jones, and clicker training. T.E.A.M. work uses a system of touches and groundwork exercises to teach horses confidence, relaxation, and alternatives to defensive behavior. Clicker training (known as "operant conditioning" in behavioral psychology) is a method of using positive reinforcement to train desirable behaviors. Both are safe, non-forceful, and have many practical applications beyond training to clip.

Teaching a horse to accept clippers takes time and patience. Don't try this if you're in a hurry, cross, or impatient. If you breathe deeply and talk quietly with a soothing tone, it will help her relax; yelling, jerking, or punishment will only confirm her fears.

TEACHING TRUST AND HEAD LOWERING

The first step is teaching the horse to lower his head, because lowering the head goes with calmness, trust and acceptance, while a high head is on the defensive, ready to flee. Reach up and rest your hand on his neck just behind the ears, and apply pressure downward with your fingers; be tactful, but clear and insistent. When he makes the slightest move to lower his head, instantly relax the pressure, praise, and reward. Gradually he will learn to lower his head when you press down on the top of his neck; you may teach him a command like "Head down."

When the horse will lower his head, gently rub his neck, poll, and the base of his ears, to get him used to having these parts handled comfortably. If he's afraid of having his ears handled, he'll be twice as scared if you try to clip them!

Next, introduce the clippers. Let him sniff the clippers (unplugged, with the cord wrapped up); rub his neck, cheek, and head with the clippers as if they were a brush. Then let the cord dangle as you continue. If he gets nervous, use the "head down" signal, back off to a stage that he's comfortable with, and then repeat the next step.

The next step is to get the horse used to the noise of the clippers. Have someone switch on the clippers a little distance away. If the horse is nervous, have your assistant remain where he is, with the clippers running, while you ask the horse to lower his head and reassure him, and only bring the clippers closer when he's calm. Don't rush this stage of training, but don't turn the clippers off if he's acting up, or he'll learn that acting up makes the noise go away; turn them off only when he is standing quietly. Sometimes it helps to leave the clippers running outside the stall during feeding time, until the horse no longer reacts to the noise.

Once the horse is unconcerned or merely interested in the running clippers, move the clippers around; turn them on and off, and bring them close enough to touch him. Place your hand against his shoulder and hold the running clippers against the back of your hand, which muffles the vibration. Then hold the housing of the clippers against his shoulder and let him feel them running (but not clipping hair). Work down the legs, up the neck, and gradually up to his head until she tolerates the clippers on all the places you plan to clip. If he gets tense, ask him to lower his head; reward with praise, rubbing, and a tidbit when he complies.

When the horse accepts the clippers, you can begin trimming. It often helps to trim the front legs first, then work on the head. Your assistant can ask the horse to lower his head if he gets tense or fidgety, and can help

FIGURE 70. Introducing clippers quietly.

keep him still by holding up a front foot. Be careful not to jab the horse with the corner of the blades, and stop before the blades become uncomfortably hot.

This process may go better if spread out over several days. Work with the clippers a little each time you groom, always insisting on lowering the head and finishing on a good note. Perhaps you can trim the front legs one day, the hind legs the next, then work on his head and jaw, and finally do the bridle path and ears.

When body clipping, start on a less sensitive part of the body, such as the shoulder. Once the horse has become accustomed to clipping, you can proceed to more sensitive areas like the belly, flanks, and head. If a horse has been trimmed on the head and legs without fuss, he will usually accept body clipping with less trouble.

RESTRAINTS FOR CLIPPING

While it is always best to train a horse to accept clipping without fuss, there are some horses that are restless or difficult to clip. You may have to use a restraint in order to protect yourself, your helpers, and the horse and to get the job done safely. Always use the least restraint that will do the job, stay calm but aware, and protect yourself in case a horse resists or acts up.

One of the simplest restraints is holding up a front foot, using a toe hold. Pick up the foot on the side you are working on, and hold it with your hand over the sole of the foot, and your fingers gripping the toe. In this position, if the horse leans on you or tries to take his foot away, you can flex his ankle a bit more and move with him; if you have to let him go, you can safely get out of his way.

The most common restraint is the lip twitch; it will keep many horses quiet for ear clipping or similar procedures. When properly applied, a twitch causes the horse to release brain chemicals called endorphins, which have a calming effect. However, some horses fight the application of a twitch, so use this only if it works for that horse.

To apply a twitch, the loop is placed over the upper lip and tightened by twisting the handle toward the lip. "Humane" twitches look like a pair of aluminum tongs—these are squeezed on the lip and then snapped to the halter. A "one-man" twitch can be made by snapping a large double-end snap into a 6-inch loop of rope. The loop is tightened around the lip by twisting the snap, which is snapped to the side ring of the halter.

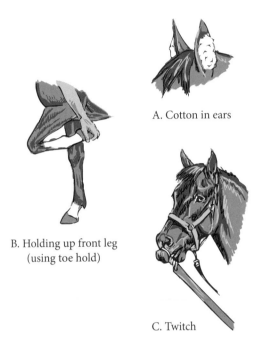

A. Cotton in ears

B. Holding up front leg
(using toe hold)

C. Twitch

FIGURE 71. Restraints for clipping.

If you must use a twitch, apply it quietly, remove it as soon as possible, and rub the horse's lip after removing it so that he does not learn that every time you handle his muzzle you put a twitch on it! *Never* apply a twitch to any part of the horse except the upper lip. Besides being brutally painful, using a twitch on an ear or elsewhere can cause permanent injuries.

Many horses are easier to clip if a ear plugs or cotton are stuffed gently into each ear. This deadens the clipper noise and prevents hair from getting into the ears. A handler can take a firm hold on the base of the ear, squeezing it shut to deaden the noise and steady the head but *not* twisting it or hurting it. A hand cupped over the eye may also help when clipping near that area, and protects the eye from being bumped by the clippers if the horse should toss his head.

If despite your best effort, a horse will not stand for clippers with a simple restraint humanely applied, it is better to tranquilize him than to fight him. Tranquilizers are best administered by a veterinarian, who can give the correct dose so that it acts quickly and safely. If you use a tranquilizer, do so well in advance of any competition and check the USEF Medications pamphlet to learn how long to allow for the drug to clear his system to avoid a positive drug test and penalties.

Chapter 8

Blankets and Horse Clothing

Blankets, sheets, rugs, and other horse clothing are used to keep horses warm, dry, and clean and to protect them from flies and the elements. They can also be used to induce horses to maintain a short coat instead of growing a winter coat. Blanketing is a common practice in cold climates and in show stables. However, using blankets and horse clothing is one of the more artificial things we can do in keeping horses, and it requires knowledge, expense, and daily work. It's important to know what purpose you want horse clothing to serve, how to select, fit, and maintain it, and how to manage a blanketed horse.

Why Blanket? Nature versus Nurture

Horses are naturally adapted to handle cold weather. Many horses live well outdoors even in harsh climates if they are allowed to grow a full winter coat and have adequate nutrition and shelter. Most horses will adapt to cold or warm climates by growing more or less winter coat, but this process may take a year or longer. However, some horses always have a thin coat and are less able to withstand extreme cold.

WHEN A BLANKET MAY BE NEEDED

Even if you don't routinely blanket, there are some reasons to keep a stable blanket on hand. Horses that are old, thin-skinned, debilitated, or lacking a full winter coat may need blanketing during extreme cold or when turned out in cold or wet conditions. Foals born during extreme cold may require extra warmth, and a sick horse may need blanketing to prevent chills. Horses being shipped may require blanketing because of the cold draft of a moving vehicle (however, it is important not to over-blanket a horse in a trailer, as this can make him sweat and then become chilled). A horse whose coat is wet with sweat must be protected from drafts and chills until he is dry, and sometimes you may want to use a sheet or blanket to keep a horse clean overnight. And if you clip your horse, blankets and other clothing replace the coat removed by clipping.

Winter Care

Horses that live, work, or are turned outside in winter conditions need good management and careful observation. Harsh weather requires extra calories and can deplete horses' reserves of fat, so they need shelter from wind and freezing rain to conserve energy and body heat.

A horse's winter coat keeps him warm because of its *loft* or air spaces between the hairs, which insulate the skin like a down comforter, and the natural skin oils which resist wetness. In order to stay warm, his coat must be dry and fluffy. Blankets flatten down the hair, reducing the loft so the coat loses its insulating qualities. A blanket must be warm enough to make up for this; a light sheet that flattens the coat may actually leave a horse colder than no blanket at all.

Some horses fail to grow enough coat or are less robust and need extra warmth and protection, especially in severe weather. Cold wind can penetrate the coat, and continuous exposure to cold, wet, and muddy conditions may lead to breakdown of the skin, resulting in rain-rot or mud fever (scratches). Dirty, scurfy skin provides an ideal environment for bacterial or fungal infections and opportunistic parasites such as lice, which can further debilitate a horse. Early signs of weight loss may not be obvious under a winter coat. Some horses need the extra protection of a turnout rug to keep them warm and dry.

It's important to notice how much a long-coated horse is sweating during work, because he can easily get overheated, and a wet coat exposes him to chills and takes a long time to dry. This is one reason for clipping horses that work hard in cold weather.

Drying a Wet Coat

When a long-coated horse gets wet and sweat-soaked, he must be protected from wind, cold, and chills. Scrape the sweat away and rub the wet spots with a towel or a handful of straw. Allowing a horse to roll in dry sand or sawdust will blot up the sweat and hasten drying; you can brush him clean later. Cover the horse with a cooler and keep him in a draft-free stall until his coat is dry. Don't put on his regular blanket until he is dry, or the lining will become damp and clammy from sweat. His coat must be dry and brushed out before it will keep him warm again.

An open-weave "fish-net" cooler underneath a sheet or light blanket can help dry the coat; so can the old horseman's practice of *thatching*, or stuffing a thick layer of straw up under a blanket or sheet. Both the straw and the open-weave cooler trap air next to the horse for warmth, allow moisture to evaporate, and absorb wetness. You can also use a hair dryer or the warm air blower of a horse vacuum cleaner to dry a wet coat.

BLANKETING FOR A SHORT COAT

One reason for blanketing is to induce a horse to retain a short, fine coat instead of growing a winter coat. An unclipped coat is softer and richer in color, so many showmen prefer to blanket horses and keep them under lights, making their systems believe it is summertime even in the dead of winter.

When his coat is clipped or kept artificially short by blanketing, a horse becomes a "hothouse flower" who is more vulnerable to chills and drafts and needs extra care. He is sensitive to cold, yet he needs fresh air and good ventilation. His blankets must fit, be kept clean and properly adjusted, and must be added or taken off as the temperature changes. During exercise he should be kept warm, protected from cold wind, and covered when he is not working. Since blanketing requires more work, daily attention, and expense, it is better to leave a horse natural unless you need him to keep an artificially short coat and have the time to care for him.

BLANKETING AND LIGHTS

To keep his coat short, a horse should begin wearing a sheet whenever the temperature dips below 60 degrees at night. As the weather becomes cooler, the sheet is replaced by a light blanket, then a medium weight blanket, and in very cold weather a warm insulated blanket, blanket liner, and a full hood may be necessary. He will also need a turnout rug. Blanketing must be adjusted according to the weather; warm weather requires lighter blankets and when the temperature dips, warmer clothing must be added.

In addition, as daylight shortens, stall lights (200 watts per stall) are kept on from 6 A.M. to 9 P.M. to simulate long summer light. The stable temperature should be regulated to between 45 degrees and 50 degrees Fahrenheit. This process acts on the horse's hypothalamus (the part of the brain which reacts to changing seasons) which makes the horse maintain a short coat or, if it is begun in January, stimulates him to shed his winter coat early. It will also bring mares into their spring reproductive cycle.

BLANKETING A BODY-CLIPPED HORSE

If you plan to body clip, it is best to avoid blanketing and allow the horse to grow his winter coat. After he is clipped, blankets and other clothing take the place of his winter coat; if he is used to being blanketed he will need even warmer blankets after clipping.

A fully clipped horse will usually need a warm stable blanket, turnout rug, lighter stable blanket and a cooler. A nylon under-sheet or shoulder protector may be necessary to protect against rubs. Depending the climate and on how he is kept, he may also need a hood, a warm blanket liner, and a quarter sheet if he is ridden outside in cold weather.

Types of Horse Clothing

STABLE BLANKETS AND SHEETS

Stable blankets are worn in the stable, for warmth, cleanliness, and protection of the coat. They come in light, medium, and heavy weights, and a variety of linings and outer materials, including nylon, polyester, cotton, canvas, and Cordura; some blankets contain a layer of insulation. A good stable blanket should be washable and of a breathable material. The lining should be smooth, so it will not rough up the coat; nylon is the least likely to rub.

Stable sheets are lightweight, unlined clothing shaped like a stable blanket, made of washable cotton, polyester, nylon, or Cordura. Sheets provide much less warmth than blankets and are used to keep the coat clean in the stall or during travel.

Dress sheets or day rugs are formal wear that display the owner's stable colors and monogram and are often used as awards. They are used in the stable or to keep a horse warm and clean while waiting to show, especially in cold weather.

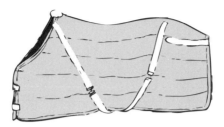

A. Stable blanket

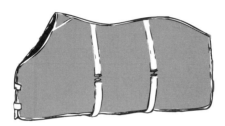

B. Sheet

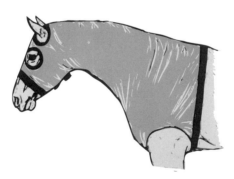

C. Lycra shoulder protector

Figure 72. Stable Blanket.

UNDERCLOTHING

Underclothing is used under clothing for extra warmth or protection against rubbing. *Shoulder, head, and neck, or full body protectors* (called "sleazies"). are made of a stretchy nylon material that is smooth against the coat and allows blankets to slip over it without rubbing. *Blanket liners* are usually made of synthetic fleece and add an extra layer of warmth.

Turnout Rugs and Sheets

Turnout rugs are sturdy blankets used during turnout; they have hind leg straps to keep them secure when a horse rolls and plays. They are made of waterproof or water-resistant materials that should breathe, allowing water vapor to escape, and must be impervious to mud, rain, and wind, and resistant to tears and damage. Canvas, nylon, and Cordura are popular materials. Turnout rugs or blankets come in heavy, medium, and light weights; winter turnout sheets do not contribute as much warmth and are used primarily to keep a horse clean and dry.

Summer turnout sheets (also called *fly sheets*) are made of a sturdy open-weave material that allows the horse to stay cool but keeps flies off his coat. Many models also protect against the ultraviolet rays of the sun, to prevent bleaching of the coat.

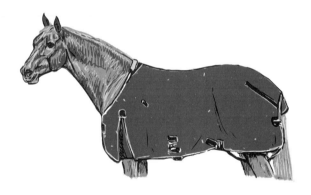

A. Turnout rug

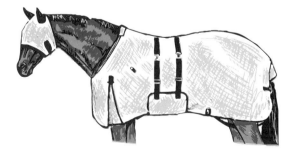

B. Summer turnout sheet and fly mask

Figure 73. Turnout rug.

OTHER HORSE CLOTHING

Hoods and neck covers are worn to protect the neck and head from cold, and to protect the mane. They should be attached to the blanket with an elastic fastening, so that they cannot shift over the horse's head. Neck covers, which do not cover the horse's head, are safer for turnout, as they cannot shift over a horse's eyes.

Coolers and walking covers are used to protect a horse from chills when his coat is wet with sweat or after a bath. Coolers are usually made of wool, acrylic or acrylic fleece; lightweight cotton or scrim walking covers are sometimes used in warmer but breezy weather. Open-weave "fishnet" or Irish knit coolers trap air next to the horse and keep him warm while his coat is drying; in cold weather they should be used under a sheet or

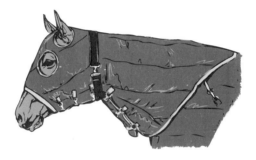

A. Hood

B. Neck cover

Figure 74. Hood, neck cover.

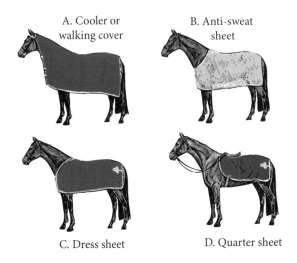

A. Cooler or walking cover

B. Anti-sweat sheet

C. Dress sheet

D. Quarter sheet

Figure 75. Walking cover, open-weave cooler.

blanket. Some modern fabrics are designed to wick moisture away from the body, which enables faster drying while keeping the horse warm.

Rain covers are usually waterproof nylon, sometimes lined for warmth; they are used to protect the horse and tack during inclement weather.

Quarter sheets, made of wool or synthetic fleece, are used to protect a clipped horse's back and hindquarters from chilling during exercise. They fasten to the girth of the saddle, and have a fillet string around the hindquarters to keep them in place.

Putting On and Taking Off Blankets

Putting On a Blanket

To put on a blanket, place the folded blanket across the horse's neck and withers. Fasten the chest fastenings first, then unfold it and slide it back into place. Then fasten the surcingles and/or leg straps. Hind leg straps may be crossed through each other to prevent them from rubbing the insides of the hind legs.

Removing a Blanket

To remove a blanket, always unfasten the hind leg straps and the rear or belly surcingles first. Fold the back half of the blanket forward over the

A. Undo surcingles and hind leg straps first.

B. Unfasten front, fold blanket forward, and remove.

Figure 76. Removing a blanket.

withers. Then unfasten the chest fastenings, and slide the blanket off the the horse's back.

BLANKET SAFETY

Horse blankets may be kept in place by surcingles that go under the belly or hind leg straps. Some horses are sensitive about being touched in this area and may kick or act up if they are irritated by having a blanket put on, taken off or pulled about. It is safer to put on, remove, or adjust blankets when a horse is tied up or restrained by a halter and lead rope.

Never remove a blanket or pull it forward without first unfastening the hind leg straps or belly straps. This can cause the straps to pinch the horse in the flanks like a bucking strap on a rodeo bucking horse, which may provoke a rodeo bucking performance!

Blankets that are too big or improperly fitted may shift when a horse lies down. The horse may then get a hind leg caught in the blanket and injure himself or damage the blanket. Stacking on too many layers makes blankets more likely to slip; a single warm blanket is safer. Some horses need a shaped blanket or one with hind leg straps to keep it in place, especially for turnout.

Fitting a Blanket

MEASURING FOR A BLANKET

To measure a horse for a blanket, run a measuring tape from the center of his chest to the center of his buttock. The number of inches is the size of the blanket, but when in doubt, go up a size. It may also help to measure the "drop," or the distance from the center of the back to the top of the legs. Stoutly built horses may need blankets with extra long drop.

FITTING BLANKETS

Blankets must fit well or they may slip or cause rubs or pressure sores. A blanket should cover the horse's body completely, from his chest to the sides of the tail and well down his sides. There must be adequate room at the shoulders to prevent shoulder rubs and allow freedom or movement, especially in a turnout rug. The neck opening must not be too large and should be around the neck in front of the shoulder; if the opening is too large the blanket will slip back, rub the shoulders, and may cause pressure sores on the withers.

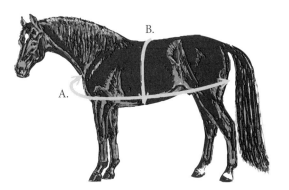

A. Length : Measure from center of chest to back of thigh.

B. Drop : Measure from center of back to a line even with the belly.

Figure 77. Measuring for a blanket.

Blanket Care and Maintenance

Blankets and horse clothing are a big investment, so it makes sense to take care of them. Whenever you remove a blanket, it should be brushed clean, folded, and hung up. If you notice a rip or a tear, it should be mended promptly; dental floss can be used to sew up a tear.

CLEANING BLANKETS

Blankets get very dirty, so they require periodic cleaning. The ammonia found in urine and manure acts like acid on fabric, causing it to deteriorate. Different blanket materials require different cleaning methods; it is best to save the washing instructions that come with a new blanket or check the fabric care tag. Most blankets and sheets can be washed in a heavy-duty washing machine, but some require a large commercial washer. Because washing horse blankets is a smelly job that is hard on the washing machine and may require several wash and rinse cycles to complete the job, you may prefer to take your blankets to a laundromat or use a horse blanket laundry service.

Before laundering, a blanket should be spread out and precleaned, hosing off heavy soil, spot-cleaning especially dirty areas, and brushing or vacuuming the inside to remove loose hair. Any buckles or metal fastenings that cannot be removed should be protected by covering them with an old sock, fastened with a rubber band. This protects the inside of the washing machine, too.

Blankets should be washed with mild laundry soap or a product made especially for washing horse blankets. Use cold water, as hot water may shrink the blanket or the straps and fittings. It is best not to put blankets in the dryer, as they may shrink and straps and fittings may be damaged by the heat. Instead, they should be hung up and allowed to drip dry.

Sheets, fly sheets, synthetic fleece items, and nylon under-sheets may be machine washed in cold water with a mild liquid detergent and may be tumble-dried on a low setting or dried outdoors. They should not be exposed to bleach, high dryer heat, or direct sunlight.

Wool coolers and dress sheets should be dry-cleaned, although some owners wash them in cold water with Woolite.

Turnout rugs can be hung on a fence and the mud and dirt hosed off, then allowed to drip dry in the sun. Some water-repellent blankets and sheets may lose their water repellent qualities if they are machine washed with laundry detergent.

WATERPROOFING

A water-repellent blanket may need occasional treatment to renew its waterproofing treatment. Scotch-Guard and Nikwax Rug Proof are two products that may be applied to turnout rugs and other outdoor blankets for this purpose.

STORAGE

Blankets should be always clean and dry before being stored. If blankets are stored dirty, especially in a closed container during a hot summer, the ammonia from manure and urine breaks down and weakens the fabric and stains become permanent. Blankets should be stored in bins or tack trunks to protect them from mice and other rodents that will chew holes in blankets and make nests in them. Woolen items should be stored with mothballs or other moth repellents.

Chapter 9

Final Touches

Whether turning out a show horse for the ring or presenting a horse in public or to a prospective buyer, little things can make the difference between a first-class appearance and a mediocre presentation. While you cannot change a horse's basic structure or make up for a complete lack of preparation, there are many small extras that can give you an advantage. A rather ordinary looking horse can be made to appear handsome through good grooming and presentation. Attention to details is the hallmark of the topflight stable, showman, and groom.

Coat

The coat should be clean and well groomed, but may be enhanced with a conditioner or coat polish. The coat product is sprayed on the clean coat after grooming, or it may be applied after a bath while the coat is still damp. Spray the coat thoroughly, allow it to dry, and then brush lightly with a soft brush to lay the hair in place. It can be applied to the face with a dampened rag, as most horses hate to have anything sprayed on their heads. Silicone products should not be used beneath the saddle pad, as they can make the saddle slip.

Apply fly repellent, especially if the horse must stand still in a halter class or for a photo session. There are coat products that contain fly repellent; these are better than oil-based fly sprays, which will pick up dust.

Face and Skin

The face, muzzle, eyelids, ears, and any other places that have fine hair and show the skin should be cleaned with a sponge, damp towel, or disposable baby wipe. Highlighter applied to these areas makes the skin

1. Wipe rider's boots and tack.
2. Wipe horse's face and bit.
3. Paint feet.
4. Whiten white markings.
5. Pick out tail; remove tail bandage.
6. Remove stains or sweat marks.
7. Apply coat polish and fly repellent.

FIGURE 78. *Applying the final touches.*

appear darker and finer, reflects light, and enhances the expression and refinement of the head. Highlighters are available in clear, brown, or black. Only clear highlighter should be used on white face markings, but black highlighter will make the eyes appear larger and accents the contours of the face more dramatically on horses with dark skin. Brown is best on chestnuts or horses that fall between the extremes of very light and very dark.

To apply highlighter, rub it on the face, muzzle, eyelids, and ears (including inside the ears, if they have been clipped) with a rag dampened with the highlighter gel. Wait five or ten minutes for it to dry, then wipe off any excess with a clean towel. Highlighter is preferable to baby oil or Vaseline, as it does not pick up dust and dirt.

FIGURE 79. Highlighting face.

The fine skin beneath the tail and under the belly should also be cleaned with a damp towel or a baby wipe. The chestnuts should be cut off level with the skin and may be rubbed with highlighter or Vaseline, or darkened with hoof polish if the leg around them is dark. Any cuts, scars, or blemishes should be treated so as to minimize their appearance. On dark-coated horses, a touch of gentian violet on a scrape will darken it as you treat it and will minimize the problem, but on a grey or a palomino it would make it more noticeable. Avoid using scarlet oil to treat minor wounds—it looks like blood! A bit of Vaseline applied to a scab or scar helps to soften the scab and also minimizes the blemish.

Stain Removal and White Markings

White markings should appear dazzling white and spotless. They should be shampooed if necessary, and carefully dried. Using a whitening shampoo or spot-cleaning with Wisk laundry detergent helps to get white legs perfectly white. White legs and face markings are sometimes clipped closely so the hair will pick up less dust and appear whiter, but this should be done far enough in advance that the hair is slightly grown out and shows no clipper tracks.

Polo wraps can be used to keep a horse's legs clean while she warms up in a muddy or dusty ring, and removed just before going into the ring. Don't forget to take off polo wraps and tail bandages; in some classes (especially dressage competition), bandages are prohibited and a forgotten bandage can cause the entry to be eliminated.

To make white leg and face markings extra white, you can dust them with cornstarch, baby powder, or French chalk just before showing. The powder is dusted onto the leg and sifted into the hair with the fingers, working against the lay of the hair. The excess is then lightly brushed off with a soft brush. Whitening sprays are also available for white legs, but use whitening agents sparingly, especially on the body. It can be embarrassing to have your horse leave his white markings all over the judge's hand!

A. Dusting with baby powder
or cornstarch

B. Cosmetic whitener for
white markings

C. Grooming chalk

FIGURE 80. Whitening markings.

Mane and Tail

The mane and tail should be neatly braided or picked out by hand until all the hairs are untangled and free of dust, bedding, or other debris. The skin of the mane and tail should be clean, especially on horses that are braided, as braiding exposes the roots of the hair.

Some horses, especially Arabians, have a thin, fine tail that needs more body. A tail can be made to look fuller by braiding it into tiny pigtails or "crocheting" small strands into figure-eight-shaped loops and then treating the hair with setting gel or hair spray. The braids or loops are removed just before show time, and the tail hair should be carefully picked and separated. This has the same effect as setting human hair—it gives the tail more body, with a wavy look.

When a horse is presented with an unbraided mane, the mane should be laid on the correct side by brushing the roots with a damp brush. Setting gel can be used to make cowlicks or fly-away areas lie down. A mane-tamer may be applied for an hour or so before the class, with the mane wet down with setting gel to lay it flat and smooth on the desired side.

FIGURE 81. *Picking the tail by hand.*

The forelock should be picked carefully and smoothed into place. Some horses look best with the forelock tucked down neatly beneath the browband; others are flattered more by a free forelock.

The top of the tail should appear smooth and slimmer than the skirt. On sport horses, a tail bandage may be applied to the dampened dock for an hour or so before showing, to lay the hairs of the dock and shape the tail. Don't forget to remove the tail bandage before the horse is shown!

If the horse wears a tail extension or tail wig, this should be applied securely and the tail hair arranged over it so that it is not obvious. (For directions on applying tail extensions, please see chapter 5).

Feet

Hoofs should be cleaned out just before going into the ring and hoof dressing or hoof polish may be applied. The outside of the hoof may be scrubbed clean with a nail brush or a vegetable brush. In some breeds it is a common practice to sand the walls of the hoof smooth; if this is done, a protective hoof sealant must be applied to protect the hoof against moisture loss.

The type of hoof dressing or hoof polish used depends on what is conventional for that breed or type of horse, and also what looks best on the individual horse.

Oil-based hoof dressings give the feet a dark, uniform appearance and have long been preferred by hunter and sport horse exhibitors. One disadvantage is that the oil is quickly obscured by mud, dirt, and dust; the feet must be painted again before each class.

Hoof polishes are similar to nail polish. They are painted onto the clean, dry hoof wall and allowed to dry. Hoof polishes come in clear, black, and brown, and give the hoof a higher shine than oil dressings. They do not need to be renewed for each class, but may last for a day or even longer. Hoof polish is more commonly used on saddle and harness horses, Arabians, Morgans, and in breed halter classes; it has often been used by western showman, but some western showmen now prefer oil-based hoof dressing instead. Appaloosas should be shown with clear hoof polish, as their striped feet are a breed characteristic that should be visible. Horses with light feet usually look best with clear polish—black polish beneath a white leg sometimes makes the hoof appear larger and gives the impression the horse is wearing galoshes! Using brown polish on the

I. Stand horse on mat to polish feet.

A. Hoof with cracks and defects

B. Cracks filled with filler

C. Hoof sanded smooth and sealed

D. Dark hoof polish hides defects.

II. Hoof finishes

A. Dark hoof oil

B. Black hoof polish

C. Brown hoof polish

D. Clear hoof polish

E. Glitter polish
(only for parade horses!)

FIGURE 82. *Hoof polishing.*

feet of a chestnut tends to minimize the size of the feet and draw attention away from them. When a horse has one white foot and one dark one, it should usually have both feet darkened. Sometimes the contrasting coloration can make the stride appear uneven. It's best to try various colors at home and use the one that looks the best for that individual.

After showing, hoof polish should be washed off; hoof polish remover makes the job easier. The hoof can then be treated with a good moisturizing hoof dressing. Today's hoof polishes are formulated for use on horse's feet; they do not dry and crack the feet as did the shoe polish that was used in the past. Most drying and cracking is due to overenthusiastic scrubbing or sanding of the hoof wall, rather than hoof polish.

Hoofs that have cracks or blemished places can be improved cosmetically by filling the gaps with epoxy glue or with acrylic putty. While this will not make the hoof stronger, it does present a more even appearance, and when covered with hoof polish, the crack or defect will be hidden.

Quarter Marks

Quarter marks are sometimes used on formally turned out hunters and sport horses. They call attention to a well-turned croup and wide, well-muscled hindquarters, as well as highlighting the gloss of the coat. Quarter marks look especially nice under the lights in an indoor class at night.

Quarter marks should be used only on horses with especially good conformation of the croup and hindquarters, as they draw attention there. They act as artificial dapples, and are best used on solid-colored horses. In order to make quarter marks, the hair must be very clean, shiny, and short. Quarter marks are usually made in a checkerboard pattern, which may be square, triangular or another simple design. The pattern should start above the point of the hip and should not extend too far back and down the side; this give the appearance of a longer croup and hip.

How to Apply Quarter Marks Using a Comb:

1. Break off a one-inch section of fine-toothed comb.

2. Wet down the hair of the croup, using a sponge brush or water brush dipped in setting gel. Sponge or brush straight backward, in the direction of hair growth.

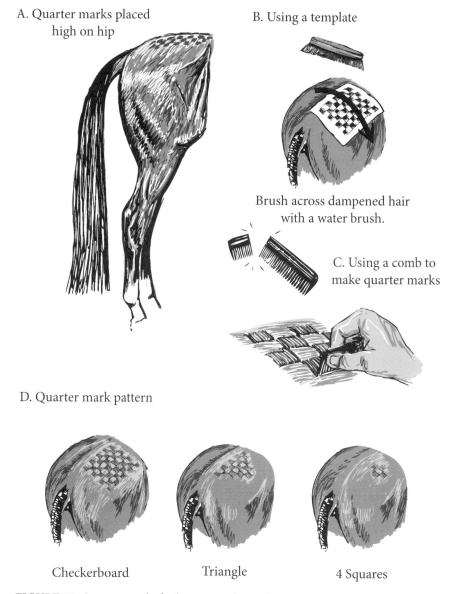

A. Quarter marks placed high on hip

B. Using a template

Brush across dampened hair with a water brush.

C. Using a comb to make quarter marks

D. Quarter mark pattern

Checkerboard   Triangle   4 Squares

FIGURE 83. *Quarter marks for hunters and sport horses.*

3. Starting along one side of the center line of the croup, comb downward, across the direction of hair growth, for exactly the width of the comb section to form a square. Skip a section of exactly the same width, then make another square. Continue along the line of the croup.

4. Start the next line by making squares in alternate sections along the bottom of the first line to form a checkerboard pattern.

5. The pattern should be placed in high on the hip between the hip bone and the tailhead. Don't place it too far back.

Plastic templates are available to make quarter marks with checkerboard, triangle, or other patterns. To use a template, first wet down the hair and brush it toward the tail. Place the template firmly over the wet croup, and using a body brush or a water brush, brush straight downward across the direction of hair growth. Carefully remove the template and the design will be left on the hair.

Tack

The bridle, saddle, girth, breastplate, or martingale, and the rider's boots (including the soles of the boots, as these will be visible) should be clean and shiny when the horse goes into the ring. You can wipe over exposed leather parts with Lexol (however, don't overdo wiping the reins, as it can make them slippery). The rider's boots should also be gone over with Lexol and a rag, and any mud cleaned off the stirrup tread. If the horse's mouth is foamy, the bits should be wiped off, except in dressage competitions, where foam is considered a desirable sign of acceptance of the bit. Check that all parts are correctly adjusted and all strap ends are secured by their keepers. A last-minute check should also be made of the rider's clothing and hair, and the number should be firmly secured and easily visible to the judge.

The One-Day Makeover

Top show presentation comes only from good health and condition, and there is no substitute for regular care, grooming, and conditioning. However, there are times when a horse must be cleaned up and made presentable quickly. Here's a procedure for a quick all-over clean-up:

- First, get him clean: bathe the horse (weather permitting), or if it's too cold for a bath, groom thoroughly, vacuum, and clean him with a hot towel bath or with a towel and waterless cleaner.

A. Before : straight from the pasture, covered in mud, dirt, and burrs

B. Cleaned up and trimmed, ready for a public appearance

FIGURE 84. *One-day makeover.*

- Pick or brush out the mane and tail; shampoo the tail. Apply mane and tail conditioner. Coat polish may be applied over a clean coat to enhance the shine.

- Use shampoo, spot cleaner, or stain remover to remove stains and scrub white markings clean.

- Scrub the hoof walls clean, remove any bot eggs, and trim the chestnuts even with the skin.

- Trim a bridle path (according to breed or type of horse). Trim excess hair from the fetlocks, jaw, edges of the ears, and whiskers (trim whiskers only if the horse will be stabled). Extra long hairs can be removed from the legs and body by lightly brushing the clipper blades over the area, being careful to avoid cutting into the hair coat.

- Pull, thin or shorten the mane as necessary for the appearance of the mane, according to the horse's breed or discipline, and lay the mane over to the correct side of the neck with a water brush. The tail may be pulled, thinned, banged off, and/or shaped with a tail bandage, according to the requirements of the breed or discipline.

- Using a sheet or blanket will cause the hair coat to lie down smooth and flat.

- If time and circumstances permit, expert body clipping, followed by a hot oil treatment to restore the shine of the coat, can sometimes transform a horse's appearance. However, you'll have to blanket him afterward.

Chapter 10

The Show Hunter

Today's show hunter is usually a Thoroughbred, warmblood, or of Thoroughbred type; hunter ponies exhibit similar conformation and type in a smaller size. In the early days, Thoroughbreds were usually braided, both in the hunting field and when racing, while cold-blooded hunters had their manes hogged or roached off. Hence braiding came to denote "blood" or quality. Today braiding is used to complement and emphasize the line of the neck when a hunter is presented in hand, moving on the flat, or using his neck well when jumping. The lines of a show hunter are long, smooth, and clean, and his trimming, braiding, and turnout should emphasize and reflect these qualities.

Like any quality show horse, a hunter should have all long hair trimmed from the fetlocks, lower legs, jaw, face, and muzzle. Ears should be trimmed outside and the inner hair trimmed short and neat if not completely removed. It is not mandatory to braid either the mane or tail when showing hunters, but it is customary to braid at least the mane. A horse may have only his mane and forelock braided and the tail left free, but if the tail is braided, the mane and forelock must be braided also.

A hunter may be shown with quarter marks, a small, neat, well-placed pattern of diamonds or checkerboard pattern, placed high on the hip, to emphasize the conformation and gloss of the hindquarters. These are only used on the most formal occasions, when both the mane and tail are braided and the horse and rider are formally turned out in every other respect.

Hunters may be body clipped for winter shows. A full clip is more formal and is preferred over a hunter clip or trace clip.

187

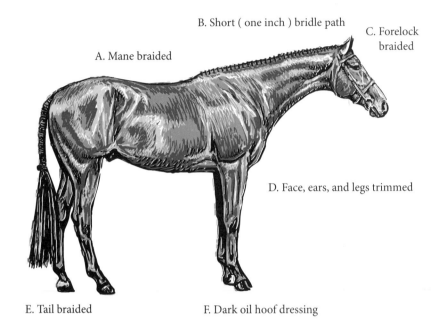

B. Short (one inch) bridle path

C. Forelock braided

A. Mane braided

D. Face, ears, and legs trimmed

E. Tail braided

F. Dark oil hoof dressing

FIGURE 85. Show hunter—formal turnout.

HUNTER MANES

A hunter's mane should be pulled to a short, even length of about three and a half to four inches, and should lie evenly on the off side of the neck. A shorter mane will produce smaller, neater braids; a slightly longer mane looks better when unbraided and is less likely to stick straight up. The mane should be pulled by hand, never cut, for a natural appearance when unbraided and to provide the right length and thickness for neat braiding. A hunter mane is always braided on the right side of the neck, regardless of which side the hair tends to fall on, so grooms usually train the unbraided mane to lie on the right side. The forelock should be fairly short and thin so that it makes a neat braid that is not excessively bulky.

A hunter's bridle path should be very short—only long enough to remove the hair that lies beneath the crownpiece of the halter or bridle—about one inch. The first braid, or the edge of the mane when unbraided, should begin as close to the poll as possible and continue in an unbroken line as far back as possible. This gives the impression of a long neck and

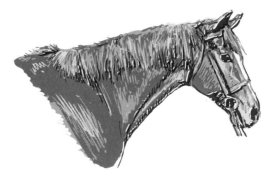

A. Unpulled mane

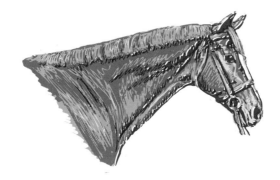

B. Pulled hunter mane

FIGURE 86. Pulled mane.

long, well-set back withers, which go with a sloping shoulder. If the bridle path is clipped too long, it breaks up the line of the neck and gives the illusion of a shorter neck. If the mane is removed or left in an unbraided fringe at the withers, it not only makes the neck look shorter but gives the impression of high withers and a straight shoulder.

HUNTER TAILS

The tail is usually left as long as it will grow, or it may be banged off (cut off square at the bottom of the skirt) at the height of the pasterns. Some tails look better with a natural point (a "switch" tail), especially those that are rather thin. The hairs at the top of the dock, especially those at the edges, should not be broken off or shortened, as these will be used in braiding the tail. While it is permissible to show a hunter with a tail pulled as for a dressage horse, this is uncommon in this country and makes it impossible to braid the tail, as the braiding hairs are pulled short. A pulled tail is more commonly seen on show jumpers, dressage horses, or eventers than on show hunters, though it is an alternative to consider if the tail hairs have been so damaged that braiding is impossible.

With the trend toward warmbloods in the hunter ring, fuller tails have become the norm. Some hunter exhibitors augment a thin tail with a tail extension or hairpiece made to blend with the tail. This can be secured and the attachment covered better if the tail is braided. (See chapter 5, page 99 for more on tail extensions.)

Braiding the Mane

Hunters' manes are customarily braided to display the line of the neck and to keep the mane from blowing and tangling in the reins and the rider's hands. Braiding is not mandatory—in fact, certain horses may look better with a well-pulled and unbraided mane, especially those with a large head or a thin or ewe neck. However, good braiding can flatter good conformation or subtly play down defects; a short neck can be made to look longer by using many small braids, and an excessively long or heavy neck can be balanced by using fewer and larger braids. Braiding also shows that the exhibitor cares about his turnout, and is considered a mark of respect for the show and the judge.

The number of braids varies with the size of the horse or pony and the length and thickness of the mane, but a good average number is about thirty braids. Good mane pulling will result in a mane of even thickness, tapering slightly as the ends, which can be put up into uniformly spaced braids of about the width of a cigarette. Slightly heavier braids are acceptable if neatly done, especially on large horses. Very thin braids are harder to put in and may not lie straight. The segments from which the hair is gathered for each braid should be about a half to one inch and evenly spaced, which means that it is rare to put in fewer than twenty braids. While the traditional custom in England is to make seven to nine larger plaits, American hunter show customs call for many more and smaller braids. Purists claim that the number of braids should be odd for a stallion or gelding and even for a mare, but few judges have the time or patience to count the braids!

BRAIDING YARN AND EQUIPMENT

While the braids can be fastened with rubber bands or sewn in with thread, yarn is universally used in top-class hunter shows today. Yarn is available in all colors; it's easy to apply and tie, holds securely without breaking off hairs, and is easy to remove. It is always correct to use yarn the same color as the mane; some exhibitors prefer a subtle color contrast such as dark blue or hunter green for a black mane, light blue for a grey mane, or dark brown for a light chestnut mane. Keep in mind that any color contrast draws attention to the braiding and to the neck—it must be extra neat and used only a neck with excellent conformation and perfect braids. Some judges dislike contrasting yarn, considering it flashy and untraditional, especially colors like red, yellow, bright green, or white. Since the object is to make a correct and formal appearance, it's best to be conservative.

To braid a mane, you will need a comb to part the hair, a sponge to wet it down, a braid puller or latch-hook to pull the yarn ends through, a clip to keep the unbraided hair out of the way, and scissors. You can wet the mane with plain water, but spray-on braiding products such as Quik Braid hold the hair together better. The horse should be cross-tied in a well-lighted area; you will need a stool to stand on. An apron with pockets or a small braiding kit that attaches to your belt will keep your equipment within easy reach. A seam ripper is necessary for taking out the braids without cutting the hair.

To cut braiding yarn to the proper length, wind the yarn around your hand and elbow about twenty times. Slip the wound-up yarn off your elbow and cut it at the top and bottom. If you want longer yarn pieces, cut only once. You will need about thirty-five yarn pieces twelve to sixteen inches long.

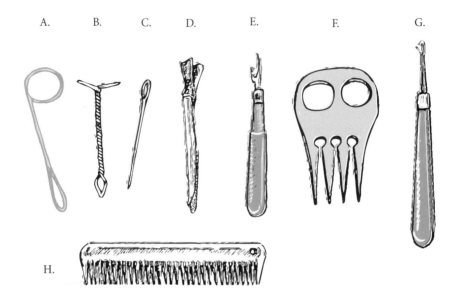

A. Plastic pull-through
B. Wire pull-through
C. Braiding needle
D. Hair clip
E. Seam ripper
F. Braid-Aid comb
G. Latch hook
H. Mane pulling comb

FIGURE 87. Braiding tools.

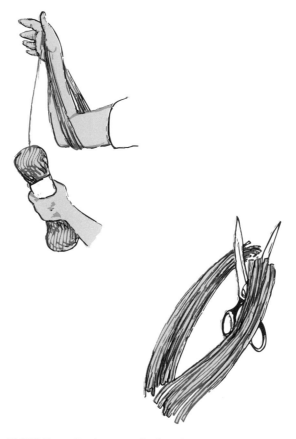

FIGURE 88. Cutting yarn for braids.

How to Braid a Hunter Mane, Using the Basic Yarn-Braid Method

1. Part a section of mane about a half to one inch wide, using a comb to part it straight. Wet down the section with warm water.

2. Use a beauty parlor clip to keep the unparted mane out of the way.

3. Divide the section into three equal strands and begin to braid. Pull the hair across the neck and braid down the side of the neck, keeping the braiding very tight.

4. When you have braided an inch or more, place the center of a twelve- to fifteen-inch piece of yarn behind the braid. Add each end of one of the braiding strands and continue braiding to the end of the mane hairs.

5. At the end of the braid, separate the tiny ends of the hairs, from the two yarn ends pinching them tightly. Pass the yarn ends around the braid and pull them through, creating a doubled slip knot around the end of the braid. Usually the entire mane is braided this way before pulling up and tying off the braids.

A. Wet down the hair.

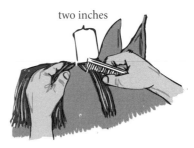

two inches

B. Neatly part a two-inch segment for the first braid.

C. Divide into three equal parts and clip mane out of the way.

D. Begin to braid.

FIGURE 89. Beginning to braid.

A.

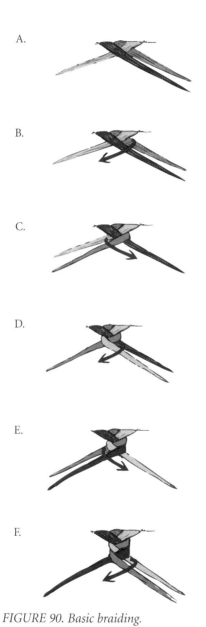

B.

C.

D.

E.

F.

FIGURE 90. Basic braiding.

G. Pull and twist each strand to the side to keep the braid tight.

H. Pulling downward away from the neck results in a loose braid.

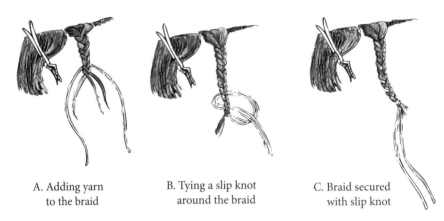

A. Adding yarn to the braid

B. Tying a slip knot around the braid

C. Braid secured with slip knot

FIGURE 91. Braiding with yarn.

6. To pull up the braid, push the loop end of the braid puller or latch-hook down through the hair at the top of the braid, keeping it close to the skin of the neck. Double the yarn ends and push them through the loop of the braid puller or latch hook, then pull them through so the end of the braid is tucked tightly under, against the edge of the crest.

TYING OFF BRAIDS

There are two basic methods of tying off braids—the basic method and the "knob" method, which is preferred for dressage braids. The basic method is quick and easy to put in and works best on a short mane; the knob method is extra secure and works better on a mane that is slightly longer.

How to Tie Off Braids Using the Quick and Easy Method

1. Separate the yarn ends above the crest and bring them down on each side to cross beneath the braid.

2. Bring the ends to the front of the braid and press the braid with your thumb to make it "turn the corner" at the crest.

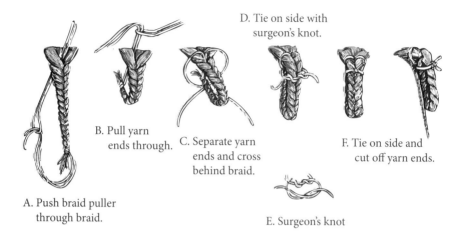

D. Tie on side with surgeon's knot.

B. Pull yarn ends through.

C. Separate yarn ends and cross behind braid.

F. Tie on side and cut off yarn ends.

A. Push braid puller through braid.

E. Surgeon's knot

FIGURE 92. *Tying off braids—basic flat braids.*

3. Tie the yarn ends in a square knot about a half inch down on the side of the braid. (If you give the first wrap of the knot an extra twist, it will form a "surgeon's knot," which holds more securely. The second part of the knot is tied as an ordinary square knot.)

4. Cut off the ends of the yarn, leaving about a fourth-inch ends to prevent the knot from coming untied.

How to Tie Off Braids Using the Knob Method

1. Separate the yarn ends above the crest and bring one down on each side of the braid to cross behind the braid.

2. Bring the ends to the front of the braid and press the braid upward with your thumb to make it "turn the corner" of the crest and create a knob that sticks up about a fourth to a half inch. Cross the yarn ends below this knob, keeping the yarn tight.

3. Cross the yarn ends underneath the braid again, then tie them on top of the braid, just above the knob. Pull the ends very tight and tie them in a square knot or a surgeon's knot (see figure 92).

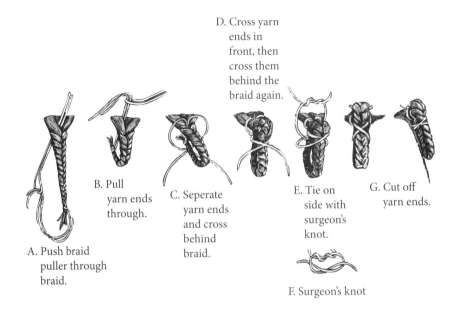

D. Cross yarn ends in front, then cross them behind the braid again.

B. Pull yarn ends through.

C. Seperate yarn ends and cross behind braid.

E. Tie on side with surgeon's knot.

G. Cut off yarn ends.

A. Push braid puller through braid.

F. Surgeon's knot

FIGURE 93. *Tying off braids—knob-style braids.*

4. Cut off the ends of the yarn, leaving them about a quarter inch long. Knobs should be uniform and should not stick up high above the crest. This method results in a line of colored yarn that is visible from both sides, so it must be very neatly tied off.

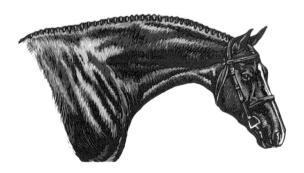

FIGURE 94. *Hunter man braided.*

BRAIDING THE FORELOCK

The forelock must be braided whenever the mane is braided (jumpers, dressage, and sport horses are sometimes shown with a braided mane and the forelock left free, but this looks sloppy and incorrect on a hunter). There are two basic methods of braiding the forelock. The simplest way is to part the forelock hairs into three sections, braid to the end, pull the braid under and tie it off as for a mane braid. This looks fine if the forelock is fairly short and thin. For a bushy forelock, a French braid (similar to a miniature tail braid) will contain the hair all the way down and create a neater and fancier effect. The French braid can be done in either the "outside" or "inside" style, just as in braiding a tail, but the "outside" braid looks fancier.

How to Braid the Forelock with an Outside French Braid:

1. Divide the topmost half inch of forelock into two equal strands. Cross the right strand over the left.

2. Separate another strand on the right side below the first. Bring it into the center behind the end of the left-hand strand.

3. Bring the topmost strand (upper left strand) around behind and into the center. Part another section (about a quarter inch or less) from the left side and add it to the strand just braided, from behind. Keep the strands tight.

4. Continue to braid by braiding the topmost strand around the back and into the center, adding an extra a quarter-inch strand from the same side each time you braid. This will result in a raised, braided ridge that gathers in the hair from the sides of the forelock.

5. When you reach the end of the forelock, divide any remaining hair among the three braiding strands and continue to braid. Place the center of a fifteen-inch piece of yarn behind the braid and add one end to one of the braiding strands. At the end of the hair, tie off the braid in a double slip knot as described in mane braiding.

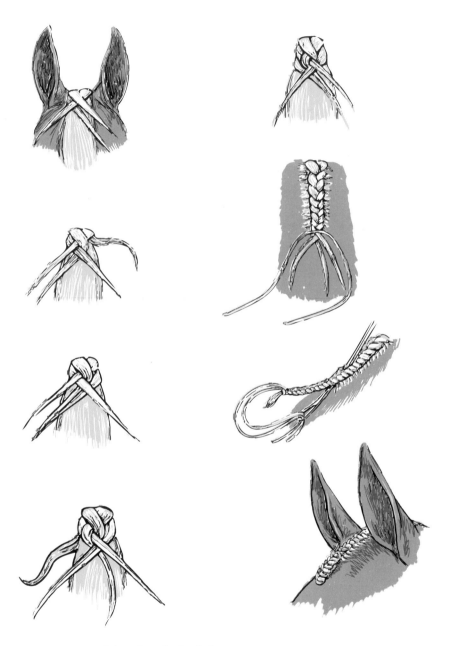

FIGURE 95. French braiding the forelock.

6. Push the braid puller down underneath the French braid from the top. Double the yarn ends and push them through the loop of the braid puller, and pull the braid up until it is the same length as a mane braid. (The braid can even be pulled up inside the French braid if it is too long.) Tie off and trim the yarn ends as you would for a mane braid.

SEWN-IN OR BUTTON BRAIDS

Sewn-in braids or button braids were more popular in the past and are not often seen on show hunters today; they are more often used on eventers. They are more time-consuming to put in and take out, but the tiny round "buttons" are flattering to some horses, especially those with a rather thick crest. Button braids are sometimes used when the rider is apt to grab the mane, as they are the most secure type of braid. They are also one way to put up a long mane (such as a Morgan's or Arabian's) into an acceptable hunter braided mane, although the braids will be larger than usual. This is useful for a long-maned horse that must make an occasional appearance in a hunter class, particularly a hunter class for his own breed, but cannot have his mane pulled short enough for conventional hunter braiding. For directions on button braids, please see chapter 11, page 228.

THE SCALLOPED MANE

Another method of braiding hunter manes is the scalloped mane. This is not as common as conventional hunter braids, but is sometimes seen on formally turned out conformation hunters in Canada as well as in the United States, and has even been used by the Olympic team. It draws attention to the line of the neck and can make a thick crest appear thicker, so it should only be used when a horse's neck conformation is particularly good and it must be done especially neatly. Scalloping looks especially nice when the mane contrasts with the color of the neck, and it works best with a mane that is a bit longer than usual—about four to four and a half inches. While unusual, scalloped braids are acceptable for hunter or hunter seat equitation classes and can be used for jumpers or dressage horses as well.

How to Braid a Scalloped Mane

1. Braid the mane into individual braids, using sections about one to one and a half inches wide, with matching color yarn or thread braided in.

2. The first braid of the neck is passed behind the second and pulled up underneath the base of the third braid. This can be done with a braid puller or using thread and a braiding needle. The ends are separated, crossed underneath the third braid, and tied in a square knot on the top, about a quarter inch down on the side of the braid. The ends are trimmed short.

3. The next braid is passed underneath the one next to it and pulled up and tied off under the next braid. This is continued down the neck. The scallops will look best if the braid is given a slight twist so that it turns and lies flat.

4. At the end of the neck, the last braid is looped under and fastened as a regular mane braid. The last two braids are fastened underneath this braid.

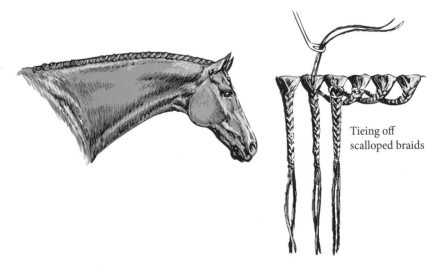

Tieing off
scalloped braids

FIGURE 96. Scalloped mane braids.

Braiding with Rubberbands

Braiding with rubberbands is quicker than sewing in yarn or thread but it is not acceptable for high-level competition, and it will break off hairs and damage the mane. Rubberband braids should be reserved for times when it is necessary to put a mane up in a hurry, or for less formal occasions. The rubber bands should always be the same-color as the mane hair. Rubber bands in black, white, gray, brown, and chestnut are available in most tack stores. Because the hair is easily broken off or pulled out when using rubberbands, they should be removed by cutting the band with a seam ripper—don't try to save the bands, save the mane!

How to Braid a Mane Using Rubberbands:

1. Part and braid a section of mane about half to one inch wide. Braid all the way to the ends of the hairs. The mane should be wet down before braiding.

2. Fold the end of the braided strand upward, with the ends of the hairs on top, pointing up toward the neck. Fasten a rubberband around this tiny loop, wrapping it around until it is tight.

3. Turn the braid under, up against the underside of the braid and the edge of the neck. Use a second rubberband to fasten it, bringing the rubberband up higher with each twist.

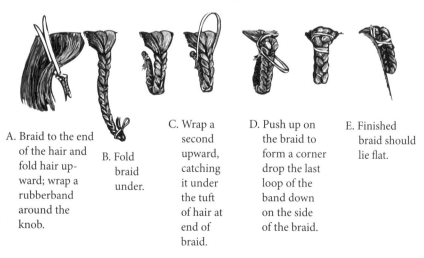

A. Braid to the end of the hair and fold hair upward; wrap a rubberband around the knob.

B. Fold braid under.

C. Wrap a second upward, catching it under the tuft of hair at end of braid.

D. Push up on the braid to form a corner drop the last loop of the band down on the side of the braid.

E. Finished braid should lie flat.

FIGURE 97. Rubberband braids.

4. The final twist of the rubber band is dropped down about ¼ to ½ inch on the side of the braid to make it "turn the corner" and lie flat against the neck. This can create the effect of a "knob" if you push the top of the braid up a bit before starting to wrap the braid with the second rubber band.

TIPS FOR A NEAT, PROFESSIONAL LOOKING BRAID JOB

Neatness is all-important when braiding. If each braid is not started tightly and kept tight, it will loosen and spread out when it is fastened, creating a sloppy, bulging appearance. This can happen if you pull out away from the neck while braiding; thinking you are keeping the braid tight. To make a tight braid, each strand must be twisted tightly against the last instead of pulling outward on the whole braid.

Braids must be evenly spaced and of a uniform size. This requires good mane pulling as well as good measuring when braiding. An uneven mane or poorly divided hair sections results in uneven spacing of braids, with some braids too large and others too thin. The finished braids should always lie straight and flat against the neck.

The under line of the braids must be straight and uniform, with no braids sticking up, out, sideways, or longer or shorter than the rest. All braids should be tight, neat, and securely fastened, and the yarn or other fastening should be almost invisible. Good tying off makes a great difference, especially if the braids are large or thick. All braids should lie down tightly against the side of the neck—if they are tied on top or fastened loosely, they will stand out as if caught in a stiff breeze and will bounce and flop with every stride.

Stand on a stool or hay bale when braiding—not only is it tiring to work upward, but this often causes the mane to be tied off improperly so the braids stick out. Don't take too much in one braid, especially if the mane is stiff and wiry, but don't make braids so tiny that they look like little wiggly wires. If the mane is too thin, you can add yarn of a matching color right at the beginning of the braid; you can even add double yarn strands to give the braid some body. Remember that American hunters are *always* braided on the right side—a mane braided on the left is a sure sign of a greenhorn!

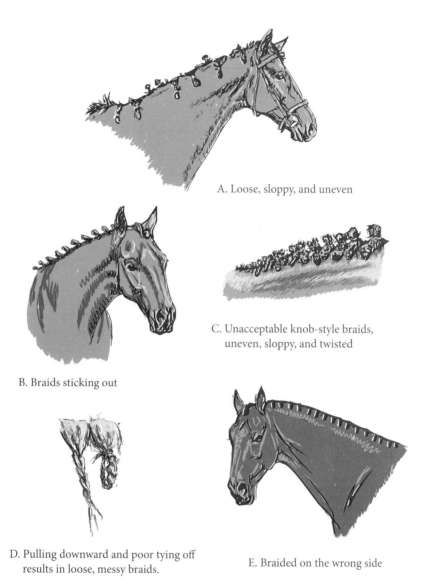

A. Loose, sloppy, and uneven

C. Unacceptable knob-style braids, uneven, sloppy, and twisted

B. Braids sticking out

D. Pulling downward and poor tying off results in loose, messy braids.

E. Braided on the wrong side

FIGURE 98. Bad braiding.

Exhibitors with long-maned horses sometimes wish to show in a hunter class. In hunter classes in shows for their breed, they may be presented with hunter braids, button braids, a French braid (running braid), or even with a long free mane, but not with unconventional braids such as a lattice braid or Continental braid. However, this type of presentation is unconventional at best in open hunter shows. If you are competing seriously in hunter shows, your horse should have a properly pulled mane and correct hunter braids.

MAINTAINING A BRAIDED MANE

Ideally, the mane should be braided on the day of the show. Sometimes it is necessary to braid the night before, but the braids will not be quite as neat and bedding may get into the hair. A possible compromise is to braid the mane but not to pull the braids up or tie them off until the next morning. However, some horses dislike the feeling of the tight braids and will rub their manes on the side of their stall door, so it may not be worth the time saved to try to leave a mane braided overnight. Professional braiders always braid the day of the show and take the braids out as soon as the horse's last class is over, as the longer a mane stays braided the greater the risk of breaking off the braiding hairs. If even a few hairs are broken off each time the mane is braided, the horse will soon have an unsightly fringe of hairs too short to braid that sticks up above and around the braids. For this reason, professional grooms braid only when the occasion is formal enough to require it, in order to preserve the mane for the most important championship shows at the end of the season, and they never leave a mane braided overnight.

TAKING OUT BRAIDS

When taking braids out, it helps to wet the mane down thoroughly first. This stretches and loosens the yarn and makes the hairs uncrimp, so the horse will not have a kinky mane when the braids are removed. Use a seam ripper instead of scissors to cut out the yarn, as it is easier to cut accurately without accidentally snipping some hairs. To cut out a braid, first clip the tied portion at the side of the braid, then lift the braid up and cut the X formed by the yarn or thread where it crosses underneath. When the braid is extended, slip the blade of the seam ripper through the slip knot, cutting outward. This frees the hairs; if they are still tightly braided, the back of the seam ripper (the non-cutting edge) can be used to pick the braid out until it unravels freely. Rubber band braids are easily removed by clipping the band with a seam ripper; sewn-in thread braids require careful cutting of the thread until they can be straightened out.

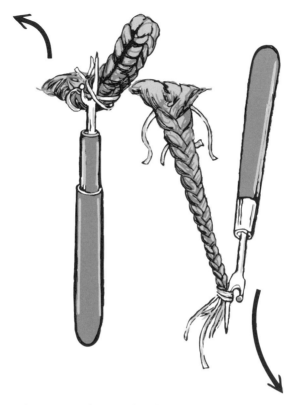

FIGURE 99. *Taking out braids with a seam ripper.*

Braiding the Tail

A braided tail is the final touch to a formal turnout for a show hunter. The custom originated in England, where hedges and thorn fences were common in the hunting field and tails were either cropped short or braided to keep them from picking up brush or thorn branches. The slim, braided dock is an extension of the spine and draws attention to a horse that uses his back well over a jump or when moving on the flat, and makes the width and muscling of the hindquarters more noticeable. Tail braiding is not required in hunter classes, but it is customary to braid the tail for formal occasions. The mane should always be braided when the tail is done.

A hunter's tail may be put up in a mud knot (less formal but permissible on muddy days), a mud braid, or a braided stick—a braided tail with the skirt braided and tucked up inside. The last style is more formal and sometimes is used to show off good hindquarters, especially on hunter ponies.

The upper hairs of the dock should be left as long as they will grow if the tail is to be braided. A few hairs are broken off or pulled out each time a tail is braided, so it is preferable to braid the tail only on formal occasions that warrant it, saving the tail hair for the most important shows at the end of the season. If a tail has had many hairs broken off short from tail rubbing, excessive braiding, or other causes, it may be too short to braid neatly. Horses with brittle tail hair can have a hot oil treatment and other conditioners applied to condition and strengthen the hair, but this must be done at least a week or two before braiding, or the hair will be too slippery to hold and braid. If the hair is so short as to make braiding impossible, the upper tail can be pulled in the manner of a dressage horse, but this means that the hairs will be too short to braid for at least a year.

Before braiding a tail, it should be clean, as the underside of the hairs will be exposed. The tail should be shampooed several days before the show—if it is shampooed or conditioned the day you braid, the hairs will be too slippery. The tail should be brushed or hand picked out so that all the hairs are free and there are no tangles.

METHODS OF BRAIDING THE TAIL

A hunter's tail is braided in a French braid for the full length of the dock. The three basic strands are braided down the center of the dock, with small strands added from each side of the dock each time a strand is braided. The tail is wrapped up in its own hair. This makes the center braid grow larger as the braid progresses, so the strands should be quite fine with only a few hairs added each time. There are two methods of making the French braid: the over-braid or "inside" braid, in which the braiding strands are passed over and into the center, with the braid on the inside, and the under-braid or "outside" braid, in which the braiding strands are braided under each other to produce a braided ridge on the outside. The over method is easier to learn, as it is more closely related to the way most people braid rope, twine, or hair. Learning the under method is confusing at first for some people, but the resulting braid is more attractive and sometimes more secure.

How to Braid a Tail Using the "Over" Method for an Inside French Braid

1. Part one strand from the left top of the tail and two strands from the right.

2. Bring the left strand across the tail between the two right-hand strands.

3. Braid the topmost strand (the upper left strand) into the center over the middle of the next highest strand. Part a strand from the left (about a quarter-inch wide) and bring it over into the center, adding it to the strand just braided.

4. Continue braiding the topmost strand (upper right will be next) over and into the center, parting and adding a strand from the same side each time you braid.

5. Continue down the tail, keeping the braiding hairs pulled tightly across the tail. The strands added from the side should stay horizontal, and the tail should be tightly wrapped with an even center braid. Keep the strands you add small and thin, so that the center braid does not grow too large.

6. You are wrapping the tail in its own hair, holding the hairs together by braiding them down the center of the tail. You will begin to see the center braid, which is on the inside of the wrapping hairs.

7. Braid all the way down to the end of the dock, then see "Finishing the Braided Tail" for ways to complete and secure the finished tail braid.

   Finished inside braid: The braids are neat and tight; strands from the side are even and horizontal, about a quarter inch wide at the edge. The center braid is inside, even and not too large.

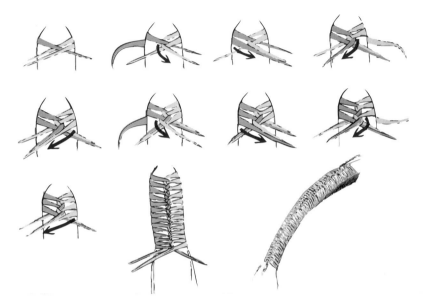

FIGURE 100. Braiding a tail with a French "inside" braid.

How to Braid a Tail Using the "Under" Method for an Outside French Braid

1. Part one small strand from the top left of the tail and two strands from the right.

2. Bring the left-hand strand across the tail between the two right-hand strands.

3. Begin braiding by bringing the topmost strand (upper left) into the center by passing it around behind the middle of the next topmost strand. Keep it pulled straight across the tail and very tight.

4. Part another small strand from the left side of the tail and add it to the strand just braided, passing it behind the middle of the next topmost strand.

5. Braid the next topmost strand (upper right will be next) by bringing it around behind the center of the next highest strand, and add a strand from the same side each time you braid. Keep the strands added from the side small (about a quarter inch), as the center braid will grow as you work down the tail.

6. You are wrapping the tail in strands of its own hair, holding that hair by braiding it down the center. Because you are twisting the hairs under the braid, the braided ridge is on the outside of the strands that wrap the tail.

7. Braid all the way down to the end of the dock, then see "Finishing the Braided Tail" ways to complete and secure the finished tail braid.

   Finished outside tail braid: The center braid is neat and tight and should be about the width of a pencil. The strands are small (about a quarter inch) and are pulled horizontally, not up or down at a slant, which loosens the braid.

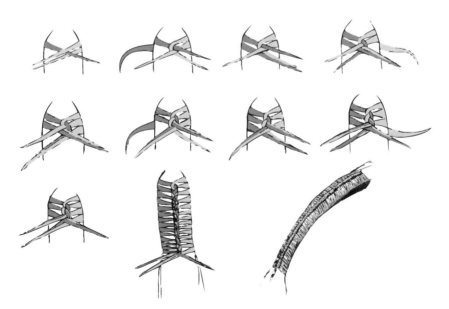

FIGURE 101. Braiding a tail with a French "outside" braid.

TIPS FOR BRAIDING TAILS

When braiding by either method, it is fairly easy to keep the braid tight on the upper part *of* the dock, where the tail is bald underneath. When you reach the point where hair grows from the bottom of the tail, it becomes harder to part the hairs from the back and keep the braid tight and neat, with the wrapping strands horizontal. Be sure to keep an even tension on both sides as you braid—if you pull harder on one side than the other, the center braid will begin to slant off to one side. Remember to add a strand from the side each time you braid and to braid the strands in order—right, left, then right again—as a missed strand will throw you off your braiding. The tail should be braided all the way to the end of the dock, or you can stop an inch or two above the end of the dock, but don't braid only a few inches at the top of the dock. Only draft horses are shown with a partially braided dock, so if you only braid partway down you might be implying that your horse belongs in front of a cart! When you reach the end of the dock, simply stop adding strands from the side and continue braiding the central braid for five or six inches before finishing the tail off.

FINISHING THE BRAIDED TAIL

There are several methods of finishing the braided tail. The quick-and-easy method uses two rubberbands; the sewn-in pinwheel is the most formal, and the wrap-around tail finishing has recently become popular. If you want to tuck the skirt up inside for a braided stick, it should be braided into two pigtails, which are then pulled up inside the French braid. If you plan to wrap the skirt up in a mud knot over the braided tail, a simple rubber band fastening is best. Never leave a long braided loop hanging below the dock, as this detracts from the neat appearance of the braid and can catch on things.

How to Finish a Tail with the Rubberband Method

1. Braid out about five or six inches. Double the braided end up, with the unbraided hairs on top, pointing up toward the dock. Fasten a rubberband around the braided loop at the end.

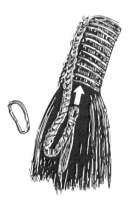

FIGURE 102. Finishing a tail with rubberband method.

2. Turn the braid under and push it up underneath the French braid until the loop that remains is about the size of a mane braid. The unbraided part of the hair will blend with the skirt of the tail.

3. Fasten a rubberband around the small loop at the bottom of the French braid. To remove the braid, find the short unbraided hair ends and pull them; as the braid straightens out, the rubberbands will pop off.

The rubberband finish is quick and easy but less suitable for formal turnout than the next two finishes.

How to Finish a Tail with a Formal Pinwheel

1. Braid the central braiding hairs out to the ends. About two inches from the ends, add in a fifteen-inch strand of braiding thread in a matching color. Tie off the end with a double slip knot and thread the ends through a large-eye needle.

2. Roll the braid back up toward the dock, keeping it very tight. At each complete turn, take a stitch through the center of the braid.

3. When the pinwheel is rolled up against the dock, take a stitch through the center of the pinwheel and through the French braid. Tie it off to the central braid and trim off the ends of the thread.

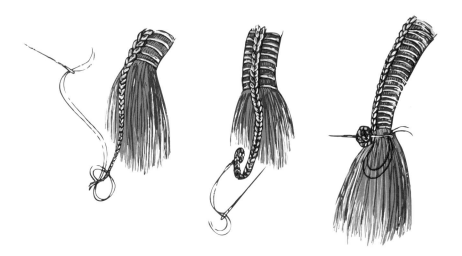

FIGURE 103. Finishing a tail with pinwheel method.

How to Finish a Tail with the Wrap-Around Method

1. Finish the French braid down to the end of the dock, then continue with a regular three-strand braid for about eight to twelve inches.

2. Braid in a twelve to fifteen inch strand of braiding yarn or heavy braiding thread (same color as the tail hair) and tie it off.

3. Fold the braid at a right angle so it lies perpendicular to the tailbone. Use a braiding needle to stitch the braid to the French braid, carefully sewing all the way around the tail. Keep the first stitch loose, but the rest taut.

4. Use a latch hook to pull the end of the braid down under the part that's already sewn-in, as if you were tying a knot around the end of the dock. The loose hair at the end of the braid should lie down and blend with the hair of the skirt of the tail.

5. To secure the wrap, loop a strand of yarn around the spot where the braid is tucked in and tie in a square knot. Or use a braiding needle to stitch through and around the knot and tie the ends off. Clip the yarn ends short.

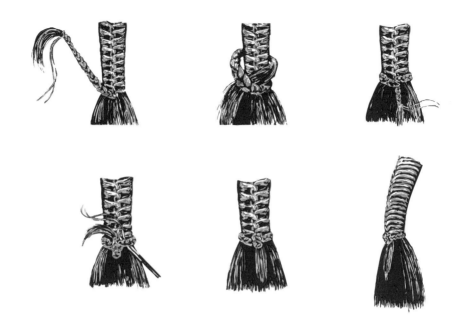

FIGURE 104. Finishing a tail with wrap-around method.

How to Put up the Skirt of the Tail in a Braided Stick

1. Braid to the end of the dock, keeping the braid slightly looser than usual but not so loose that it will not hold the braid. At the end of the dock, divide the skirt hair in two equal sections. One section is separated into three equal strands and braided along with the central braid hairs to the very end. The other section is divided into three segments and braided similarly. Each braid should have a piece of strong thread or yarn about thirty inches long, in a matching color, braided into it and used to tie off the end.

2. An extra-long braid puller is worked carefully down the length of the dock underneath the right side of the braiding strands. Thread the yarn ends through the braid puller and carefully work the braided pigtail up underneath the right side of the French braid.

3. Repeat with the left-hand braid, working it up under the French braid.

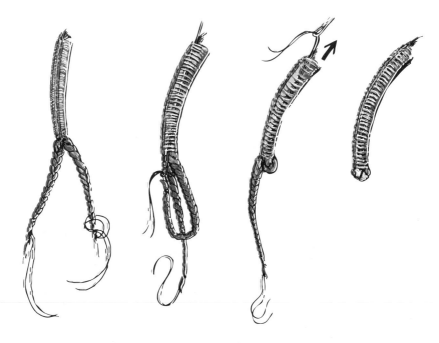

FIGURE 105. Putting up a tail in a braided stick.

4. Thread the yarn ends into a large-eye needle. Stitch from the top down to fasten the skirt braids to the center braid, and tie off at the bottom of the dock.

PROTECTING A BRAIDED TAIL WITH A TAIL WRAP

A braided tail should be protected with a tail bandage until the horse is ready to show. A tail bandage can be applied over slightly dampened hair, or setting gel can be applied to the short hairs at the side of the tail to make them lie down with the braided hairs. Never wet the bandage—it may shrink into the tail and cause tissue damage. A soft cotton stockinette or "track" bandage is the safest type to use on a tail, but some professional grooms prefer an Ace bandage. If you use an Ace bandage, do not apply it at full stretch. The next-to-last wrap is lifted up and the extra roll of bandage can be tucked underneath to secure the bandage. Don't forget to take the tail bandage off before the horse goes into the ring!

A tail should not be braided until the day of the show, and should be taken down as soon as possible to avoid breaking off the braiding hairs. It is not a good idea to try to keep a tail braided overnight, even if the braid is covered by a bandage. Keep the horse protected from flies by using a scrim fly sheet and fly repellent, so that he will not need to switch his tail incessantly, which can loosen the braid. If he is wearing a tail wrap, check it for comfort from time to time—a bandage that is shrinking or wound too tight can cut off circulation in the dock in a matter of hours, leading to great discomfort if not permanent damage.

If you show on a muddy day, you may want to keep the skirt of the tail clean, especially if your horse has a light-colored tail. A mud knot keeps the skirt of the tail up out of the mud. It also keeps the horse from switching a muddy tail and covering his hindquarters, his tack and you with mud. If you are foxhunting, competing over a cross-country course or just hacking out on a wet day, you may want to put the tail up in a mud braid, which is more secure although it does not look as formal. The mud braid is derived from the method used to fasten up polo ponies' tails so that they will not spoil a player's aim by switching their tails into the mallet.

How to Put the Skirt of the Tail up in a Mud Knot

1. Divide the hair of the skirt into two equal sections.

2. Pass the right-hand section around behind the dock.

3. Pass the left-hand section around behind the dock, crossing it over the right-hand section.

4. Give each section a twist to make it into a rope; continue wrapping each section alternately, crossing at the front and the back of the dock. Wrap up the dock until the hair is too short to go around again.

5. Separate one of the strands into two sections and pass the other single strand into the center between them. Braid the three sections very tightly to the ends and fasten with a rubber band or braid in a piece of yarn and tie off.

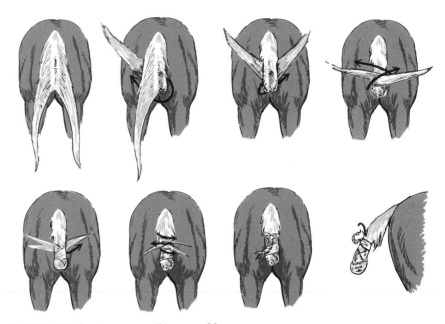

FIGURE 106. *Putting up a tail in a mud knot.*

6. The small braided tab can be tucked down inside the last wrap of hair. A piece of plastic tape in a color close to that of the tail hair (black, white, or brown) should be used to reinforce the mud knot, especially if it is needed to stay in for a long time.

7. To release the skirt of the tail, release and unbraid the small braid and give the dock a shake. The skirt will fall free.

How to Put up the Skirt in a Mud Braid or Polo Tail

1. Divide the skirt into three sections.

2. Braid to the end and fasten with a rubber band.

3. Tuck the braid up under the skirt, turning the end under. Alternatively, the braid may be folded up on top of the dock.

FIGURE 107. Putting up a tail in a mud braid or polo tail.

4. Fasten the braid up with three to five pieces of plastic tape or elastic adhesive tape. Electrician's tape and plastic mending tape work well and are available in black, white, or brown. Do not pull the tape so tight that it indents the skin of the dock.

Chapter 11

Sport Horses: Turnout for Dressage, Show Jumping, Eventing, and Driving

Sport horses include horses and ponies competing in the three Olympic equestrian disciplines: dressage, show jumping, and eventing, plus combined driving competitions. Even if the occasion is a small local competition, the styles and turnout expected in these disciplines reflect the international influence, particularly that of Europe.

Sport horses are often massive, especially the European warmbloods that are popular in these sports. Good trimming and attention to details is necessary to make a good impression. While any good horse looks beautiful in action, the heavier legs, larger feet, and often Roman-nosed head of some warmbloods may appear coarse if they are not well trimmed. A clean, sharp turnout and good trimming and braiding can make even a heavy horse look impressive, and finer-boned horses also benefit from good presentation as well. And in driven dressage and carriage presentation classes, perfect braiding and turnout is essential.

In Europe it is not customary to trim muzzle whiskers, ears, or even bridle paths as is done in North America; frequently the fetlocks are also left untrimmed. The mane is braided on the side to which it falls—either the right or the left—and the braids are usually larger and fewer in number than would be acceptable in an American show stable. The top of the dock is pulled or sometimes clipped with electric clippers, which can make it uncontrollably bristly as it grows out. While the European look is becoming more common as more horses are imported, American show ring standards prefer a cleaner look with more attention to trimming and fine details. The influence of the hunter show ring is evident in the presentation of American show jumpers and is felt to some extent in the turnout of dressage horses, while. eventers often follow British presentation standards.

Turnout and Braiding for Dressage

Dressage competitions are the epitome of formality, the direct descendant of command performances before royalty in the courts of Europe. Horse and rider are judged on the perfection and purity of each movement, so turnout and braiding should never distract or be disturbing to the eye. Besides, most dressage judges are conservative in outlook and are unfavorably impressed by an untidy or flamboyant turnout. Dressage competition rules prohibit ribbons, bangles, or any kind of decorations except for a braided mane, which may be accented with white tape. An impeccably turned out horse, sparkling clean, with clean, conservative, and well-fitted tack and a rider equally well presented, makes the best impression.

TRIMMING FOR DRESSAGE HORSES

Dressage horses should be trimmed as neatly as any other breed, with fetlocks and lower leg hair closely trimmed and the coronary band hair trimmed to an even line. The legs may be booted up, especially if the horse has heavy leg hair or white markings, but close-clipped areas should be carefully blended. Long hair should be trimmed from the jawline and the first few inches of the throat, and a short bridle path should be clipped (one to two inches). The outside edges of the ears may be trimmed to give them a neater appearance, but it is not necessary or even advisable to clip the hair from the inside of the ears. If the inner hair is removed and the horse is bothered by flies or gnats attacking his unprotected ears, he may start tossing his head and spoil a performance. Horses with large ears are not flattered by removing the inside hair, anyway—this can make the ear appear larger. In this country, the muzzle whiskers are usually clipped closely, but this practice is not followed in Europe and some American dressage competitors choose to leave muzzle and eye whiskers natural.

FIGURE 108. Dressage horse correctly turned out for show.

Dressage Manes

The mane of a dressage horse should be pulled to a uniform length of three and a half to five inches; it is usually braided for competition. The braids may be done as flat hunter braids, knob-style braids, sewn-in button braids, or Euro-style banded braids. Dressage braids are often thicker than hunter braids and may be fewer in number, averaging about twenty to twenty-five braids instead of the thirty or more on a hunter mane; however, some exhibitors prefer more smaller braids. Unlike hunter braiding, the forelock may be left unbraided, which sometimes is more flattering to a horse with a large or Roman-nosed head. In this country it is more common to braid the mane on the right, but in Europe the mane is braided on either side, whichever way the mane naturally falls, and this is acceptable although less usual in American competitions.

Taped Braids

Mane braids may be accented with white tape, which is either wrapped around each braid on the side, over the fastening or around the "knob" so that it is visible above the neck from both sides. The tape should be no more than a quarter-inch wide and only white should be used. Narrow white plastic tape especially for braiding is available in tack shops. If the forelock is braided, it should also be taped. You can braid with yarn or rubber bands as for hunter braids and then apply tape over the braids. If the mane is to be taped, the yarn should match the color of the mane. A dark mane may also be braided with white yarn, which gives a little accent but a less noticeable effect than white tape.

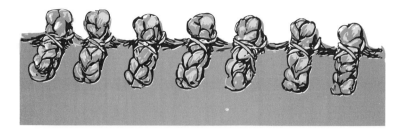

A. Knob style braids, untaped

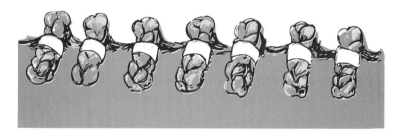

B. Braids taped on side

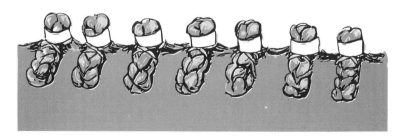

C. Tape around knob

FIGURE 109. Taped braids with knobs.

FIGURE 110. Making banded braids.

Euro-Style Banded Braids and Button Braids

The most common style of dressage braiding, which is rapidly gaining in popularity, are Euro-style banded braids. These braids are done with rubber braiding bands, which makes them quick, secure, and easy to take out. They may be secured with white braiding bands, which results in a narrow line of white on each braid; this may be taped over or left untaped. However, as with all rubber band braiding, they may cause some breakage and damage to the mane hair.

Sewn-in button braids are also appropriate, stay in well, and look nice whether taped or not. (For instructions on basic braiding, see chapter 10.)

How to Do Euro-Style Banded Braids:

1. You will need a comb or mane divider, sponge, water, or Quik Braid, a hair clip, and braiding bands in the same color as the mane hair. You may also use white braiding bands to secure the final braids.

2. Dampen and measure off a section of mane (approximately one inch" wide) and part it into three strands. Clip the rest of the mane hair out of the way.

3. Braid the three strands tightly to the ends of the hairs, then fold the ends of the hairs upward. Wrap a braiding band tightly around the tiny knob.

4. Fold the end of the braid under a third of the way up the braid. Then fold the braid under once again, resulting in a small loop of triple thickness.

5. Using a second band (a white band), wrap the whole braid together, keeping the band as close to the crest as possible. Wrap the band at least three times, depending on the thickness of the braid. Do not leave any gaps of mane showing between wraps of the band.

6. Be careful to keep the braids uniform, with the band at the same place on each braid.

FIGURE 111. Euro-style banded braids.

To sew in button braids you will need heavy braiding thread (button and carpet thread will do) in a color to match the mane, scissors, and a large-eye metal or plastic needle. A yarn needle (available in knitting shops) works well, or some tack stores sell braiding needles.

How to Do Sewn-In Button Braids

1. Separate, wet, and braid a section of mane to two-thirds of its length, as you would for a conventional yarn braid. Place the center of a fifteen-inch piece of thread behind the braid and add it in, as you would add in a piece of yarn. Tie the ends off with a double slip knot, as in using yarn.

2. Thread the ends of the thread through the braiding needle. This is easier to do if the ends are cut off together.

3. Use the needle to pull the braid up, stitching up through the braid at the crest of the neck.

4. Stitch back down through the braided loop, using large stitches. The thread ends should come out the end of the braided loop.

5. Turn the doubled braid under again and stitch up through, close to the crest. Bring the thread around the braid to the right and stitch up through the braid again.

6. Bring the thread around to the left and stitch up through the braid once again.

7. Unthread the needle and separate the thread ends. Cross them behind the braid and wrap them around the braid once or twice, tying them in a square knot about a quarter inch to a half inch down the braid on the side, then trim the ends short. The finished braid should be short, tight, and rounded, resembling a braided button.

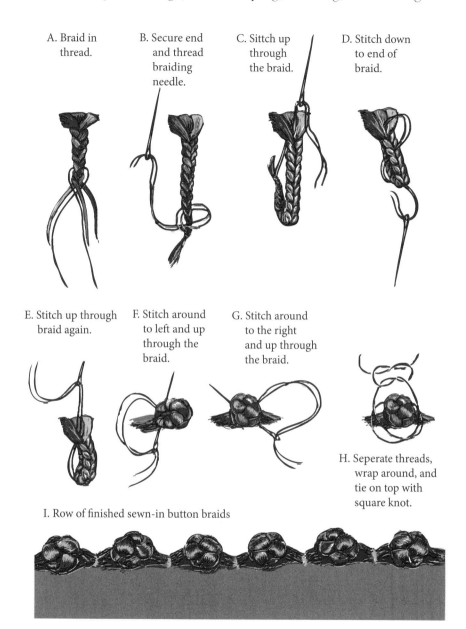

A. Braid in thread.

B. Secure end and thread braiding needle.

C. Sittch up through the braid.

D. Stitch down to end of braid.

E. Stitch up through braid again.

F. Stitch around to left and up through the braid.

G. Stitch around to the right and up through the braid.

H. Seperate threads, wrap around, and tie on top with square knot.

I. Row of finished sewn-in button braids

FIGURE 112. Button braids.

Other Types of Braiding

While taped braids are the most commonly seen, other styles are permissible for dressage shows. Although it is customary to pull the manes of dressage horses, long-maned horses like Arabians or Morgans may show in dressage without pulling the mane. They may put the mane up in doubled and sewn button braids or Euro-style banded braids, or leave it free and natural, according to the custom and standards of their breed. However, there are two special mane styles that are used on long-maned horses.

French Braid or Running Braid

The French braid (or running braid) is a long, single braid that runs along the crest. It encompasses all the hair much like a tail braid, except that the strands are added from one side only. A French braid may be done as a high, tight line of braiding along the crest, or as a "dropped" braid, which falls several inches below the crest. One disadvantage of a French braid right along the crest is that it will loosen and buckle as the horse flexes and stretches his neck; this is not a problem with the dropped French braid.

To Put the Mane up in a French Braid

1. Part three strands at the front of the mane, with each strand about three quarters-inch wide. Cross the center strand over the right-hand strand.

2. Bring the third strand (left-hand strand) behind the end of the first strand. (The first strand is "sandwiched" between the second and third strands.)

3. Bring the highest strand (the end of the first strand) down behind the end of the second strand. This begins the braid.

4. Part another strand about three quarters-inch wide from the edge of the mane and add it to the strand just braided, passing it underneath the braid. Keep the braiding tight and close against the neck.

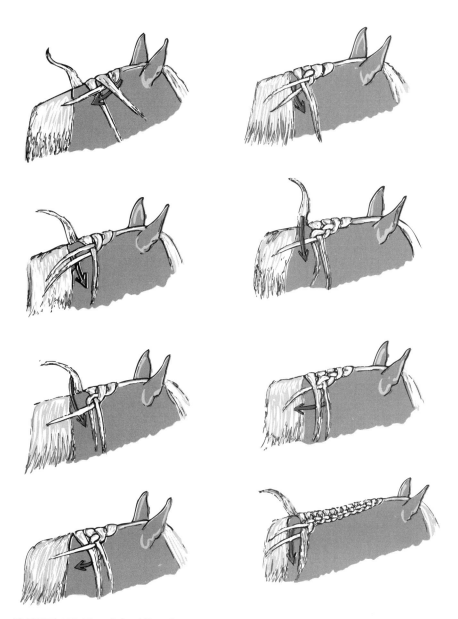

FIGURE 113. French braiding the mane.

5. Bring the strand at the far right around behind the braid and into the center.

6. Continue to braid by bringing the highest strand (upper left) around behind the braid and into the center, then parting and adding a strand from the edge of the mane. Then bring the upper right strand around behind and into the center.

7. Keep the braid tight and well up against the crest of the neck. Continue along the crest to the withers. The thickness of the strands may need to be adjusted to keep the strands perpendicular to the neck and the braid even.

8. At the end of the neck, stop adding hairs from the crest and braid the remaining hairs out into a short pigtail. This can be fastened with a rubber band or turned under and fastened with yarn as in a hunter braid.

To Do a "Dropped" French Braid

1. Begin in the same way as a regular French braid (see directions above).

2. Each time you part and add a strand from the mane, bring it down three to four inches before adding it to the braid. This should result in a braid that hangs in a smooth even line, three to four inches below the crest of the neck.

3. Keep the braiding strands of an equal length, so the dropped braid stays smooth, even and level. Finish the dropped braid in the same way as a regular French braid.

4. A dropped braid may need to be reinforced by weaving braiding yarn (in a color to match the mane) into the braid with a braiding needle, especially at the beginning of the braid.

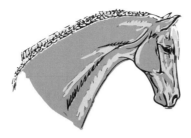

A. French braid

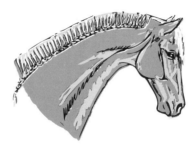

B. Dropped french braid

FIGURE 114. French braids.

Continental or Lattice Braid

The Continental braid (or lattice braid) is some-times used on Arabians, Morgans, Andalusians, and other long-maned horses. It does not really involve braiding, but creates a striking pattern of diamond shapes by parting, banding, and reparting the mane. It looks particularly attractive when the mane color contrasts with that of the neck.

To put the mane up in a Continental braid, you will need braiding bands and plastic mending tape a half-inch to one-inch wide. The tape may be either white or black, but colored tape is not appropriate for dressage competition.

To Put up the Mane in a Continental or Lattice Braid

1. Part the mane into one-inch segments. Apply a rubberband around each segment about one inch below the crest, keeping the mane pulled down against the side of the neck. The bands should all be the same distance from the neck.

2. Cover each band with a piece of tape. (Do not try to tape the mane without securing it with a rubberband first, as the tape will not hold securely alone.)

3. Part each segment below the tape into two sections. Band each half-section to the half-section beside it. This forms the first row of diamonds. Cover each band with a piece of tape.

4. The end sections are not divided, but are banded to the half-section next to them.

5. Continue the process as above to make two or three rows of diamonds, depending on the length of the mane. Too many rows distract the eye from the top of the crest and can distort the diamond shapes. The hair below the bottom row of diamonds is allowed to hang free.

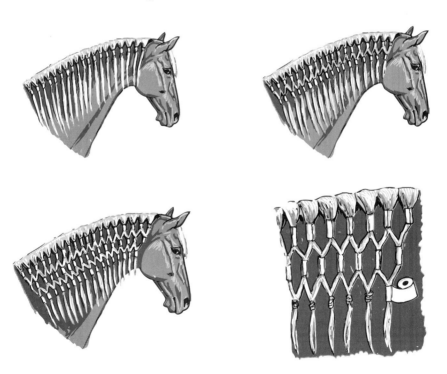

FIGURE 115. Continental or lattice braid.

BANGING THE TAIL

The tail of the dressage horse is important, as it is an extension of the spine and its carriage gives the judge an indication of how well the horse uses its back. While tail braiding is permissible under the rules, this can cause a horse to carry its tail stiffly and lose points, so tails are seldom braided for dressage. Instead, the hairs at the top of the tail are pulled or trimmed with clippers to slim down the line of the dock to the point where the dock turns over when the tail is carried in motion. The skirt of the tail may be banged off square or left in a natural point. While English grooms tend to favor a shorter tail, banged off level with the bottom of the hocks, in North America a longer tail, reaching to the bottom of the fetlock joint, is preferred. A bang tail is not a requirement; some horses may look better with a natural switch tail.

The term, "banging a tail" comes from the old method of squaring off the skirt of a horse's tail. The bound tail hair was laid across an upturned blade and given a "bang" with a block of wood, cutting the hair off squarely.

When squaring off a tail, always have a helper raise the tail to the angle at which the horse carries it when he is moving. The skirt should be cut straight across at a slight angle, so that the bottom of the tail hangs level when the horse is in motion. Electric clippers do the best job of squaring off a banged tail—run your fist around the hairs down to the bottom of

A. Tail untrimmed   B. Tail pulled, trimmed, and banged

FIGURE 116. Banged tail.

the skirt and hold it firmly, and trim the ends of the hairs level with the clippers. You can bang a tail by cutting the ends with heavy scissors, but it is more difficult to get it exactly square and level.

PULLING THE TAIL

The upper part of the dock may be pulled or trimmed to give it a slimmer appearance, which emphasizes the tail carriage. The hair is pulled short along the sides of the dock for a distance of about 4 and a half to six inches, depending on the size of the horse and his natural tail carriage. The pulling should taper off just before the "turnover point" of the tail, and it should be done mostly along the sides and hardly at all on top. If the pulled area is extended too far down the dock or the hair is pulled too short, the contrast between the short-haired dock and the long hair of the skirt gives an ungraceful "broom-handle" appearance. A well-pulled tail looks natural when it is carried in motion, but the lower side hairs are thinned and shortened so they do not obscure the underline of the dock.

When pulling the tail, you can use a metal pulling comb or your fingers; you may wish to protect your fingers with a wrapping of duct tape. Pliers may be used to pluck out short hairs that are too short to grasp with the fingers. Work from the top of the dock down the edge, pulling the hairs very short for a quarter-inch strip along the hairless side of the dock; this pulled strip should taper off to the point of turnover. When you have pulled a quarter-inch strip from each side for about six to eight inches, begin at the top and pull another quarter-inch strip, blending this strip in a little earlier. Continue until the hair at the sides of the dock is shortened but not completely stripped bare, and stop to hold up the tail and check your work frequently. The pulling should not extend up onto the top of the tail, and it should not be obvious when looking at the tail from the side. It is better to leave the hair a little too long than to pull it too much and have the tail look bald.

If the hair on the top of the dock is thick and bushy, you may carefully thin it by pulling out a few hairs—just enough to make the hair lie down more easily. Be careful not to pull too many hairs form one spot, creating an obvious short patch of hair.

TRIMMING THE DOCK

An alternative method is to trim the sides of the dock with clippers. Use #15 or #30 blades, which must be very sharp. Starting at the top edge of the dock, run the clipper blades downward with the hairs, pressing lightly and evenly to thin and shorten the side hairs for only about five or six inches. Taper the trimmed area smoothly under the top hair, to just above the turnover point. Trim the sides of the dock until they are even with the width of the tailbone, but do not use the clippers on the upper side of the dock. This trimming will have to be repeated every two weeks, or whenever the trimmed hair begins to get too long and bristly.

Some horses do not enjoy having their tails handled, much less pulled, and a horse can register a very effective protest! If you pull only a very few hairs at a time and pull them out with a swift jerk straight out (not a long pull down or sideways), most horses don't object. If the horse is sensitive, pull only a few hairs each day until you get the tail sufficiently short, or use the clippers to trim him instead of pulling. When pulling tail hairs, you may see tiny points of blood on the skin. This is harmless and is not painful, but it should be wiped away with a baby wipe or a clean sponge.

Horses that have had their tails pulled or trimmed should have a tail wrap applied to the dampened hair of the upper dock for an hour or so before they show. This smooths and shapes the hair of the dock and enhances the shape of the tail. Make sure to remove the tail bandage before the horse enters the ring, as the rules forbid all bandages, including tail bandages, in competition. Should you forget to remove the tail wrap, the entry would be eliminated.

Pulling or trimming the top of the dock is not mandatory. Some horses, especially Arabians and others with a naturally high tail carriage, or horses that carry their tails crookedly, look best with a natural, untrimmed tail.

Dressage horses should be cleaned and finished off as other show horses before entering the ring, but with one exception—do not wipe the foam from the horse's mouth or the bit. In dressage, foam is considered a desirable sign of a relaxed and responsive mouth; in fact, some dressage riders feed their horses sugar before warming up to encourage the horse to chew the bit and make foam!

Hair at the sides of the dock is trimmed or pulled short.

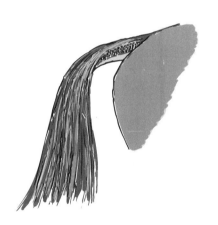

Dock pulled to breakover point   Dock trimmed too far down

FIGURE 117. Trimming dock.

Some additional final touches include applying silicone coat spray to the coat and the skirt of the tail; putting on dark hoof oil or hoof polish, and using highlighter gel on the face, muzzle, eyelids, and ears. Fly repellent should be used on the face and ears, but be sure that it is not strong enough to burn the fine skin of the head. Since the horse must remain obedient, attentive, and on the bit throughout her test, the distraction of flies or gnats can be a hindrance to his performance.

Turnout for Show Jumpers and Eventers

Show jumpers and eventers are judged solely on their performance, and their turnout is not judged specifically as long as their equipment is legal under the rules of competition. Nevertheless, any serious competitor will want to appear well turned out as a courtesy to the audience and the judges, and to reflect her pride in her horse, her stable, and sometimes her team. While perfect braids or a clean coat won't make a horse jump higher, these and other points of turnout indicate the rider's and the stable's attention to detail—or lack of it. The best competitors get all the details right!

In the athletically demanding world of show jumping and three-day eventing, the groom's job is directed primarily toward the aspects of grooming that affect the horse's and rider's safety and ability to perform at their athletic best, and only secondarily concerned with appearance. A groom must be thoroughly familiar with each piece of equipment the horse wears and its correct adjustment. He must check the strength and security of each strap and buckle, the fit of boots and bandages, the adjustment of noseband, martingale, and breast-plate, and the security and balance of the weight cloth. The correct studs must be put into the shoes according to the ground conditions. The groom must also be familiar with the rules and know what could disqualify or penalize a rider—for instance, if an eventing competitor carries a whip into the dressage arena, he will be eliminated. During an event or between rounds of a class, the groom may have to help both horse and rider recover as quickly as possible from their exertions and be ready to go on with the next phase or into a jump-off calm, refreshed, and ready. In addition, the demands of these events often mean that the groom must contend with a horse that is extremely hot, tired, and stressed, and requires expert skill and knowledge in cooling out and after-care. This requires more knowledge than can be adequately conveyed in this chapter. Event grooming in particular is best learned through apprenticeship to an experienced event groom, or by going to events and learning on the job by helping as one of the "pit crew" volunteers. An excellent book on grooming for eventers is *The Event Groom's Handbook* (Event Books International, 1983) by Jeanne Kane and Lisa Waltman.

SHOW JUMPERS

The standards for trimming and braiding show jumpers and event horses are similar to those for dressage horses. Show jumpers' manes are often braided as hunters, with many small flat braids put in with yarn, or they may use sewn-in button braids or Euro-style banded braids. The braids are never taped for show jumping; the forelock may be braided or left free. Some jumpers wear a slightly longer mane (about five to seven inches) and are left unbraided, but most have their manes pulled to the shorter length appropriate for hunters: about three and a half to five inches.

Many show jumpers wear a decorative ear cover, to protect their ears from flies, reduce noise, and sometimes to retain the ear plugs used to further block the noise of the crowd. The forelock is usually left unbraided underneath the ear cover.

Show jumpers' tails, especially Thoroughbreds, may be braided as a hunter tail but are often left free. If the tail is never braided, it may be pulled like the tail of a dressage horse, or it may be left natural. Some warmbloods have large, thick docks and thick, coarse tail hair; their tails are usually pulled short as they do not braid as easily or look as nice when braided as most Thoroughbreds.

FIGURE 118. Show jumper correctly turned out for competition.

EVENT HORSES

Event horses are usually presented as for dressage horses, with a pulled mane and pulled and banged tail. For the dressage phase of an event, they are turned out as for a formal dressage show. They are also braided and turned out beautifully for the formal veterinary inspection required at three-day events. Because many of the top eventers have English grooms, it is common to see English show grooming details such as English plaits, quarter marks and shark tooth patterns on the quarters, and pulled and banged tails on event horses.

Appropriate mane braids for event horses include flat hunter braids, knob-style hunter braids, sewn-in button braids, English plaits (similar to sewn-in button braids, but larger and fewer), and Euro-style banded braids. Braids may be taped or banded with white for the dressage phase or formal veterinary inspection. Braiding is not required and is often omitted in lower-level competition, but the mane should be evenly pulled, clean, and neat.

Event horses usually go unbraided for the cross-country phase. However, a single braid is sewn into the mane just behind the ears; a shoelace is attached to the bridle crownpiece and securely braided into it. This prevents the bridle from coming off in case a horse should part company with his rider over a cross-country fence. If time permits, the mane may be braided for stadium jumping, but the braids are not taped and tail braiding is seldom seen.

FIGURE 119. *Event horse correctly turned out for formal veterinary inspection.*

COMBINED DRIVING AND OTHER DRIVING COMPETITIONS

Combined driving is a relatively new sport, similar to three-day eventing, but done with a carriage and a single horse or pony, a pair, or a four in hand. A Combined Driving Event or CDE involves a driven dressage test, requiring formal turnout, a marathon, including varied terrain and obstacles (similar to the cross-country phase of eventing), and a cones competition. There are also carriage driving and pleasure driving competitions, in which the turnout of the horse, whip (driver), and vehicle are important factors in the judging. Driving classes are also offered in horse shows for various breeds, but turnout for these classes is covered under their respective breeds.

In carriage driving, horses or ponies should be presented with trimming and braiding appropriate for their breed and type. For instance, Friesian horses would be shown with long manes, tails, and feather on the legs, while a sport horse or pony would have a pulled and/or braided mane. The type of vehicle also matters; horses shown to a draft cart would be braided and trimmed as draft horses, while those put to a gig or sporting vehicle would be trimmed and braided accordingly. Because there are great variations in requirements according to the vehicle, breed of horse or pony, and the class or competition, it is essential to check the details of correct turnout with an expert. This is too large a subject to cover in detail here.

Combined driving is one of the international equestrian sports, so the horses and ponies that compete in it are usually turned out as sport horses. Most have pulled manes and tails and are shown in dressage or formal presentation classes with braided manes. The braids are usually sewn-in button braids (often very small and neat) or Euro-style banded braids, though flat hunter style braids are also acceptable. Tails are unbraided and may be pulled and banged or natural.

For the marathon, manes are usually unbraided; some competitors put the tail up in a mud tail so it is less likely to switch mud or water over the whip (driver) or get caught over the reins. It's also a good idea to attach a shoelace to the crownpiece of the bridle and braid this into a securely sewn-in braid at the poll, to prevent the bridle from coming off in case of an accident on course.

Horses and ponies are turned out more formally for the cones competition than for the marathon. While it is not required to rebraid the mane for the last phase of a one-day event, they are usually braided for the cones competition on the third day of a combined driving event.

Chapter 12

The Western Show Horse

The purpose of western trimming styles is to show off the characteristic features of the western horse and to contribute to the best overall picture of horse and rider.

Old-time cowboys trimmed their horses purely for practical reasons if they trimmed them at all. The tails of working cow horses were shortened to keep them from picking up a stray piece of cactus, which could have immediate and violent consequences! The mane was sometimes roached to keep the rider's rope or fingers from getting tangled when roping—an accident that could cost a cowboy a finger. A roached or shortened mane made it easier for the reined cow horse to respond to the "rustle of the rein" along his neck. Traditionally, trimming also allowed a cowboy to tell at a glance whether a horse was broken to ride or unhandled. The vaqueros of California cut a single tuft of mane at the withers to indicate a finished horse that worked "straight up in the bridle"; two tufts indicated a green horse, still working in a hackamore, and an untrimmed mane meant an unbroken horse. While few of today's western show horses ever actually work cattle, western tradition still influences our thinking about what looks right on a western horse.

The outstanding characteristics of the stock-type horse are full, broad and well-muscled hindquarters; a compact and powerful appearance without extreme height or legginess; clean and athletic legs and feet, and a neat, wedge-shaped head radiating intelligence and cow sense. The conformation and type of the western show horse has evolved into a taller, slimmer, more refined, and longer-legged horse than the early "bulldog" type. The roached mane and shortened tail that was seen on the shorter, stouter horses of years past is not as flattering to the taller, more streamlined modern western show horse. In addition, some western horses are also shown in English classes such as Hunter Under. Current styles favor a long, full tail and a shortened, pulled, and "banded" mane with a medium-long bridle path. Western performance horses usually have a long, free mane, especially in reining, working cow horse, cutting, roping, and speed events.

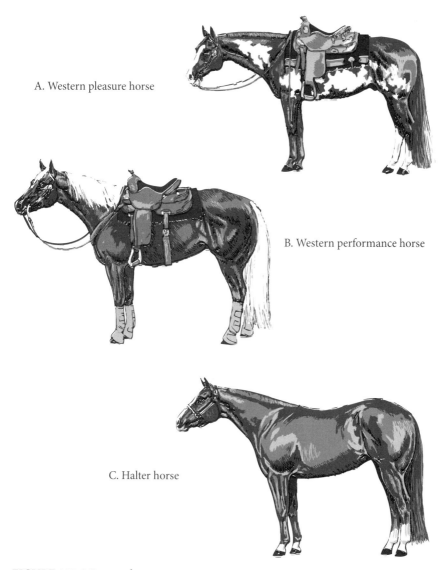

A. Western pleasure horse

B. Western performance horse

C. Halter horse

FIGURE 120. Western show types.

One place where western competitors let their imagination run wild is in barrel racing and similar speed events. Along with colorful tack and running boots in red, white, and blue or bright neon colors (even pink and turquoise barrel racing saddles), glitz and glitter have become popular accents to the excitement of speed events. Some barrel racers apply colored glitter stencils of an American flag or other design to the horse's hindquarters, or wipe glitter gel onto the mane or the top of the tail. Please note that this is *only* for barrel racing and similar speed events—never use glitter or fancy designs on any other type of show horse, or the judge may show you the gate!

Trimming the Western Horse

The finer points of the stock horse head can be emphasized by careful trimming. All long hair should be removed from the lower jaw, and the whiskers should be trimmed off closely. The characteristic "fox" ear of the Quarter Horse and related breeds is emphasized by closely trimming the hair of the outside edges and clipping it clean inside. For top-level halter competition, the inside hair is completely removed, sometimes by using a depilatory cream such as Nair. A tiny "diamond" is left at the inside tip of the ear, which gives it a natural sharp point. (Since this removes the horse's natural protection from flies, he must be protected with fly repellent and a fly mask with ear covers.)

Horses that grow a heavy hair coat may have their muzzle, jaw, and face clipped closely, but the hair on the jowl should be left natural except for trimming the lower edge of the jaw. This looks best on greys, roans, or Appaloosas, which show less obvious color difference where the hair is clipped. Large white markings such as a wide blaze or bald face are often clipped to make them appear whiter and finer, but they should not be cut so closely that they appear pink and "scalped." The #10 clipper blade usually works best. Since clipping the muzzle and face removes much of the horse's natural sun protection, he will need sunscreen ointment applied to the white areas to prevent sunburn.

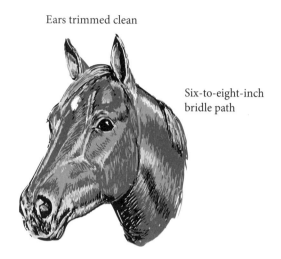

Ears trimmed clean

Six-to-eight-inch
bridle path

Face, jaw, and muzzle
trimmed clean

FIGURE 121. Western horse head, showing trimming.

BRIDLE PATH

A well-trimmed bridle path sets off the head and neck of the western horse. Western bridle paths are usually longer than those of hunters, averaging about six to eight inches. A large horse or one with a heavy throat looks more refined with a longer bridle path, but don't extend the bridle path too far or the mane will appear out of proportion, as if it started halfway down the neck. If the horse is to be shown in English classes as well as Western, you should compromise with a shorter bridle path—the braids should start as close to the ear as possible to give a long, smooth unbroken line of the neck. A four- to six-inch bridle path is more acceptable in this case.

THE MANE AND FORELOCK

It is traditional for a western horse's mane to fall to the left side, originally to prevent it from getting in the way of the rope, which is handled on the right. English manes usually fall to the right, which leaves the versatile horse caught in the middle! However, changing the side to which the mane falls is difficult, especially if the mane is pulled short. If a mane naturally lies smoothly all on one side, it is often neater and easier to leave it on that side. If part of the mane crosses over or if a cowlick stands up, this part must be trained to lie down on the correct side. Few judges take much notice of which side the mane falls on, as long as it is well pulled, neat, and lies smoothly all on one side.

Pulled Manes

The mane is usually pulled to a length of three and a half to six inches. The length should complement the length and shape of the neck of the individual horse, and the type of hair should be taken into account. The mane should be long enough to lie smoothly all on one side. It will need careful pulling (as described in chapter 5) to make the mane appear even yet natural and thin enough to present a refined appearance. A short, fine mane makes the neck appear longer and more refined; a massive neck can carry a longer mane, which would be out of proportion on a thin, slim neck.

Long Manes

Western performance horsemen, especially those competing in reining, barrel racing, and speed events, increasingly prefer the look of a longer mane, which accents the line of the neck when the horse is working at speed. A thick or uneven mane may be thinned or trimmed to give it a better appearance. AQHA Versatility Ranch Horse competitions and

FIGURE 122. *Quarter horse with banded mane.*

FIGURE 123. Longer mane for Western performance horse.

Foundation Quarter Horse shows require a more traditional working ranch horse appearance, banning braided or banded manes, tail extensions, and coloring of the mane or tail. Arabians, Morgans, Palominos, and other pleasure breeds in Western classes generally adhere to the standard for these breeds, which is a long, natural tail and a full mane grown as long as nature will allow, with a six- to eight-inch bridle path.

Banded Manes

Most western pleasure and halter horses are shown with a banded mane. The hair is wet down and parted into small segments about a half-inch wide. Each segment is combed and pulled down flat against the correct side of the neck and a rubber band is wound around it close to the roots. Banding must be done neatly, evenly, and with uniformity, and the bands should match the color of the mane. As with a braided mane, banding should be done on the day of the show and the bands should be removed at the end of the day. The easiest way to remove the bands is to cut them with a seam ripper, with the point downward.

How to Band a Mane

1. You will need a comb, hair clip, bands, and setting gel. Dampen the hair before banding.

2. Part a half-inch section of hair, starting behind the ears; clip the rest of the mane off to the side.

3. Wrap the band several times around the section of hair, keeping the band close to the neck.

4. Repeat until the entire mane is banded, then apply setting gel to the banded mane. (Using setting gel before banding may make the hair too slippery to band neatly.)

5. Pull on the bottom hairs of each banded section to make them turn under and lie close to the neck. Any extra long ends of hair should be snipped off with scissors.

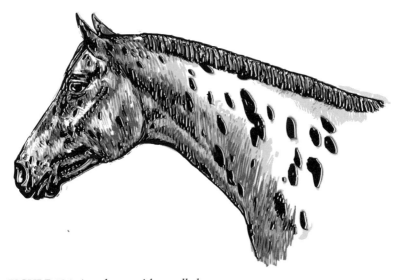

FIGURE 124. *Appaloosa with a pulled mane.*

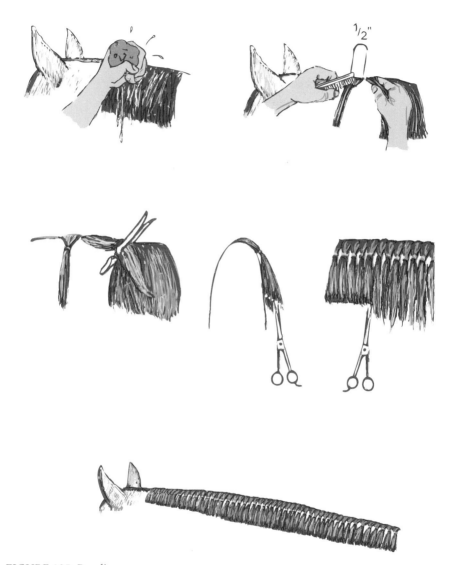

FIGURE 125. Banding a mane.

CRIMPING THE MANE

Some exhibitors use a butane-heated curling iron to crimp or turn a mane under on the desired side, instead of banding the mane. This works well on very short manes of three to four inches, and is one way to make a wiry mane lie down neatly. A crimped mane will stay neat for a halter class, but may not lie down as neatly as a banded mane for a long day of showing or if it's windy. The mane should be curled under with the curling iron, one section at a time, and setting gel is applied to keep it flat and smooth during the class. Do not use too hot a setting or apply the iron for too long or it may damage the hair.

THE FORELOCK

The forelock should be in proportion to the horse's head. For a fine-headed horse, the forelock should be fairly thin and not too long. A horse with a large or plain head usually looks better with a longer, fuller forelock—a very thin, short forelock emphasizes a convex profile, giving the horse the sloping-forehead look of a Neanderthal! If a horse's forelock is excessively thick and bushy and pulling it does not solve the problem, you can carefully clip a strip of half an inch or so from each side and from underneath, leaving a reasonable amount of forelock. This clipping will have to be repeated at least once a week or it will form an unsightly stubble as it grows out. The horse must be held very still when clipping—if he tosses his head, you could remove his whole forelock!

Some exhibitors prefer the look of a braided forelock, especially when the horse has a fine head and a pretty face marking or small, shapely ears. The dampened hairs are gathered into a single braided pigtail and fastened with a single rubber band of the same color as the mane. Sometimes the end is fastened with a tiny silver barrette in the shape of a concho. Check your breed rules, however—Quarter Horse rules prohibit braiding of any kind in halter or showmanship classes.

Western Tails

A long, full tail is prized as one of the chief beauties of a western show horse, and the natural tail is grown as long as possible. The skirt of the tail should be long and full, reaching to the pastern area, while the hair of the dock should be flat and smooth, not bushy, to emphasize the width of the hindquarters. Horses with thin, short, or damaged tails often have hair extensions added to supplement their natural tail hair.

The skirt of the tail should be well picked out, clean and full; conditioner or a detangling product can be used to make the hair silky, shiny, and free of knots or tangles. To make the skirt fuller and slightly wavy, it can be braided into several pigtails and sprayed with hair spray or setting gel; when unbraided and carefully picked out, it will have more body and a slight crimp or wave. If a tail is particularly bushy at the top, a little careful thinning can be done to reduce the thickness, but the hair should not be noticeably shortened. A tail wrap applied over the dampened hair of the dock for an hour or so will make the hair of the dock lie flatter and trimmer.

Because a single tail hair can take several years to grow to ground length, all possible measures should be taken to prevent loss and breakage of the tail hair. The skirt of the tail should be protected by keeping it clean, conditioned and protected in a braid, tail bag, or tail cover. Some exhibitors simply keep the skirt in a single long braid; others use a tail cover or tail bag over the braid, or divide the skirt into three strands, which are inserted into lycra tail tubes and braided. The braid or tail cover cannot make the hair grow faster or longer, but it preserves the hairs so they do not break off or pull out as they naturally would if unprotected.

Braids or tail covers are less effective than a natural tail for swishing off flies, and some horses hit themselves with the bag or braid and become upset. If a horse is turned out with his tail in a braid or tail protector, a length of "fly fringe" should be attached to the end to swish off flies, and a fly sheet and fly repellent are recommended for extra protection.

A long, full tail can get dirty or damaged during ordinary riding, exercise, or warmup. If the skirt is very long, a horse may even step on his own tail while backing up, which can hurt as well as spoiling the looks of his tail. For this reason, the tail is usually kept in a braid or in its tail bag or tail protector during exercise, schooling, and turnout. The tail should be trimmed to pastern level; always check the length of the skirt and any tail extensions by backing the horse, as the horse's hindquarters and tail drop lower when backing up.

TAIL HAIR EXTENSIONS

With the recent trend toward longer and fuller tails, tail hair extensions have become a popular way to augment western horses' natural tail hair. AQHA and most other stock horse breed rules state that tails may be lengthened only with natural horsehair, using a hair-to-hair attachment with no attachment of any kind to the tailbone. It's important to check the rules for your breed and show division before purchasing a tail extension. (For details on selection, application, and care of tail hair extensions, see chapter 5.)

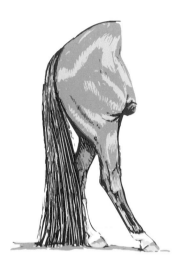

Tail should just touch the ground when the horse backs up.

FIGURE 126. Checking height of tail extension.

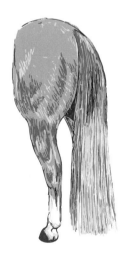

A. Short, thin tail

B. Natural loop style tail hair extension

C. Tail extension in place

FIGURE 127. Tail extension.

A. Part hair two inches above end of tailbone, twist, and secure with hair clip. Separate three braiding strands.

B. Slide loop over one strand and braid it in.

C. Make two small security braids with tail hair and extension hair.

D. Let down hair and comb over extension.

FIGURE 128. *Applying loop-style extension.*

Legs and Feet

A western horse should have clean, well-defined legs without an excess of hair. Chestnuts should be cut off close to the skin and smoothed with Vaseline; they may be darkened to the color of the leg. The fetlocks and any hair at the back of the knee and lower leg should be trimmed closely, clipping with the hair so the hair is thinned and shortened evenly but no obvious clipped zone is visible. The coronary band should be trimmed evenly, and the ergot may have to be cut off close to the skin so that the fetlocks may be trimmed closely. Horses with white legs or that grow heavy hair on the legs may be booted up using a #10 or #15 clipper blade, but the clipping must be very neat and even, without scalping, leaving clipper tracks, or clipping so closely that surface scratches are visible.

The hoof wall should be scrubbed clean with a nail brush or a vegetable brush before hoof polish or hoof dressing is applied. Some exhibitors sand the outer wall of the hoof to make it clean and smooth, but this removes the *periople,* the hoof's natural protective outer coating. If you insist on sanding the feet, you must immediately apply a hoof sealant to take the place of the periople and prevent the hoof from drying and cracking. If the hoof wall has cracks or other surface defects, these can be filled in with acrylic putty; an opaque hoof polish will hide the repairs

Hoof polish gives an even, opaque, and glossy finish to the feet. Horses with white feet usually look best with clear hoof dressing, as black dressing below a white leg makes the hoof appear larger. Appaloosas wear clear hoof polish, as their striped feet are a breed characteristic which should be visible to the judge. Horses with dark legs may use black, brown, or clear hoof polish or a dark oil hoof dressing. Brown hoof polish often looks better on a chestnut or sorrel, as it provides less contrast than black. Some western exhibitors have adopted the dark hoof oil dressing long preferred by hunter exhibitors; this type of dressing gives the foot a dark but natural-looking shine and is better for the condition of the hoof, but it picks up dirt and must be repainted before each class.

Hoof polish should removed by using hoof polish remover after the show.

Show Halters

When showing western horses in halter or showmanship classes, a leather halter is used, usually trimmed with silver. A show halter should fit in such a way as to follow the contours of the face and jaw and flatter the horse's head. The throatlatch is rounded and shaped to lie along the back edge of the jaw, outlining the jowl; the cheekpieces should lie just below and parallel to the upper edge of the cheekbone. The noseband lies high on the face, one to two finger widths below the corner of the cheekbone; it should be buckled snugly beneath the jaw without a large gap. A noseband fitted high and closely makes the horse's head appear shorter and more wedge-shaped; a low or loose noseband gives the illusion of a longer and less refined head. The center stay (which runs from the chin ring to the throatlash) should be adjusted so that it fits closely under the jaw without hanging loose.

Show halters come in a range of sizes, widths, and prices. The width of the leather and the type of decoration should flatter the individual horse. A horse with a massive, plain, and solid-colored head can carry a wider, heavier, and more ornate halter than a horse with a finer, smaller head or one with flashy face markings. When the halter has been custom fitted, the ends of the straps should be cut off so they will tuck neatly into their keepers without excess length sticking out.

A western show halter typically comes with a matching leather lead shank with a chain end. The chain may be doubled through the central chin ring or may be run through the left side ring, under the chin and snapped to the right ring. If this leaves too much chain on the left side, the chain can be passed through the right side ring and run along the right cheekpiece to fasten to the upper ring. The shank should always be held by the leather portion, not by the chain, so an excessively long chain is a nuisance. A chain over the nose is frowned upon in showmanship classes, although it may be necessary in order to have complete control of an unruly horse.

FIGURE 129. Western show halter, properly adjusted.

Chapter 13

The Pleasure and Versatility Breeds

Arabians, Morgans, Pintos, Palominos, Haflingers, and some other horses and ponies often present a trimming problem because of their versatility. How does one correctly trim a horse that may be shown in halter, western pleasure, English pleasure, driving, dressage, and perhaps in trail classes, speed events, or over fences too? Owners of pleasure horse breeds such as Arabians, Morgans, and Halflingers point to the versatility of their horses with pride. But while an owner-rider may become a quick-change artist in switching from English to western in three minutes or less, you cannot change trimming or braiding styles as easily as you can change your tack.

The Tail, Mane, and Forelock

The answer is a basic universal trim for pleasure horses that is acceptable in both English and western classes and in most breed show classes as well. A long, natural mane and tail, with a medium-to-long bridle path, is the norm for pleasure breeds, especially when shown in saddle seat English pleasure, western pleasure, or pleasure driving classes. It is also acceptable in Open English Pleasure classes and on pleasure-type horses shown in Hunt Seat classes.

The pleasure breeds are shown with a natural mane and tail as long and full as it will grow. The tail must be carried in a natural position without the help of tail sets, ginger, or artificial appliances. The horse's natural tail carriage is considered a conformation point in Arabians especially, and any interference with Nature in this area is considered an illegal and unfair

256

practice in showing. Neither the mane nor the tail should braided when showing these breeds, except when competing in hunter, jumper, dressage, or roadster classes in which braiding is customary.

A. Arabian, show trimmed

B. Morgan, show trimmed

C. Saddlebred, show pleasure trimmed

Figure 130. Pleasure breeds.

The mane and forelock are grown long and should be thinned or shortened only if necessary to give the mane a graceful slope from the front of the neck to the longest point above the point of the shoulder. It then tapers back up toward the withers. The mane should all lie on the same side, usually the right. A mane that tangles easily may need to be kept in long braids to protect it (see chapter 5 on mane and tail care).

The forelock can be quite long but is sometimes thinned if it appears too thick and bushy to complement the horse's head. Since a long forelock is usually considered a complement to a beautiful head, it should not be shortened. If a forelock is too thick and bushy to be tamed by careful pulling, a narrow strip (about half-inch wide) may be clipped closely along each side to reduce the bulk of the forelock. This must be done very carefully to avoid clipping too much, and it must be retrimmed every week or it will grow out into unsightly stubble.

BRIDLE PATH

A pleasure horse's bridle path is usually medium to long; this shows off the refinement of the ears, head, and throat, and keeps the mane neatly out of the way of the bridle. One way to measure a bridle path is to follow an imaginary line about 30 degrees back from the line of the back of the jaw. The point where this line intersects the crest is where the bridle path should begin. This will usually be no more than six to eight inches from the poll on the average horse. The bridle path may be cut slightly shorter or longer to flatter the individual horse, but a bridle path cut too far back breaks up the line of the crest and gives the impression that the horse is missing half his mane. The bridle path should be trimmed very closely, using #30 or #40 blades. Do not touch the hair coat next to the bridle path with such fine blades, as they will remove the hair right down to the skin!

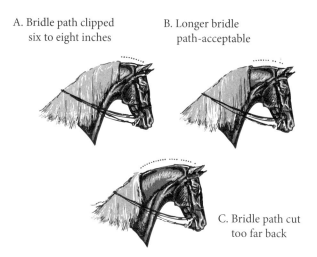

A. Bridle path clipped
six to eight inches

B. Longer bridle
path-acceptable

C. Bridle path cut
too far back

FIGURE 131. Bridle paths.

TO BRAID OR NOT TO BRAID?

Some pleasure breed exhibitors wish to show their horses or ponies in hunter or dressage classes, in which braiding is customary. A long, unbraided mane is perfectly acceptable in any dressage class, and is also allowable in hunter classes, even if the pulled and braided hunter mane is more conventional. A clean, well-brushed mane that lies on one side, with the forelock tucked neatly under the browband, is always appropriate for a pleasure horse or pony whether shown in Saddle Seat, Hunt Seat, Dressage, or Western tack. For driving classes, the forelock is sometimes braided and tucked back under the browband, to keep it out of the way of the browband and blinker stays.

A long mane can be braided for hunter or dressage competition by putting it into a French braid (running braid) along the crest. If the mane is not too long and thick, it may be braided into slightly larger button braids, doubled and sewn-in, or Euro-style banded braids. However, if the mane is too long or thick to make neat, uniform braids it should be put into a French braid or left unbraided; nothing looks worse than enormous sloppy braids!

The Continental braid (or lattice braid) is sometimes used on Andalusians, Arabians, Haflingers, and other long-maned horses for dressage competition, drill teams, and exhibition rides. It is not actually braiding, but creates a pattern of diamond shapes by parting, banding and reparting the mane The Continental braid is *not* appropriate horse show turnout for horse show pleasure or halter classes, and especially not for hunter classes. (For directions on French braiding and the Continental or lattice braid, please see chapter 11.)

TAIL CARE AND MAINTENANCE

A pleasure horse's tail is kept as long as it will grow, and a full and slightly wavy tail is considered a beauty. The skirt of the tail is usually allowed to grow to a natural point, although "banging" or squaring it off at pastern height is optional. The long hair of the tail and mane should be carefully hand-picked, never combed or brushed. Spraying the long hair with a conditioner or silicone coat product makes the hairs slippery, which makes it easier to pick the tail clean of bedding and tangles without breaking off or pulling out hairs. The skirt of the tail should be shampooed and treated with hair conditioner to strengthen and smooth the surface of the hairs so they do not tangle or catch on things and break off. The skirt is usually kept in a braid, tail cover, or a tail bag when the horse is not showing; the braid may be doubled up and protected with a Vet-rap bandage or with a cotton tube sock taped in place with duct tape.

ADDING BODY TO THE TAIL

Some horses, particularly Arabians or Half-Arabs, have very fine tail hair that may appear limp and stringy. Most pleasure breeds prohibit hair extensions, but the tail hair can be treated to give it the maximum fullness and body. If a tail is too thick, bushy and wiry, it can be tamed by applying a conditioner and by wrapping the upper dock with a bandage over the dampened hair for an hour before showing.

The skirt of the tail may be braided into several small, tight pigtails, which are treated with setting gel and left in overnight. When the braids are removed, the tail hair will have a slight crimp and will appear more full and wavy.

The tail hair can be done up in "rings" and treated with hair spray or setting gel, much like women setting their hair. When the "rings" are picked out and the tail hair is carefully picked free and teased a little, it gives the appearance of more fullness and body.

How to Put in "Rings" for More Body in the Skirt of the Tail

1. Part several strands of hair from the skirt of the tail and make a loose overhand knot. The "ring" you form should be about three inches in diameter.

2. With the long end of the hairs, make a second three inch ring intersecting the first. Make a third ring by passing the next ring through the second. Continue on until you reach the end of the strand.

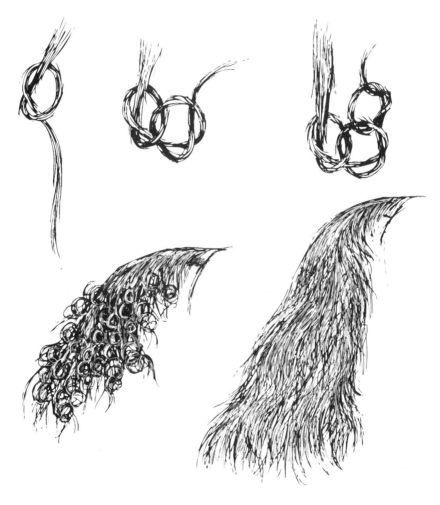

FIGURE 132. Making "rings" in tail hair.

3. The entire skirt is treated this way, making a series of rings from the dock down to the end of each strand. The smaller the rings, the more full and fluffy the skirt will be.

4. Spray the chains of rings with hair spray. Another method is to put in the rings while the hair is wet. The chains and rings may be left in for an hour or more, until the hair spray is dry.

5. Carefully undo the chains and pick out the tail. The skirt will be full and fluffy. If it is too full, spraying it with a little water will remove some of the curl.

Trimming and Touching Up

Pleasure horses and ponies usually have small, refined, and expressive heads. Good trimming around the head, ears, and muzzle is important to emphasize the short face, chiseled head, and expressive eyes and ears.

TRIMMING THE FACE

The muzzle, jawline, face, and eye area should be clipped closely and all whiskers removed, using #15 blades on the fine-skinned areas around the eyes and #10 blades on the face, jaw, and muzzle. The hair above and below the eyes may be clipped closely to give the impression of a larger eye, but the eyelashes themselves must never be cut. The outside edges of the ears are trimmed and the inside hair is removed and clipped clean; a small "diamond" is left at the tips of the ears to leave a sharp natural point. Using #40 (surgical) clipper blades will give a razor-sharp line to the edges of the ears, but the clipper must be handled smoothly or it will leave unsightly marks and irregularities. The hair may be removed from the inside of the ears by applying a depilatory cream such as Nair. If the inside ear hair is removed, the skin should be cleaned with a baby wipe and protected against flies by a fly mask with ear covers during turnout.

The muzzle and face may be clipped closely, or if the horse has a large blaze or other extensive white markings, they may be clipped with #10 or #15 blades to make them appear whiter and finer. The underside of the jaw and the first few inches of the throat may need to be clipped closely in order to give a clean, sharp appearance, but if clipping would create an obvious color contrast, it is better to trim with the hair instead. In winter, pleasure horses may receive a face clip, full head clip, or apron clip if they are not body-clipped. (See chapter 7 for more information on show trimming and clipping the head.) Keeping a jowl wrap or a hood on the horse helps to keep the throat slimmed down and the hair of the neck and head fine and shiny.

TRIMMING THE LEGS

The legs should also be closely trimmed, removing all long hair from the lower legs, fetlock joints, and coronary band. The legs are often booted up to make them appear cleaner and more slender and to keep white markings from picking up ring dust. Booting up must be carefully blended so that it does not show a dividing line between the clipped and unclipped hair. The chestnuts are cut off close to the skin and smoothed with Vaseline or darkened with hoof polish if the leg is dark colored.

HIGHLIGHTER AND COAT POLISH

Before showing, highlighting gel is applied to the fine skin of the muzzle, face, eyelids, ears, and bridle path. The highlighter dries to a shiny, reflective but soft coating that makes the details of the face stand out. Clear highlighter should be used on white or light-colored hair, but brown or black can be used to emphasize dark skin on the eyelids, muzzle, and ears—this makes the eyes appear larger and the nostrils look thinner and finer. Silicone coat polish or a light oil dressing may be applied to reflect light from the body, muscles, and coat. Spraying the lower legs with silicone coat spray will help them to repel dust, stains, and ring dirt, keeping white markings whiter.

HOOF POLISH

The feet should be scrubbed clean with a nail brush or a vegetable brush before hoof polish is applied. Many exhibitors sand the outer wall of the hooves in order to make them clean and smooth, but this removes the *periople*, the hoof's natural protective coating and can lead to dry, cracked feet. If you insist on sanding the feet, you must immediately apply a special hoof sealant to protect the hooves from loss of moisture.

Light hoofs are usually painted with clear hoof polish, and black or brown polish is used for black or chestnut legs. Black polish under a white leg tends to make the hoof appear larger. However, a horse that has one white leg and one dark leg may give the impression of an uneven stride—in this case it may look better to use black polish on both feet.

The horse should be stood on a mat or a piece of cardboard while his hoofs are painted with hoof polish and until the polish dries; if he stands on a dirt surface, the polish will pick up dust. Hoof polish dries to a glossy finish and can remain on the hoof for the duration of the show. A touch-up with extra polish or a polish enhancer gives the hooves an extra gloss before showing. After the show, the polish should be washed off with hoof polish remover.

Show Halters

Most pleasure breeds, when shown in halter or in-hand classes, are handled in a show halter, an in-hand bridle or a bridle. Mature saddle seat type pleasure horses are usually shown in hand in a show Weymouth bridle. The curb reins are brought over the horse's head and the horse is handled on the curb. The bradoon sliphead, including the bradoon (snaffle bit) and snaffle rein are usually removed for in-hand classes. Alternatively, the bradoon may be left in place and the snaffle rein left up over the horse's neck, resting across the withers. The horse is always posed, run out in hand, and controlled with the curb reins.

Hunter type pleasure horses and ponies are usually shown in a hunt type snaffle bridle.

A show halter usually consists of a noseband and headstall with a matching browband. A throatlatch is required so that the horse cannot slip out of the halter during a class. Show halters often employ colored vinyl or patent-leather browbands and nosebands with a contrasting bead around the edges; the chin strap is formed by a fine chain that passes from the halter ring under the jaw to the far ring.

A show halter should fit the lines of the horse's face, with the noseband lying high and close to the point of the cheekbone and the cheekpieces parallel to the line of the cheekbone. The browband should complement the size and shape of the head; the forelock is usually tucked back under one side of the browband. All billet ends should be confined in keepers and any excess length cut off so that it does not hang loose and distract from the clean and elegant appearance.

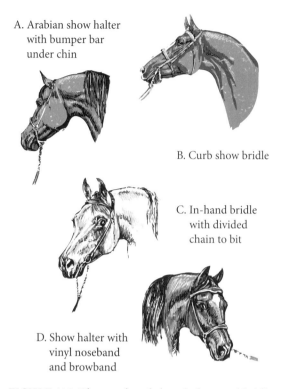

A. Arabian show halter with bumper bar under chin

B. Curb show bridle

C. In-hand bridle with divided chain to bit

D. Show halter with vinyl noseband and browband

FIGURE 133. Pleasure breed show halters and bridles.

Arabian show halters are sometimes made ultra-fine, using a narrow but strong cable covered with leather, vinyl or a metallic finish to enhance the line of the head. A fine chain may form the throatlatch, and the halter is held together by a silver or jewelled concho. The chain underneath the chin gives control and keeps the halter securely in place.

An in-hand bridle is a fine headstall equipped with a snaffle bit. The lead shank chain is usually equipped with a divided chain end that can be snapped to both bit rings to equalize the pressure on the mouth. Some in-hand bridles do not have a noseband and may or may not have a browband, but a throatlatch is mandatory; these are used on Arabians, Half-Arabians, and National Show Horses. A sturdier version of an in-hand bridle, with leather noseband, browband, and throatlatch, is used when showing pony stallions.

Chapter 14

Other Breeds

Many other breeds and types of horses and ponies have become popular for pleasure riding, driving, and show competitions. Some breeds that are rapidly gaining in popularity are Friesians, Iberian horses (Andalusians and Lusitanos), Gypsy cobs (Gypsy vanners), and gaited breeds, including Paso Finos, Peruvian Pasos, and Icelandic horses. (American gaited breeds such as Tenessee Walking Horses, Plantation Walkers, Rocky Mountain Horses, Racking Horses, and Missouri Fox Trotters are covered in chapter 15.) Apologies to any breed that has been left out—there are more breeds than one book can cover in detail, and more appearing all the time!

Long-Maned Breeds with Feather

Long-maned breeds with *feather* (long hair on the lower legs and fetlocks, extending to the ground) include Friesians, Welsh cobs, and Gypsy cobs, vanners and "drum horses." These horses are prized for their long, beautiful manes, tails and the abundant "feather" that accentuates their characteristic action, especially at the trot. The fetlocks and long hair of the legs (called "feather") is never clipped or trimmed, and is allowed to grow as long as possible. The profuse growth of feather is considered a beauty in these breeds, and it emphasizes their characteristic action, particularly at the trot.

A. Friesian

B. Gypsy cob

FIGURE 134. Long-mane with feather.

MINIMAL TRIMMING

The long-maned feathered breeds are kept and shown with minimal clipping and trimming, especially Gypsy cobs and vanners. These horses often grow a profuse but silky coat, with long hair under the jaw and below the neck, chest, belly, and buttocks, as well as abundant feather on the legs. Gypsy cobs may be shown body clipped (without touching the feather, one of the chief beauties of the breed) or in natural coat, including full facial hair.

Friesian show rules call for horses to be shown "in their natural splendor, with full mane, tail and feathering." Friesians may be clipped over their muzzle, jaw, and cheekbones, but only guard hairs may be trimmed from the ears, and if a bridle path is clipped, it may not exceed two inches. Manes, tails, and legs may not be clipped on purebred Friesians, but a small amount of pastern hair may be removed to prevent scratches. Braiding is optional for Friesians shown in hunter, dressage, or sport horse classes.

MANES AND TAILS

Manes and tails should be long, full, and natural. Many of these horses have a natural crimp or wave in the mane and tail hair, which can make the long hair prone to tangles. (Knots and tangles in a long mane were once feared as "witch locks," a sign that witches had been riding the horse in the night!) The long hair should be protected by occasional shampooing and applying detangler and conditioner, then carefully picking the hair out by hand. It's a good idea to put the mane into working braids during exercise to prevent the mane from becoming sticky with sweat.

Both mane and tail hair may be protected by keeping it braided and contained in a tail bag and mane covers (mane bags). Keeping the mane in many long "pigtails" is another way to protect the hair and allow it to grow as long as possible; this also produced a shimmering wavy look when the mane is unbraided for show. (Please see chapter 5 for specific directions on mane and tail care, working braids, and the use of mane covers.)

CARE OF FEATHERED LEGS

Feathered breeds need extra care, as the long hair of the legs and fetlocks must be preserved and kept clean and silky. White markings should be clean and shimmering white for a striking appearance at a show or presentation.

The feather of various horses ranges from coarse to silky, and the skin may be inclined to become greasy underneath, especially in winter. Feathered legs should be carefully brushed out daily. If burrs or other debris become caught in the hair, the feather can be sprayed with Showsheen or baby oil, which makes the hair slippery and makes it easier to slide the burrs out without pulling or breaking the hairs.

Feathered horses kept outside in wet, muddy conditions may lose some of their leg hair, a condition called *bog burn*.

The legs may be washed in warm weather, but it is important not to allow the skin to become chapped and cracked, which can happen when feathered legs are washed with cold water and left wet in cold weather. Shampoo should be mild and thoroughly rinsed out, then followed with a conditioner. The feather can be dried with a hair dryer or the warm air blower of a horse vacuum.

Long-feathered horses are especially vulnerable to skin problems, especially when their legs get damp, cold, and dirty. The skin beneath the feather should be inspected daily, as it is much easier to cure a developing problem if it is caught early.

Scratches or Mud Fever (Grease Heel)

This is a common condition found in the pastern area, in which the skin becomes chapped, inflamed, and develops sore, crusty, weeping scabs, and cracks that ooze serum. It is usually caused by the invasion of a bacterium called *dermatophilus congolensis,* which penetrates the skin following exposure to wet or mud. Cracked skin in the pastern areas can be difficult to heal since the area is always flexing as the horse walks Horses with white legs often have more sensitive skin and are more susceptible to scratches.

To prevent scratches, it's important to check the legs daily, protect horses from the wet and mud as much as possible, and to begin treatment at the first sign of cracks or weeping.

Heel Mites or Chorioptic Mange

Heel mites (also known as leg mange or *chorioptic mange*) is a problem of the feathered breeds, caused by a mite called *Chorioptis bovis.* The mites feed on the scurf and dandruff beneath the hair and irritate the skin, causing thickening of the skin, sores, crusts, and patches of ulceration around the foot, pastern, and fetlock region. Because of the severe itching caused by the mites, horses will stamp their feet and rub their legs incessantly. Horses suffering from heel mites may become hypersensitive and may resist shampooing, clipping, or having their legs handled

Chorioptic mange is often mistaken for scratches (mud fever), but can be diagnosed by a skin scraping taken by a veterinarian. It may require clipping of the legs and treatment to kill the mites. Heel mites can live in infected stalls and stables for two months or longer, and can be passed to other horses through contaminated stables and bedding

Iberian Horses

Iberian horses include Andalusians (also called PRE or Pura Raza Espanol) and Lusitanos. These horses are characterized by strong, balanced conformation, elastic gaits, and a long, noble head.

Show rules require that the Iberian horse "be shown in its natural splendor, with a full mane and tail in the Andalusian style." The mane and/or tail may be braided for certain classes such as hunter, show hack, dressage, and long reining, but glitter, decorations, and hair extensions of any kind are not allowed. Bridle paths should not exceed four inches.

In breeding classes, young horses manes and tails may be trimmed in traditional Andalusian style, as described below:

> **Weanlings:** Forelock and all tail hair shaved; mane roached and shaped to enhance the line of the neck.
>
> **Yearling fillies:** Forelock shaved, mane as shaped above, tail hair shaved to below the vulva, with a short "bob" (two to four inches), banged off square above the hocks.
>
> **Yearling colts:** Forelock shaved, mane as above, tail permitted to grow but banged off square for neatness.
>
> **Mares 2 and older:** Shown with or without a forelock, roached or shaped mane, dock shaved to below vulva; tail hairs allowed to grow long but banged off square for neatness.
>
> **Stallions and geldings, 2 years and older:** Forelock, mane, and tail long and natural.

MANE CARE

The long, silky mane of the Iberian horse is one of its chief beauties. Some horses grow extremely long manes, but this requires meticulous preservation and care of the precious mane hair. Because the hair is fine, silky, and easily damaged, it should be treated carefully and picked out only with the hands, never combed or brushed. Occasional shampooing and use of a good hair conditioner will keep the long hair clean, soft, and supple and avoid tangles.

A long mane may be put up in a braid to protect it from sweat during exercise, and kept in loose braids to prevent damage in the stable or during turnout. These braids may be fastened into individual mane bags or mane covers for extra protection. The better the care and protection of the mane and tail, the longer and fuller it will grow. (Please see chapter 5 for specific directions on working braids and the use of mane covers.)

TAIL CARE

The tail hair should also be kept clean, conditioned, and protected against damage and breakage. The tail may be kept in a braid or a tail cover to protect the hair and keep it clean and free of tangles.

A. Full mane and tail

B. Traditional trim for breeding stock

Mare with roached mane and clipped dock

Foal with mane and tail clipped short

FIGURE 135. Iberian horses.

The skirt of the tail is allowed to grow as long and full as possible, but it should be banged off squarely at the level of the pasterns.

Paso Finos, Peruvian Pasos, and Icelandic Horses

Paso Finos, Peruvian Pasos, and Icelandic horses are naturally gaited breeds, though their gaits, appearance, and origins are different. Paso Finos and Peruvian Pasos are of Latin and South American origins, while Icelandic horses come from Iceland. These breeds are shown as naturally as possible, with minimal trimming and without braiding, cosmetics, artificial alterations, or hair extensions of any kind. Manes and tails are grown as long and luxurious as nature will allow, and the use of coat polish and cosmetic coat products is discouraged. A bridle path up to four inches is acceptable for Paso Finos, but Icelandic horses are preferably shown with no bridle path at all, and their fetlocks and facial hair are left untrimmed.

A. Plantation Walking Horse
(pleasure trimmed)

B. Paso Fino

FIGURE 136. Gaited.

FIGURE 137. Iclandic horse.

American Pony Breeds

In North America, a pony can be defined in several ways, by height, by breed and type, or by the job he does. The horse show definition of a pony is by height alone: any animal that measures less than 14.2 hands (58 inches) at the withers maturity may compete in pony classes, regardless of its breeding. (Western shows often set the height limit for ponies at 14 hands, or 56 inches.) Animals under that height may compete in their regular breed classes, especially in breeds such as Arabians in which often produce small though purebred animals. Ponies shown in pony hunter, western, dressage, saddle seat, or driving classes are presented in the same style as for a horse shown in that division.

Some of the oldest and most popular North American pony breeds are the American Shetland, Welsh, Connemara, and Pony of the Americas.

The American Shetland Pony is trimmed and presented as a miniature sized harness horse or roadster, with a long mane and tail, a long bridle path, and the forelock and the first lock of the mane braided with colored ribbon. The tail may be natural, set or may be held in a humane tail brace or spoon crupper.

Welsh ponies may be presented as hunter ponies with pulled and braided manes and tails, or when shown in Welsh pony breeding classes, with a natural, unbraided, or evened mane and a natural, unset tail.

Connemara ponies are usually presented as hunter ponies, with hunter braided manes and tails optional, but they may be shown as native ponies, with a full, natural mane and tail.

Ponies of the Americas (POAs) are shown as miniature Appaloosas. They usually have a pulled mane, which may be banded for western classes, braided for hunt seat classes, or left unbraided.

Chapter 15

The Saddlebred, Walking Horse, Parade Horse, and Other Set-Tail Horses

The show ring saddle horse or fine harness horse exhibits the height of formality and elegance in show grooming. Even in formal hunter classes a workmanlike appearance is expected, but the saddler is all "show biz" while being shown, even using wigs, glitter, and makeup! Gaited riding and fine harness driving evolved from formal riding and driving parties often held as social events in the Gay Nineties; saddle-seat attire for evening classes is patterned after the tuxedo, and ladies driving in Fine Harness classes wear long formal gowns. Tennessee Walking Horses, racking horses, and parade horses are presented in a similar style, as are Shetland ponies and long-tail harness ponies. The combination of horse and rider or driver should always present an impeccably groomed, elegant, but somewhat dramatic appearance.

While any riding horse can be called a saddle horse, the term is used more specifically to refer to horses ridden in the saddle-seat style, especially the American Saddlebred. Morgans, Arabians, National Show Horses, and other breeds are ridden saddle seat, but the Saddlebred is the prototype of this style. In the past, Saddlebreds were shown as three-gaited horses (which perform only the walk, trot, and canter), five-gaited horses (performing the walk, trot, canter, slow gait, and rack), as fine harness horses, or in hand. Today they may compete in several pleasure divisions, including Country Pleasure, Show Pleasure, and Western Pleasure. Saddlebreds shown as pleasure horses are required to wear a long, natural mane and natural, unset tail; they must be shod without artificially built-up feet to enhance the action. Tennessee Walking Horses have a Plantation Walking Horse division that has similar requirements. Show trim for horses showing in a pleasure division is covered in chapter 9. In this chapter, the term "saddle horse" is used to refer to the three-gaited, five-gaited, or fine-harness show horse or pony, whatever her breeding.

Trimming

Like other show horses, the saddle horse is trimmed to accentuate its special conformation points and performance style. Saddle horses are ridden in high collection, with a lofty head carriage and highly arched neck. The refinement and expressiveness of the head and the line of the neck contribute to the high "front" and showy appearance. Hence perfect trimming of the head and bridle path are very important. The characteristic high action is pointed up by clean, sharp trimming of the legs and polishing the feet. A highly arched and flowing tail balances the high head carriage, and the mane and tail may be lightened or dyed or have extra hair added to match or contrast with the color of the coat.

A medium to long bridle path of six to eight inches accents the line of the crest and the shape of the ears on horses shown with a long mane (which includes all types of saddle and fine harness horses except three-gaited saddle horses). The forelock and the first lock of the mane are braided into two long, slim braids using colored braiding ribbon. Tennessee Walking Horses and parade horses may have fancier braids for some classes, sometimes adding bows, bangles, or metallic ribbons in the braids. The three-gaited saddle horse has the mane and forelock completely roached off, which draws attention to the clean outline of the neck and head.

The trimming of the saddle horse is much the same as for the pleasure breeds; the jaw, muzzle, eyelids, and ears are clipped closely, using #15 or #30 blades and carefully blending the clipped areas into the unclipped hair so there is no visible line. The ears are completely clipped inside and along the edges, leaving tiny diamond-shaped tufts at the tips to give the ears a sharper appearance. If the horse is in winter coat, the entire head and face may be closely clipped, blending into the regular coat at the back of the ears, where the tell-tale dividing line will be covered by the bridle. Another

A. Five-gaited and
Fine Harness

B. Show Walking
Horse

C. Three-gaited
horse

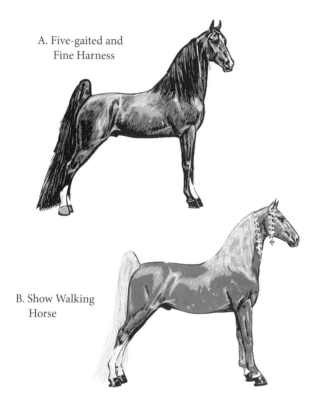

FIGURE 138. Gaited trim.

method is to clip the head and partway down the front of the throat, blending the line of the clipping along the jugular groove. This gives the horse a clean line of the jaw and throttle and makes the head more refined and expressive. If the horse's head is clipped in cool weather, he will need to wear a hood or the long hair will soon grow back in. The legs are trimmed cleanly, with chestnuts cut off close to the skin and smoothed with sandpaper. Legs may be booted up for a more refined appearance, but the clipper blades must be very sharp and a careful job done in order to avoid "stripes" or clipper tracks; #15 blades usually work well.

The hoofs of a saddle horse or fine harness horse are usually built up with weighted shoes and leather pads. Heavy shoes may be held in place by a metal band that passes across the front of the foot as well as ordinary clinches. The weight and angle of the shoes are critical to producing the horse's best action, but they can cause problems if the horse trips, stumbles, or throws its legs about when playing or on uneven ground. Horses

FIGURE 139. *Built-up shoe with band and quarter boot.*

with built-up feet are usually worked in protective boots or polo bandages and may wear quarter boots to protect the inside of the coronary band from blows from the opposite foot. Roadsters and five-gaited horses work at speed with high action and are hence more vulnerable to injuries. The groom must notice any loosening of the shoe or nails or roughness of the clinches before a shoe can be *cast,* an accident that can break off so much wall that it is very difficult to nail the shoe back on securely. Because the sole of the foot is covered with a leather pad, it would be easy for thrush to get started in the cleft of the foot or around the frog, as it cannot be picked out and exposed to the air. To avoid this, the horseshoer usually packs the foot with a protective packing, but meticulous stall cleaning and daily attention to the feet are still necessary. For showing, the feet are usually painted with a dark hoof polish—black for black legs and brown for chestnut legs. White feet may be scrubbed clean with a nail brush and painted with a clear hoof polish, as black polish beneath a white leg makes the feet look bigger. However, if the horse has one white foot and one dark one, it may look better to darken both feet. The contrasting legs can sometimes create the illusion of an uneven stride.

Mane Braiding and Trimming

The bridle path (or the whole mane and forelock on a three-gaited horse) should be freshly trimmed the day before a show, using #40 blades. When roaching a mane, it is easier to clip it closely using heavy-duty body clippers or #10 blades and then to finish it with #40 blades.

The forelock must be very fine and thin in order to be braided neatly. If the forelock grows thickly, it should be closely clipped in a U shape beside and below the forelock until a fine, narrow strip of forelock remains.

When a long-maned horse is to be braided, the ribbon color should be selected to match or coordinate with the color of the browband, the horse's color and the rider's outfit. A solid-color horse may be braided with two contrasting colors; a horse with a broken color or a flashy face marking may look better with solid-color braids. To braid the mane, you will need five-eighth-inch-wide satin braiding ribbon and sharp scissors.

How to Braid the Mane and Forelock for
Saddle and Harness Horses

1. Cut three two-foot lengths of braiding ribbon for each braid.

2. Wet down the hair and divide the forelock into three segments.
    Place the three ribbons over the forelock hairs, with about three
    inches of each ribbon protruding above the top of the hairs. An
    assistant places a finger over these ends, holding them securely
    as you begin the braid.

3. Begin to braid, incorporating one of the ribbons into each
    braiding strand.

4. Roll the ribbon so that it completely encloses the hairs each time
    you braid.

A. Braid with three   C. Secure braid   E. Adding bows to braid for Walking Horses
   sections of   with slip knot.   and Parade Horses.
   braiding ribbon.

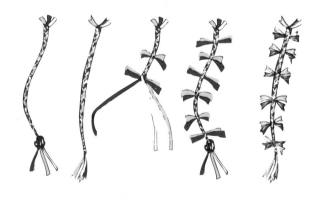

D. Completed braid
(cut ends in V shape).

B. Wrap ribbon
around hair.

FIGURE 140. Saddle-horse braids.

5. After the hairs end, keep braiding until the braid is about eighteen inches long.

6. At the end of the braid, loop one ribbon end around the others and pull it through, forming a slip knot.

7. Cut the ends of the ribbons into a "swallowtail" about one and a half inches long. Open out the ends to form a bow. The upper ends of the ribbon are treated in the same way.

8. The first lock of the mane (about a quater to a half inch of hair) is treated in the same way as the forelock.

The mane should be long, free, and clean. If the horse's natural mane is not long enough or is thin or uneven, a switch or wig can be added.

This is applied underneath the natural mane and is usually braided into the underside of the hair to hold it in place. Chestnuts often have the mane or tail lightened to provide a dramatic contrast with the coat, and darker hair that has a dull or rusty color can be touched up with hair coloring. White manes are often treated with a rinse that whitens and removes yellowing, similar to the products used by some gray-haired people. If the hair is treated or colored, it should be treated with a conditioner and cared for like human hair. If the horse's natural mane and tail color and texture are good, you may simply spray the hair with silicone coat spray to prevent it from tangling and make it float freely. Picking the hair with a little brilliantine on the fingers will add shine to the mane. The mane should be picked carefully by hand, never combed or brushed, to avoid breaking or pulling out hairs.

The bridle path or the roached mane and forelock should be clean, shiny, and free from dandruff or scurf. This can be rubbed clean with a hot towel and treated with highlighter gel or brilliantine.

If the mane is very soft and prone to become tangled or damaged, it can be kept in braids when the horse is not being shown. This gives the mane a wavy look when the braids are undone. To put the mane into protective braids, simply braid it as for show, using much larger sections of hair (about two to three inches per braid) and wide strips of cloth torn from

A. Forelock and first lock
of mane

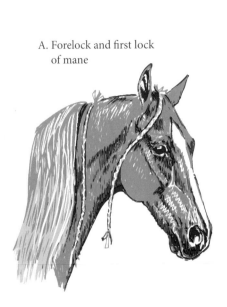

B. Bridle braid with forelock
roached

C. Braids with bows

FIGURE 141. *Types of braids.*

an old bedsheet. The sheeting strips are rolled to cover the hair as in show braiding, but the braiding is somewhat looser. The braids should be undone and the mane carefully picked out every week or two when not showing.

CARING FOR THE SET-TAIL HORSE

Tail setting is a highly controversial subject. This operation and the care and trouble to horse and handlers it entails are virtually required for some breeds and types of horses, but it is heartily condemned by many people. I do not propose to debate the question of whether or not tails should be set; the fact is that if you show or groom Saddlebreds, Tennessee Walking Horses, Hackneys, Shetlands, or fine harness horses or ponies, the chances are that you will have to deal with the care of a tail that has been set. (When shown in their respective pleasure divisions, these breeds are shown with natural, unset tails.) Remember that the results of nicking and tail setting are artificial at best, and that an improperly adjusted or neglected tail set can become a source of constant pain to the animal, as well as spoiling his appearance. If you cannot keep the horse clean, protected from flies, and the tail set comfortably adjusted, you should not be handling a tail-set horse.

Several methods are used to obtain the desirable high tail carriage of the saddle or fine harness horse. The tail is not broken, as many people think; instead, the operation of nicking is performed. The horse's tail is anesthetized and the retractor muscles on the underside of the dock are divided or "nicked." Once the incisions heal, the horse is unable to clamp her tail down closely, but the tail will not have the desired high carriage unless the muscles are trained by keeping the tail in a supporting harness and crupper, called a tail set. The tail set is kept on all the time except when the horse is being worked or shown. In the show ring, ginger salve is usually applied to make the horse hold her tail upright for the duration of the class. If the tail set is not used for a matter of months, the tail will gradually return to a natural position, as the muscles are no longer supported by the crupper.

Another method of obtaining a high tail carriage is the use of a humane tail brace or a spoon crupper. These devices are used to support the tail in the desired position while showing and do not require nicking or tail setting. Their use is limited to horses shown with long hair at the top of the tail, which is necessary to hide the brace. A special tail brace may also be required if faulty nicking or setting has disfigured the tail by causing the horse to carry it off to one side.

A. Tail set with spoon crupper

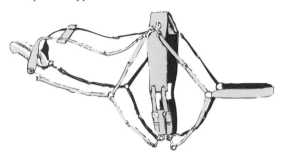

B. Tail set with bustle

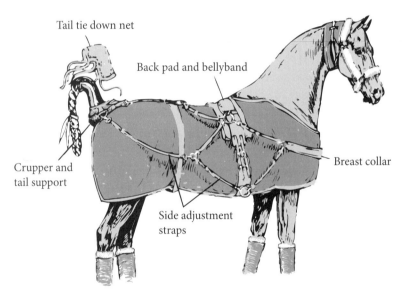

FIGURE 142. *Tail sets.*

Tail sets come in several styles and patterns; they generally consist of a bellyband and back pad, breast strap, and crupper with adjustable side straps to balance the tension on the tail. The tail set is usually worn over a sheet or blanket and additional padding may be necessary under the back pad for some horses. A tail tie-down net is worn over the top of the tail to keep the hair of the dock in place, and the hair of the tail is kept up in a braid or an old nylon stocking.

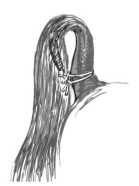

FIGURE 143. Tying the tail.

When fitting the tail set, comfortable adjustment with the right amount of support is most important. The skin of the dock area must be clean and smooth; it may be treated with baby powder. The sheet, blanket, or fly sheet is put on first. Next, buckle the bellyband and back pad around the horse's girth as you would when harnessing for driving. The girth must not be too tight and the back pad must not press on the withers. Next, fasten the breast strap across the chest so that it does not press against the base of the windpipe or drop down across the point of the shoulders. Slip the crupper under the tail, being careful not to leave stray hairs between the crupper and the skin of the dock. Some horses may need soft cotton padding for comfort. The crupper is attached to the back pad and the side straps are attached to crupper, back pad, and bellyband, taking care to keep the tension even on both sides. The tail set should fit comfortably without any points of excessive tension or strain, but firmly enough to provide support and to prevent shifting. If adjusted too tightly, the tail set can cause painful pressure sores; if adjusted unevenly or too loosely, it may shift out of place when the horse lies down or moves around.

The tail set should be removed, cleaned, and readjusted daily, with special attention to the inside surface of the crupper, girth, and any other parts that touch the horse's skin. The skin of the dock should be checked daily for irritation and sponged clean and powdered before the tail set is replaced. The skirt of the tail may be kept braided in cloth strips and protected by a bandage or tail sack; it should be taken down and picked out by hand every two weeks or so when the horse is not showing. The top of the tail is protected by a tail net, which is placed over the tail and tied underneath after putting on the tail set.

When presenting the set-tail horse in the ring, an upright position of the dock with a crimp or break-over at the end of the dock is desired. This can be achieved by a tail brace or by tying the tail with a shoelace. Since there are several models of tail brace, you should follow the directions for applying the particular brace you choose; firsthand instruction from an experienced groom is essential to get the best results. Tying the tail is simpler.

To tie the tail, you will need a long shoelace or a piece of cloth tape in a color to match the tail. One piece is wrapped around the base of the dock, keeping the wraps flat and not too tight, as the root of the dock expands when the horse raises his tail. The tape is tied in a square knot and the ends are left hanging free. Another lace or tape is applied at the tip of the dock, beneath the long hairs, care being taken not to pull the tape tight enough to cut off circulation but fastening it securely. The ends of both laces are tied together and the excess cut off. The tie should be just comfortably snug when the tail is raised. It will be hidden by the hair at the top of the dock.

FIGURE 144. Tail wig.

FIGURE 145. Tail brace.

Since a set tail doubles up the dock and raises it, it tends to make the skirt look too short. To improve the appearance of length and fullness, a tail switch or wig is often used. The hair may match, blend or contrast with the color of the natural tail hair. The wig or switch is attached by braiding a shoelace, which is attached to the top of the wig, into the underside of the tail hair and tying it securely with a tail tie as described above. The natural tail hair is teased and combed over the hair of the wig. It is essential to fasten the wig securely, as nothing is more embarrassing than to have your horse suddenly lose most of his tail in the middle of a class!

On long-maned horses, such as fine harness horses and five-gaited horses, the hair at the top of the dock is left long. This covers tail ties, tail braces, and the attachment of a tail wig or switch. Three-gaited horses traditionally have the first four to six inches of the dock (up to the breakover point) clipped, or pulled short. The hair may be roached closely with clippers, but this should only be done on a horse that carries his tail perfectly and should not be continued too far down the dock, or it may expose any defects of tail carriage and give the look of a mule's tail. When roaching the dock, it is best to use #10 blades or heavy-duty body clippers and to trim downward, in the direction of the hairs first until the length of the hairs is reduced to an even, short length. If clipping against the hair, use coarse blades that will leave a little extra length. A "feathered" tail has the upper hairs pulled slightly shorter than the long tail, but left long enough to hide a tail brace or tail tie. This style is more flattering to the horse that needs a little extra help to keep the tail in place or that has a less than perfect breakover.

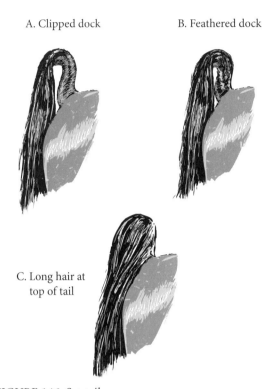

A. Clipped dock

B. Feathered dock

C. Long hair at
top of tail

FIGURE 146. Set tails.

When the horse is prepared for showing but is being warmed up or is outside the ring, the extra-long hair of the wig or switch should be loosely knotted to keep it from dragging on the ground. When the switch is removed, it can have an old nylon stocking pulled over it to keep the hairs from tangling.

Parade Horses

The parade horse is trimmed the same as a five-gaited saddle horse, with the mane and tail left as long and full as they will grow. A six- to eight-inch bridle path is cut, and the forelock and first lock or two of the mane are braided with ribbon. Often metallic ribbon is used for extra emphasis, and small bows or bangles may be added to the braid every few inches. Similar braids are sometimes added to the top of the tail to fall with the long tail hair. The tail should be full, long, and slightly wavy. The full and wavy effect is sometimes enhanced by braiding the skirt of the tail into many small pigtails and treating it with setting gel; when unbraided, it will be much fuller, with a wavy "crimp" that comes from setting the hair. The skirt of the tail may also be done up in "rings" (see chapter 10) to give it more body without obvious crimping, or it may be carefully back-combed. Using a blow dryer on the wet tail can give the skirt more body and fullness.

The parade horse's feet are cleaned, painted with hoof polish, and sprinkled with glitter while the polish is wet. The glitter and polish is removed later by using polish remover. Glitter may also be lightly dusted over the horse's croup.

Saddle horses are usually presented in hand in a show bridle with the bradoon sliphead, snaffle bit, and snaffle rein removed. They are handled on the curb rein. Young horses may be shown in a show halter, which usually has a colored vinyl or patent leather browband and noseband similar to the cavesson and browband sets found on a show bridle. The noseband of the show bridle or halter should be adjusted high up close to the cheekbone and buckled snugly. This makes the bridle or halter fit the contours of the head closely and gives the look of a shorter, more refined head.

Chapter 16

Grooming at Horse Shows

Planning and Preparation

Good planning and preparation can make the difference between a well-organized, pleasant, and successful show and a nightmare. Rider, trainer, and groom need to work together to plan, delegate jobs, and coordinate their efforts. Equipment and essential items must be assembled, checked and cleaned, repaired, or replenished before they are packed. Using checklists can help ensure that important things are not left undone or left behind when you ship out.

Before the show season, you should start a show calendar and a show information file. This should contain rulebooks of the US Equestrian Federation or any other organization under whose rules you compete, prize lists for shows, and the season's show listings or omnibus for your area. Your horse may have to be registered to be eligible for certain awards, and you may be required to produce eligibility documents such as an amateur card, membership card, pony height certificate, or registration papers, etc., when entering.

Each horse should have an individual folder containing photocopies of his registration papers, Coggins test, and any other health or vaccination certificates. These papers should travel with the horse, as you may be required to produce them on arrival at the show grounds before you will be allowed to unload. A small portable file box can keep all such information organized and safe but easily available.

You will need to know what kind of stabling to expect at each show, the time schedule, and written, clear directions to the show. This information can be obtained from an omnibus (booklet containing information and prize lists for a series of shows), the prize list, or sometimes by calling the show manager or another exhibitor.

Checklist 1: Document and Paperwork

- ❑ USEF Rule book
- ❑ Breed or other association rule book
- ❑ USEF Membership Card (membership # _____), other membership card
- ❑ Horse USEF Number _____
- ❑ Amateur Card (#_____)
- ❑ Horse's registration papers (photocopies)
- ❑ Pony Measurement Card
- ❑ Current negative Coggins test (photocopies)
- ❑ Vaccination certificate (if required)
- ❑ Prize list for show, including show schedule
- ❑ Directions to show and how long it takes to get there
- ❑ Address, telephone number, and USEF Membership number of owner, if not present at show
- ❑ Address, room number and emergency phone number at hotel for rider/trainer (on card to be attached to horse's stall door)
- ❑ Telephone number of horse's regular veterinarian

Several important chores must be done long enough before the show to allow time for repairs or other services. Certain show procedures should be done in advance to allow the horse to be at his best condition on show day.

Checklist 2: To Be Done a Week before the Show

❏ Check horse's shoeing; reset or trim if necessary.

❏ Check condition of all tack (any needed repairs made)

❏ Check supplies and obtain any needed items

❏ Have trailer and truck or van serviced and safety checked

❏ Have all required documentation on file, plus show information

❏ Trim/clip/condition coat and/or mane and tail

❏ Rider's clothes clean, fitted, and assembled

❏ Make any necessary arrangements such as ordering extra feed, transportation arrangements, etc.

A day or two before the show, bathe the horse and do a final show trim to have him looking at his best. Show tack should be cleaned and polished before it is packed and checked off. You will need to plan your schedule for shipping, arrival, and setting up at the show and will need to know the time schedule and which classes each horse is entered in. Allow time for last-minute schooling when planning shipping and arrival times.

Show Gear and How to Pack It

The equipment you need at a show will depend on the kind of horse you're showing, the nature of the competition, whether you are stabling overnight or showing from your trailer, and other variables. However, some items are important for even the simplest trip. You will develop preferences of your own about essentials and "nice-to-haves"—these should be incorporated into your own stable's checklist. The main items necessary for a one-day show or a two- or three-day overnight show will be covered here.

Packing and managing show equipment is easier if you have trunks or kits devoted to specific equipment, and each item is always packed in the same place. This saves time when you need a particular item in a hurry!

If you show a lot, you may want to keep certain items reserved for shows and permanently stored in your show trunk—for instance, "show" brushes, braiding kit, tack care kit, etc. This is easier than trying to assemble brushes, seam ripper, scissors, and sponges from all over the barn, house, and tack room and remembering to return them all after you get home. Tack trunks, tools, and other items can be painted in your stable colors to look nice and to easily identify them as yours. Portable kits that can be taken to a stall, wash rack, or the warm-up ring make preparation easier and are easier to assemble, check, and transport than a hundred individual items carried willy-nilly. Plastic totes, wooden carrying cases, a many-pocketed grooming apron, or even a plastic bucket will suffice. Plastic milk cartons are useful for carrying and storing items and are strong enough to use as a step or stool. A shoe storage bag with many pockets can hang in a tack stall or grooming area and will hold many small items neatly.

As you assemble and pack, make sure each item is clean, in good repair, and ready to go. It is much more efficient if you clean your show equipment and trunks and repack immediately after each show. Don't check an item off on your list until it's ready to use at the show and packed in its proper trunk.

SETTING UP AT THE SHOW

When you arrive at a show, your first job will be to set up your stalls (or if showing from the trailer, your trailer area) for your horses. Sometimes you may arrive after dark, so you need essential hardware and tools handy and a light to work by. When shipping a number of horses to a show, some stables send an advance crew ahead to set up stalls, tack room, feed stalls, etc.

Checklist 3: Tool Kit and Set-Up Kit

These items fit easily in a flight bag or large tool kit, which should be packed where it can be reached easily on arrival.

- ❏ Hammer and assorted size nails
- ❏ Pliers (wire cutting type)
- ❏ Screwdrivers (large and small, regular and Phillips head)

Tool Kit and Set-Up Kit *(continued)*

- ❏ Staple gun and staples
- ❏ Hand drill or cordless drill and drill bits (battery charged)
- ❏ Sharp knife
- ❏ Screw eyes (large and medium—for feed tubs, stall guards, etc.)
- ❏ Double end snaps
- ❏ Plastic electrician's tape, duct tape, baling wire, twist ties
- ❏ Coil of a half-inch rope, baling twine
- ❏ Extension cord (heavy-duty type, fifty feet long), drop light with cord
- ❏ Battery-powered lantern and fresh batteries

If you are using a stall for the day or overnight, you will need equipment for setting up and sometimes improving the stall and for hay, feed, water, and mucking out. Even if you are showing from the trailer, you must be able to water your horse, provide hay, and clean up your trailer area.

Checklist 4: Stable Equipment

Showing from trailer:

- ❏ Water bucket with snap for each horse
- ❏ Extra bucket for washing, etc.
- ❏ Tie rope *(not a chain end lead shank!)*
- ❏ Hay net
- ❏ Rake
- ❏ Shovel
- ❏ Muck basket
- ❏ Trash bags
- ❏ Bug repellent, hornet spray
- ❏ Water container; at least ten gallons

Stable Equipment *(continued)*

- ❏ Tack hook
- ❏ Portable saddle rack
- ❏ Waterproof tarp in case of rain

In addition, when using stalls:

- ❏ Stall guard
- ❏ Stall screen (stall door)
- ❏ Feed tub
- ❏ Manure fork or stall picker
- ❏ Muck tub
- ❏ Wheelbarrow or muck tub cart (space permitting)
- ❏ Broom, rake
- ❏ Bedding for two nights (minimum four bags shavings)
- ❏ Plywood panels (especially if stabling a stallion)
- ❏ Halter board, blanket rack, tack hook, etc.
- ❏ Cross-ties
- ❏ Bucket heater

First-Aid Kit

A first-aid kit with emergency veterinary supplies should be close at hand, and a human first aid kit as well. Your personal choice of first aid items and veterinary supplies depends on how much veterinary care and treatment you can handle and your own veterinarian's recommendations, but as a minimum you should be prepared to handle cuts, minor illness, or injuries. It is wise to have basic farrier tools needed to pull a shoe in case a horse should loosen or twist a shoe, but you must know how to use them. When shipping, the first-aid kit should be readily available in case of a shipping accident—not at the bottom of the least accessible tack trunk.

Checklist 5: Horse First-Aid Kit

- ❏ Chain end lead shank & twitch for restraint
- ❏ Clean plastic bucket, preferably with snap-on lid (can be used to hold first aid items and keep them clean)
- ❏ Leg wraps and cottons
- ❏ Vetrap
- ❏ Sterile gauze pads (4×4 inches)
- ❏ Bandage scissors (blunt ends)
- ❏ Penlight flashlight
- ❏ Antibacterial soap
- ❏ Thermometer
- ❏ Clean towel
- ❏ Nitrafurazone salve and/or nitrafurazone powder
- ❏ Rubbing alcohol, leg brace, and/or wrapping liniment
- ❏ Elastic adhesive tape
- ❏ Poultice and plastic food wrap
- ❏ Electrolytes
- ❏ Instant ice pack

Prescription medications, injectable syringes, and needles should be kept in a locked case. These should be prescribed by a veterinarian and should only be used on his orders. Make sure you are familiar with current regulations regarding forbidden drugs, including seemingly "innocent" drugs such as penicillin, which may contain forbidden substances such as procaine or may be an illegal "masking" drug that blocks drug tests. If you or your veterinarian administer a possibly illegal drug for legitimate purposes (such as an attack of colic), you must file a report with the show veterinarian, and you may be required to withdraw your horse from competition. Do not use tranquilizers for clipping or shipping close to the show date—this can result in a positive drug test.

Checklist 6: Farrier Tools (optional)

❏ Hoof knife

❏ Shoe pullers

❏ Farrier's hammer

❏ Clinch cutter or buffer

❏ Farrier's rasp

❏ (optional) Duplicate set of shoes, fitted by your regular farrier

❏ Screw-in studs, assorted types (if used); cotton plugs for filling screw holes

❏ Wrench for setting studs, sharp nail for cleaning threads of screw holes

Schooling Equipment

Before showing, your horse may need warm-up and schooling time. This often entails special schooling equipment such as longe lines, or boots, etc. (Add your own essentials!)

Checklist 7: Schooling Equipment

❏ Longe line

❏ Longe whip

❏ Boots or polo wraps

❏ Bell boots

❏ Martingale or other schooling device if used

Horse Clothing

The horse clothing you take will depend on the weather, the time of year, and the kind of horse you are showing. You may need a blanket rack to keep clothing clean, neatly folded, and handy.

Checklist 8: Horse Clothing

In tack trunk:

- ❑ Sheet (for keeping horse clean at night and during shipping)
- ❑ Blanket (if weather requires), with hood if used
- ❑ Anti-sweat sheet (for cooling out)
- ❑ Cooler or walking cover
- ❑ Scrim fly sheet
- ❑ Rain cover
- ❑ Paddock sheet
- ❑ Stable bandages and cottons
- ❑ Tail bandage
- ❑ Polo bandages (if used for warming up)
- ❑ Blanket rack
- ❑ Bandage rack or bandage box

Your tack should be cleaned and polished before packing it for the show, but you may need to clean up tack, boots, or bits between classes. You should also have certain spare items to make repairs or to substitute in case of breakage.

Checklist 9: Tack Cleaning, Repairs, and Spares

- ❑ Tack cleaning bucket (may serve as container for kit)
- ❑ Tack cleaning hook
- ❑ Glycerine saddle soap
- ❑ Lexol or other leather dressing
- ❑ One-Step leather cleaner (for quick cleaning jobs)
- ❑ Metal polish
- ❑ Tack sponges, turkish towels, bit scrubber, old toothbrush

Tack Cleaning, Repairs, and Spares *(continued)*

- ☐ Leather punch
- ☐ Swiss Army knife
- ☐ Extra small pieces (Chicago screws, martingale rings, rein stops, bit keepers, etc.)
- ☐ Plastic mending tape (black and brown)
- ☐ Speedy Stitcher (sewing awl with thread)
- ☐ Screwdriver
- ☐ Extra stirrup leather
- ☐ Extra halter and lead rope
- ☐ Extra rein
- ☐ Extra girth
- ☐ (optional) Rubber-covered reins for wet days

Grooming Items

Grooming items vary with the groom's individual preference and the type of horse being shown. A grooming kit should be portable, so it can easily be carried to a stall or to the warm-up ring. A separate "last-minute kit" may be taken to the warm-up ring for final touches before showing.

Checklist 10: Grooming Items

- ☐ Clippers, blades, blade wash
- ☐ Brushes, currycomb, regular grooming tools (in kit)
- ☐ Towels (several per horse)
- ☐ Scraper, sponges, hose for bathing
- ☐ Hoof pick, nail brush, hoof dressing or polish, hoof polish remover
- ☐ Mat or panel to stand horse on while applying hoof polish
- ☐ Coat spray

Grooming Items *(continued)*

- ❏ Fly repellent
- ❏ Stain remover
- ❏ Highlighter gel
- ❏ Setting gel for mane and tail
- ❏ Cornstarch, baby powder, or French chalk for whitening white markings
- ❏ Shampoo, Ivory liquid, body wash
- ❏ Mane and tail conditioner or detangler spray
- ❏ Bot block (removes bot eggs)
- ❏ Scissors, sharp knife
- ❏ Braiding kit
- ❏ Stool or step to stand on when braiding
- ❏ Mat for horse to stand on while applying hoof polish
- ❏ Tail wrapping necessities (tail bandage, cotton strips, tube sock, tape, etc.)

A last-minute kit, used for final touch-ups to horse, rider and tack just before entering the ring, might include:

- ❏ Towels (2)
- ❏ Sponges (2) 1 for Lexol, 1 dampened with water only
- ❏ Coat spray (containing fly repellent)
- ❏ Lexol or One-Step leather cleaner (to touch up leather)
- ❏ Hoof pick and hoof brush
- ❏ Hoof dressing or polish
- ❏ Cornstarch or French chalk to whiten leg markings
- ❏ Finishing brush (sprayed with coat dressing to collect dust)
- ❏ Baby oil or finishing spray for mane and tail
- ❏ Bucket for water

Comfort and Convenience Items

You will also want to plan for the comfort and convenience of your human team. You will need a place to sit down, space in which the rider can dress and make his final preparations, cold drinks, and other comforts. This may range from the front seat of a pickup truck to an elaborately appointed tack room with tack room drapes, carpets, personalized director's chairs, and a portable bar. It is essential to have a "people place" separated from the groom's working area and the horses, for the sake of safety, organization, and everyone's sanity!

Checklist 11: Tack Room and "People" Items

- ❑ Folding chairs
- ❑ Cooler with cold or warm drinks, depending on the season
- ❑ Human first aid kit
- ❑ Removable hook for clothes hangers
- ❑ Mirror and personal grooming kit
- ❑ Trash can or trash bags
- ❑ Boot jack and boot hooks
- ❑ Combination locks for tack trunks; bicycle combination lock for tack room (*Never* lock a horse in a stall!)
- ❑ Rain gear, including extra poncho and waterproof tarp
- ❑ Blanket for cold weather
- ❑ Umbrella or large parasol for sunny days
- ❑ Notebook, pencils, markers, tape
- ❑ Show schedule, posted with classes entered marked
- ❑ Work schedule (marker board or chalkboard) listing grooms' chores for each horse and any special notes
- ❑ Folding table
- ❑ Folding cot with blankets and sleeping bag (if staying overnight)

Tack Room and "People" Items *(continued)*

❑ Saddle racks, bridle racks, tack hooks, harness racks, etc.

❑ Privacy drapes for tack room (for changing clothes or if staying overnight)

❑ Battery-operated lamp for tack room (if staying overnight)

❑ Folding cart (for transporting tack, trunks, etc.)

Tack

Finally, you'll need to clean, check, and pack each horse's tack, being sure to include the correct tack for each class he is entered in. Saddle pads should be freshly laundered; it's best to have extras so that the horse will not have to appear in a pad that is dirty from earlier classes. For a two-day or longer show, have a fresh pad for each day. Tack may be shipped in trunks or in saddle and bridle cases or harness bags; it should always be covered to protect it from scratches and other damage in shipping.

Checklist 12: Tack Items

For each horse, in tack trunk or in its own case:

❑ Stable or shipping halter

❑ Tie rope

❑ Chain end lead shank

❑ Show halter and lead shank (clean, with silver polished)

❑ Saddle (clean, with metal polished)

❑ Saddle pads (freshly laundered, 1 extra pad)

❑ Breastplate (silver polished)

❑ Martingale

❑ Show bridle (clean, with metal polished)

❑ Extra bits or extra bridle

❑ Harness (clean, with metal polished)

❑ Show cart (clean, polished, with protective cover)

Tack Items *(continued)*

- ☐ Boots (clean) if worn
- ☐ Show whip or crop
- ☐ Other required appointments (list and check off!)

Feed and Bedding

When showing for only one day, you will probably take only hay and water. It's a good idea to have plenty of hay, as it keeps horses relaxed and contented when they must stand tied to the trailer or in a stall all day. Taking your own water is convenient in case the show's water source is far off or your horse refuses to drink strange-tasting water. Use 8-gallon jerrycans or large plastic buckets with snap-tight lids. Never use anyone else's buckets or feed tubs or let your horse drink from a water trough at a show—that is a way to pick up contagious diseases.

For longer shows, you will need to take hay, grain and sometimes your own bedding. While feed and bedding can usually be ordered on the grounds, it is better to come prepared with your own if possible, as you may not get the kind or quality of feed you are used to, and it may not be available when you need it.

Checklist 13: Feed and Bedding Checklist

- ☐ Haynet for each horse
- ☐ Hay (more than normal amount, as horse cannot be turned out during show)
- ☐ Feed, including any vitamins or additives
- ☐ Feed measure (or feeds may be put up in premeasured packages for a single horse that will be away only one night or so)
- ☐ Water (enough to offer horses water en route on a long trip)
- ☐ Electrolytes
- ☐ Bedding (Bagged shavings are most convenient to carry and horses cannot eat their bedding. Allow two bags or bales per stall for one night.)

How to Be a Good Horse Show Groom

Anyone who shows horses will quickly appreciate the help of a groom, whether he or she is a professional show groom, a parent, or a friend who can hold a horse for a minute or run back to the trailer for a forgotten number. Nobody can appreciate a groom more than the person who has tried to do his or her own grooming while schooling and showing, too! It is possible to groom for yourself, but it takes extra time, energy, and good organization. Ideally, the rider should be able to concentrate on the job of schooling, warming up, and showing his horse and following the advice of his coach or trainer. He should not get his clothes messy by kneeling to put on hoof dressing when he is dressed to show, and he cannot dismount in a muddy warm-up ring to pick out his horse's tail just before entering the ring. Having a good show groom can take some of the pressure off the rider and trainer and often means better care for the horse.

The rider, trainer, and groom are all equally important members of the same team, with the same goal: to get the horse to the show ring on time well prepared, and fit to do his best, and to present the best possible performance. The rider is certainly not the "lord of the manor," nor is the groom a lowly servant. Any rider who forgets this deserves to find out just how hard it is to groom for himself without good help! However, a groom must remember that most show riders are under considerable stress and should not take offense if a rider is a bit tense, flustered, or compulsive about double-checking everything. A good groom can help ease the rider's nervousness by having everything well organized and the horse ready in plenty of time, and by being there with quiet, positive support. It is not the groom's job to train the horse, criticize the rider's performance, or to discuss such things with the stable's clients or parents of junior riders; butting into these areas is bound to invite trouble and bad feeling.

Riders and trainers should remember to show their appreciation for the groom's efforts, and sometimes need to remember to curb their tongues when things are hectic. It is particularly unpleasant to hear a child rudely scolding or preemptorily ordering a parent to get the horse ready, or to fix her clothes, or whatever—especially when that parent has probably provided the horse and the outfit, trailered the horse, and has made it possible for the child to be showing at all. Show schedules and pressure are no excuse for rudeness and lack of consideration on anyone's part.

A good show groom will keep the horse's performance and needs foremost in mind. This sometimes means that a groom may not get to see as much of the show as he might like to, or have time to socialize or ride for fun. The horse is there to show his best, not for other purposes. Sometimes children want to ride their horses all over the show grounds between classes, or their friends may ask to ride, too. It is really unfair to the horse or pony to permit this, or to sit on him between classes to watch the show. Whenever a horse will not be showing for a while, he should be cooled out, unsaddled, and allowed to relax. If a groom has some free time, check to see if there is something that needs doing, such as cleaning tack or rerolling bandages, before going off to watch the show. Grooms work long hours, so they deserve a break whenever the work schedule permits, but things should be left neat and organized before going off duty, and the stable area should always have someone there to keep an eye on it.

Grooming for Yourself

Grooming for yourself takes good planning and organization and more energy. You will need to do most of your horse-care chores and grooming early, as well as any schooling, so you have time to clean up the horse and have yourself dressed and correctly turned out in time for your class. This is easier when competing in a dressage show or other show with a fixed time schedule, so you know at what time your horse must be ready. Keep in touch with the announcer and how the show schedule is running; cancellations, scratches, or combined classes can alter the schedule, and it is more difficult to cope without help.

You can save time by wearing a coverall or protective clothing over your show clothes while you groom. Female dressage riders often wear a wrap-around denim skirt over their boots and white breeches between classes; this has handy pockets for grooming tools as well as keeping the breeches clean. Set up a dressing area equipped with a mirror and toilet articles, in your tack stall, dressing room, or vehicle. If you remove and hang up your show coat, hat, gloves, and tie as soon as you dismount and clean them up with a clothes brush after your horse is taken care of, they will stay clean ready for your next class. Your grooming tools and routine should be similarly organized so that your horse is cooled down, cleaned off, and ready to go again in plenty of time before your next class. The tack can be touched up with a quick wipe-over using Lexol, One-Step cleaner, or saddle soap.

Grooming for yourself is much easier if you have an easy-going horse that will tie safely and does not require extensive schooling before showing. Even if you don't have an experienced groom, it can be very helpful to have someone along who can hold the horse for a minute or run an errand for you if necessary.

Shipping Your Horse

Horses should be wrapped and prepared for traveling so that they arrive safely and in show condition. Poor traveling protection can result in rubbed tails, scrapes, or even serious injuries, especially if a horse scrambles or does not load or unload quietly.

The legs should be protected with shipping boots or bandages that cover the coronary band in case a horse steps on his own feet while trying to keep his balance. The tendons and other structures of the leg should also be protected against kicks, scrapes or cuts that may occur during loading or shipping. Bell boots offer more protection than shipping bandages alone, especially for horses that are poor travelers. (See chapter 6 for directions for applying shipping bandages.)

The tail should be protected with a tail wrap or tail guard (see page 94 for directions) especially for horses that brace themselves against the butt bar of a trailer, as they may rub their tails raw. However, tail wraps should not be used when a horse is shipped by a commercial shipper or must be in the trailer for more than eight hours. If the bandage should slip or cut off circulation, it could cause permanent damage to the tail if not fixed in time.

The horse should wear a strong, securely fitted halter. Shipping halters are often covered with fleece to prevent them from rubbing the skin of the face. A shipping halter should be of leather so it could be cut in the event of an accident. Horses that are fearful about hitting their heads, especially when unloading, should wear a head protector attached to the halter. Make sure the halter still fits securely after the head protector is attached—sometimes a head protector makes the halter fit so loosely that it can slip off the horse's head.

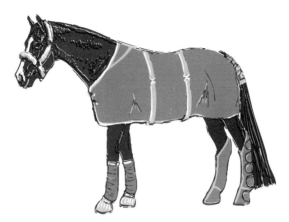

FIGURE 147. *Horse prepared for shipping.*

A horse may need to wear a blanket, sheet, hood, or anti-sweat sheet, depending on weather and the vehicle he is being shipped in. Do not underestimate the effect of a draft in a moving vehicle, especially on a clipped horse. On the other hand, a closed trailer can develop extremely high temperatures when parked in the sun—enough to cause serious dehydration and even collapse from heat exhaustion during very hot weather. It is important to monitor the horse's condition, especially on long trips and in extremely hot or cold weather. The appropriate clothing should be on hand to put on the horse if he needs it.

Horses should be fed lightly for a day or two prior to a long trip. Their grain should be cut by half, and they should not be fed just before shipping; in fact, it may be better for some horses to withhold grain entirely. A haynet in the trailer will keep them busy and contented and provides needed fiber to keep the gut moving. If a horse is to be shipped for twelve hours or longer, grain is usually withheld for a day or two days before shipping and the veterinarian may give the horse mineral oil by tube to prevent digestive upsets caused by shipping, stress, and standing idle for a long period.

Loading should be accomplished quietly, calmly, and with a positive attitude. If a horse is inexperienced at loading, he should have a practice trip before show day—never try to train a horse to load when you are in a hurry! Start early and leave extra time for loading; just knowing that you are not behind schedule will make your job easier and your attitude more relaxed and confident. Most loading problems are caused by people who are in a hurry, disorganized, and unsure of themselves or irritable. If you must load or unload in the open, attach a longe line to the horse's halter. If he should pull back while loading or unloading, he is much less likely to get away from you than if you were using only a lead shank.

Setting Up Stables At a Show

The first job on arrival is to get the stall ready, so that your horse has a safe place to be. Inspect the stall carefully before bedding it down or bringing the horse in. It may have been used as a tack room and have nails, staples or trash left in it. Remove any feed tubs or buckets—they could infect your horse with contagious diseases. If there are electrical outlets nearby, be sure that the horse cannot reach a cord and chew it. Sweep down the walls, and if the floor is dirt, dampen it before bedding down.

Temporary stalls are sometimes made of boards with open spaces between them. These can allow a horse's leg to get caught between the boards when he rolls (as horses usually do in a new stall.) Some horses, especially stallions, sniff at their neighbors, squeal and fight through the gaps. You may need to reinforce such stalls with four-by-eight-foot panels of plywood, or a heavy tarpaulin fastened at the top and bottom of the stall panel. It is a good precaution to keep horses' legs wrapped in temporary stalls, even if they are not usually wrapped at home.

The stall may have a regular stall door, a sliding board gate, or no door at all. You may need to set in screw eyes and hang a stall screen as a door, or you may use a stall guard. Only use solid stall guards, not the woven type that a horse can get a foot caught in. Some horses need two stall guards so they do not duck underneath, but be sure that they cannot get a foot through the gap.

Stall screens permit good ventilation and allow you to see the horse without going into the stall. They open inward, so they can only be used in a roomy stall. A stall screen is hung on the inside of the doorpost, and the hangers are slipped down into the screw eyes. Secure each hanger to the screw eye with a piece of heavy wire, so the horse cannot lift the door up and pull it off the hinges. A stall screen should be placed high enough to prevent the horse from reaching out and nipping passing horses, but not so high that he can injure his knees by pawing underneath the door.

Set in screw-eyes or holders for the feed tub, water bucket, and hay net. Hang buckets high enough that the horse cannot paw them. The hay net must be hung high enough that the horse cannot get a foot into it, and should be double-tied so it will not hang low enough for him to paw it when it is empty. (To double-tie a hay net, run the ties through a high ring or over the top board of the stall and then tie to the ring at the bottom of the hay-net with a slip knot, or fasten it to the bottom ring with a double-end snap.) Set in cross-tie rings or a tie ring so that you can tie the horse in the stall.

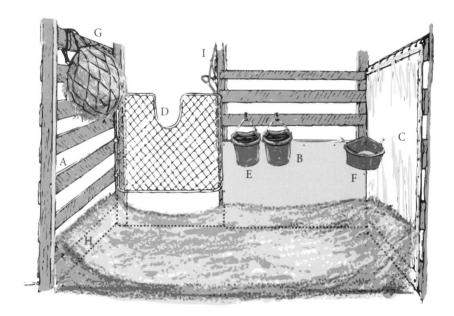

A. Check for hazards: (gaps between boards; nails and staples; electric wires
B. Plywood covers gaps between boards
C. Tarapaulin prevents contact with adjacent horse
D. Stall screen hung in doorway; hangers wired securely
E. Two water buckets (slip-on hangers)
F. Feed tub (screw eyes and double end snaps)
G. Haynet hung safely
H. Bedding banked against walls
I. Halter and lead line on stall

FIGURE 148. *Temporary stall set up safely.*

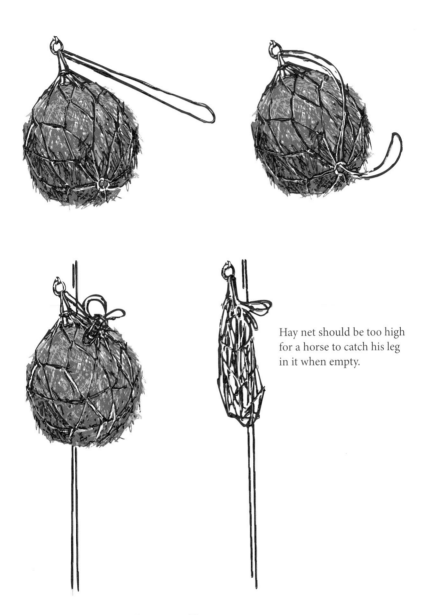

Hay net should be too high for a horse to catch his leg in it when empty.

FIGURE 149. How to tie a hay net safely.

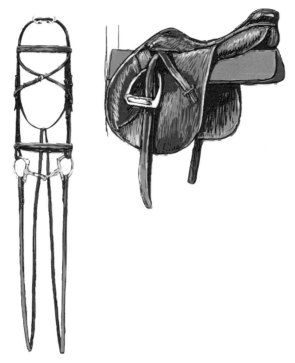

FIGURE 150. Saddle and bridle (in figure eight) on racks.

Finally, bed down the stall. Use plenty of bedding at a show; it keeps horses cleaner and encourages them to lie down and rest. The bedding should be banked well up against the walls and corners of the stall to prevent a horse from becoming cast (or stuck) if he rolls. Straw or shavings can be piled high against the walls and patted down firmly with a fork; this provides a source of clean bedding when you clean and re-bed the stall. The entrance to the stall should be swept clean so the horse will not drag bedding out into the aisle when leaving the stall. When you have filled the water bucket and tied up a full hay net, your horse can be left to investigate his new quarters.

Setting Up a Tack Stall

If you are showing several horses, you may rent a tack stall. If your stable is not large enough to rate a tack stall for your exclusive use, you may be able to share a tack stall with another exhibitor. The tack stall is your base of operations throughout the show, so it takes some planning and preparation to devise an efficient, workmanlike, but attractive setup. Professional show stables have elaborately appointed tack stalls with drapes, saddle racks, chairs, and accessories in their stable colors, with ribbons and photographs of their current champions on display. Remember that neatness and efficiency should take precedence over decoration, however.

To set up a simple tack stall, sweep down the walls and floor and put up nails or hooks for bridles, tools and clothes. Set up your saddle rack and tack trunk in a convenient place, and hang a drape or curtain for privacy when changing clothes. A piece of carpet on the floor will help keep your show clothes clean while you are changing. A battery-operated lamp or lantern or a drop light on a long extension cord makes it easier to work in the tack room and is essential after dark. You may also want an electric bucket immersion heater, but this must be used with care to avoid a fire hazard. Have folding chairs and a cooler full of cold or hot beverages for the convenience of your human helpers. Post a copy of the show schedule and underline the classes your horse is entered in; list tack changes or times when a horse may have to hurry from one ring to show in another.

It is best to keep people activities away from the horse preparation area; remember that the main purpose of the stable area is to take care of the *horses,* not for socializing, playing, eating, or entertaining. A place should be designated for horse grooming and care, for the rider to dress and fix his clothes, for tack to be hung up and cleaned, and for needed items to be stored. Put any items you have used back in their trunk or kit as soon as you are finished with them; this keeps the area neater and more organized and makes it less likely that things will be spilled, lost, or spoiled. Always have a lock and chain to close the tack room securely (a bicycle lock with a combination is handy) when you must be away from it for a while.

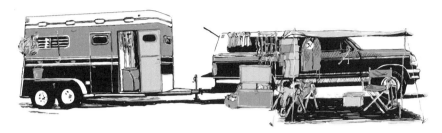

FIGURE 151. Safe set up for showing from trailer.

Showing From the Trailer or Van

When no stabling is available, you will have to tie your horse to your van or trailer, keep him in his van stall, or have someone hold him when he is not showing. If you tie to a trailer, it must be hitched to the tow vehicle and the wheels should be blocked—you'd be surprised to learn how far and how fast a frightened horse can drag an unhitched trailer! Never tie a horse to a fence board, a car door handle, or anything else he could break off or move.

Try to park your trailer so that you have convenient access to the show ring, schooling area, and entry office, but not so close you will be in the way or your horse will be disturbed by the action. Park in the shade if possible, and leave plenty of space between your rig and the next one. Be sure that you are close enough to hear class announcements.

Take a good look at your trailer's exterior before you tie your horse to it. Remember, if a horse can find a way to get hurt, he will! The trailer should have tie rings set far enough apart for horses to be safely separated, and horses should not be tied so that they could swing around and catch a leg, head, or tie rope on a door latch, ramp, or springs. Never tie a water bucket or hay net to the same ring you tie your tie rope to; if a horse should pull back and pull the tie ring loose, the water bucket would be attached to his head by the tie rope and could panic him. Make sure that he cannot paw against a sharp-edged fender and cut himself.

When you tie a horse, tie fairly short and always use a quick-release knot that can be jerked loose in an emergency. If the rope is too long, the horse may put his head down and get a leg over it or catch the rope across his poll and scare himself. Even though your horse may tie perfectly well at home, there is more excitement and more chance of his pulling back at a show. Use a strong tie rope with a sound snap, and *never* tie a horse with a chain lead shank. If a horse is carelessly tied with a chain shank over his nose or under his chin, a minor spook could result in serious injuries or even a fracture. The same goes for tying a horse by the bit or bridle reins.

Hay nets should be tied high, with the long ties run back through the center ring and then tied in a slip knot or fastened with a double end snap. If a hay net is just tied at the top, it will hang lower and lower as the hay is consumed, until it is low enough for a horse to get a foot caught in it.

If your horse doesn't tie safely, you will need someone to help out by holding him whenever he is not showing. This can be tedious, but it is far safer than leaving an excited horse tied insecurely to a trailer or having to recapture him after he has gotten loose. If you are holding a horse, it may be necessary to use a chain lead shank with the chain over the horse's nose or under his chin for control. Be careful not to let him step on the shank and when he grazes, and keep him away from hazards such as lawn chairs, wire fences, electric cables, and crowded areas around food stands and entry booths.

If your horse loads easily and your van or trailer is roomy, you may let him stand in his trailer or van stall between classes. Your trailer should be parked in the shade with ventilation windows and doors open, as the temperature inside a trailer parked in the sun can easily reach over 100 degrees. Always untack before putting a horse on the van or trailer; loading or unloading with a saddle or bridle on exposes your horse and your tack to the risk of catching a piece of equipment on the trailer stall and scaring the horse as well as damaging your tack.

Keep a full hay net in front of your horse when he must remain tied during a show. This gives him something to do and keeps him quiet and contented. Use fly repellent and scrim fly sheets if the bugs are bad, and *never* go away and leave a tied horse unsupervised.

In rainy weather, good organization can minimize the mess and inconvenience. Have a waterproof rain cover to put over your horse; you can tack and unsaddle underneath it. Other waterproof tarps can cover your tack rack and show trunk, and you may be able to set up a canopy or shelter on one side of your truck or trailer. If the ground gets muddy, a bag or two of shavings spread underfoot will make the area cleaner, if not dry. Have plenty of towels to dry off wet horses, people, and tack, and bring extra coolers so that a dry cooler can be substituted for a wet one. Your horse may need an anti-sweat sheet, especially if his rain cover keeps him warm and sweaty. Finally, don't forget hot beverages and dry towels for your wet, cold human helpers!

Duties at the Show

Once your stable area is set up, let your horse relax and settle in. He can be taken for a walk around the show grounds to see the sights, but he may be flighty and excited, so handle him with care and stay alert. He may need a chain lead shank run over his nose for control. If possible, walk a green horse or flighty horse with a calm, quiet stable mate. Stay away from other horses and watch out for hazards like guy wires, tent ropes, electrical cables, and holes where your horse could be injured.

Before it gets close to show time, your horse should be schooled and get accustomed to the warm-up area and, if permitted, the show ring. He may be longed first or schooled under saddle. Sometimes schooling over fences is permitted before the show, but don't rush a horse off the trailer and into a hasty, desperate schooling session; this can hurt rather than help the confidence of both horse and rider. Instead, plan to arrive early enough for an unhurried schooling session, with time for the horse to rest and be cleaned up before he warms up for his first class.

If your horse has been bathed, groomed, braided, and trimmed at home, you will not have much preparation to do at the show except for removing travel stains and final touches to the coat, feet, mane, and tail. If you are braiding at the show, try to get it done very early in the morning before there is too much activity around the stable area. Some horses will happily eat their grain or pick from a hay net while you braid.

Your grooming schedule will depend on how many horses you are responsible for, the kind of grooming they need, and the class schedule. The work schedule for the day should be posted prominently, showing who is responsible for what chores for each horse and for the stable area. You should keep a copy of the class schedule in your pocket, marked with your horse's classes and approximate times. Stay alert for class announcements and be aware of how quickly the show is running; remember that class changes, scratched entries or cancellations can alter the time schedule you had planned on. Keep in touch with how the classes are running and know which ring your horse will be showing in.

A typical schedule for a groom at a weekend show might go something like this:

FRIDAY AFTERNOON

Arrive ahead of horse van; set up stable area, bed stalls, hay, and water. When horses arrive, unload, remove shipping wraps, and walk them around the grounds. Feed, settle them in stalls. Post work/show schedules for next day. If horses are schooled, cool them out afterwards. Brace and wrap legs. Clean off tack. Check horses late at night. Leave area clean and secure.

SATURDAY MORNING (HORSES SHOWING AT 8 A.M.)

4:30 A.M.: Feed. Pick out stall while horse is eating. Remove wraps and check legs. Braid while horse finishes his hay. Groom and remove any stains.

6 A.M.: Tack horse for longeing or schooling and school for 45 minutes. Cool out horse and clean him up, removing stains. Clean up tack. Do final grooming, including picking tail, coat spray, quarter marks, highlighter, etc., just before horse goes to warm-up ring. Take last-minute kit to warm-up ring to touch up horse after warm-up.

After horse shows: Cover the horse with a cooler or sheet, rinse (if weather permits) and scrape him and cool him out. If he has more classes later, put him back in the stall with hay and water; plan for enough time to have tack cleaned and horse tacked up with final grooming done in time for his next class.

After last class: If the horse is sweaty or muddy, bathe, scrape, and cool him out. Remove braids and brace and wrap legs. The horse should be cool and dry for an hour after work before feeding grain. If ground is hard or he has worked hard, his legs may be poulticed or feet packed. Pick out stall, leave tack clean and area neat, and leave horse with hay, water and last feed. Check on horse late at night.

SUNDAY SCHEDULE

Chores will be similar to Saturday's schedule, but times may vary.

Midafternoon or as Last Classes Approach: Begin packing any equipment that will not be used again during the show. Take down and repack tack room items.

After Last Class: Horses must be cool and dry for at least one hour before shipping. Take out braids; wrap legs for shipping. Pack equipment in van or trailer. Load horses and ship out, with stalls stripped and stable area left tidy.

AT HOME AFTER A SHOW

Unload horses; unwrap and settle in stalls. Check for injuries. Poultice legs. Unload show equipment and replace tack and tools in proper places. Clean trailer or van. Clean tack. Launder saddle pads, bandages, etc. Check equipment for needed repairs, replacements. Make list of any supplies needed. Repack show equipment, clean and ready for next show. Horses should be jogged out in hand the next day to check for injuries or stiffness; usually they will have a day off with turnout time after a show.

AT THE RING

When you go to the ring with your horse, take along a bucket or kit with the items you need for any last-minute touches after he has schooled or warmed up. In cold weather, you may need a cooler or paddock sheet; in warmer weather, a light cover might be necessary to keep dust off his coat as he waits at ringside. If it is muddy, take along a bucket of water, sponge, scraper, and towels; the horse's tail should be tied up in a mud knot or bandaged to keep it clean while he warms up. You may need to touch up hoof polish or apply hoof oil, and the tail and mane may need to be picked out and the coat brushed and put straight. Take along Lexol, a damp sponge, and a rag to wipe over the tack and the rider's boots. Before leaving the stable area, be sure your rider is wearing the correct number and that his tack and appointments are correct.

In the warm-up ring, don't annoy the horse and rider by unduly fussing over them, but you can quickly sponge, scrape, and wipe off sweat marks, pick the mane and tail, and wipe over the tack and the rider's boots. If enough time has been allowed for a proper warm-up, these touches can be done efficiently without rushing.

After the horse has performed, he may be wanted again for further work-offs or for an award. The rider may need to return to ringside to watch his competition or listen to the judge's instructions for a ride-off. The groom should cover the horse according to the weather, scrape him down if he is sweaty, and walk him nearby, out of the way of other entries warming up but ready to go back in as soon as he is needed. Loosen the girth and noseband, but remember to readjust them when the horse is mounted again. Remember that a hunter must return to jog for a ribbon in the same complete bridle he wore when showing over the course or he could be disqualified. If the saddle is removed, tie up the martingale strap so that the horse cannot step on it; loosen the noseband but don't unbuckle it, as a horse might shake his head and hit his eye with the buckle end if it is undone. Stay clear of other horses; strange horses may be kickers.

After his class is over, the horse should go back to the stall or trailer to relax until he is needed to show again. He can be cleaned up if he has classes later, but he should be allowed to relax and not fussed over unnecessarily. He should be left with hay and water when he is cooled out; in the meantime, the groom (or the rider, if he is available!) can clean tack for the next class.

After the last class, the horse should be cooled out thoroughly and prepared for the night or for shipping. If he is shipping home, he does not need to be fed grain. If remaining overnight, he may need his legs poulticed, braced, or massaged, and protective stable wraps will probably be used as a precautionary measure. He should be fed grain only after he has been cool, dry, and relaxed for an hour, and a late-night check should be made to be sure that he is well and happy for the night.

Grooms In, Please!

You may be called into the ring to assist in grooming in certain stake classes where the horses are stripped and judged for conformation after they perform, to act as a header for harness classes, or to lead a horse in to receive a ribbon. Since you will be in the public view, you should be neat, clean, and properly dressed for the job. Even if you don't expect to be called into the ring, the way you appear around the warm-up ring reflects on yourself and your stable, so you should look professional.

Clean slacks or jeans worn with a clean shirt (tucked in) and possibly a jacket with your stable's logo are appropriate for most occasions when you have to groom in public. If you are acting as a header in a harness class or assisting in a Saddle Horse Stake class, you will look more correct if you wear jodhpurs, jodhpur boots, and a shirt and vest. Grooms who ride on a carriage in driving classes must wear the correct livery for their equipage and for the requirements of the class, as their appointments are counted in the judging.

Have a kit with a rub rag, sweat scraper, damp sponge, and soft brush to carry into the ring. Wait until the horses are lined up and you hear the call "Grooms in!"; you are not permitted in the ring until it is given. Run briskly to your horse and assist the rider in unsaddling; set the saddle neatly on end with the stirrups run up and the girth out of the dirt. Quickly scrape your horse and wipe over him with the rub rag. Use the sponge to clean the foam from his mouth and the bits; help the rider to get him properly posed or parked out before the judge comes by. It is permissible to shake your rag at your horse or speak to him to get his ears up, but do not engage in antics that attract the judge's attention to you instead! When permission is given, quickly resaddle, taking care as you do that all saddle and bridle parts are correctly adjusted. Give your rider a leg up and wipe off his boots after he is mounted; you may also have time to wipe the lather off the reins and saddle.

You may be called upon to assist in a combination class (in which the horse is both ridden and driven) or a versatility class. In these classes, the changes from harness to saddle or from one type of saddle to another are made in the ring; watching the quick transformation is part of the fun for the spectators. When unharnessing in the ring, remember that a horse must *never* be unbridled, even for a second, while it is hitched to a vehicle. When changing bridles, be sure that you have a halter secured around the horse's neck—you don't want to provide comic relief by having to recapture a loose horse! If this is a combination class, you then put the harness in the vehicle and pull it out of the ring. Whenever assisting in the ring, try to be as quick, efficient, and unobtrusive as possible; this way the entry gives a more professional impression.

If you lead a horse in to receive a ribbon, have him as clean and well turned out as when he competed. His saddle may have been removed and he should be scraped and have any saddle marks rubbed out, or he may be covered with a cooler. A hunter must return to jog for the judge in the same complete bridle in which he competed, including the martingale—substituting a halter is a violation of the rules. If the saddle is removed, the martingale strap should be knotted up so that it does not hang down where the horse could step on it as he jogs.

If you are asked to assist in a model or in-hand class, you'll need to know how to set the horse up in the correct pose and run him out in hand. This takes practice beforehand and probably some advice from the trainer. Keep your horse safely separated from other horses so that he can be seen by the judge and cannot get kicked by another entry.

Stable Security

The stable area should never be left unwatched, as there are many hazards at a horse show that would not be present at home. Most horse show spectators are horse lovers of some kind, but they may know little or nothing about horses and about safe and appropriate behavior around horses. Well-meaning strangers can upset horses by approaching too closely with balloons, baby strollers, and boisterous children or dogs, and they are apt to poke fingers, handfuls of hay, and even hot dogs into the stall for horses to nibble. You must protect the public from the horses as well as the horses from the public. Stall screens help to keep stray fingers out of stalls, and stall curtains allow the horses some measure of quiet and privacy. Another way is to set up a barrier of rope attached to standards that keeps spectators several feet from stall fronts, but be careful not to create a hazard for people who must get horses in and out.

Dogs are a mixed blessing at best at a horse show and can become a nuisance or even a real danger. A protective dog, kept tied in your tack room, can discourage uninvited visitors or thieves, but don't bring a biting dog to a horse show—it can end in a lawsuit. No dog, however cute or well behaved, should be allowed to run loose on the show grounds—*leash your dog or leave him at home!*

Be especially vigilant about smoking and fire hazards at a horse show (and at home also!), as some temporary stabling arrangements could be real firetraps. Absolutely forbid smoking in your stable area; post No Smoking signs and call attention to them; complain to the management if fire regulations are not enforced. Be very careful when using electrical appliances and extension cords; don't overload outlets or use indoor extension cords for outdoor conditions. If you do not leave a halter on your horse when he is in the stall, a halter and lead shank should be hung on his stall. Keep aisles and doorways clear for fire exits, and *never lock a horse in a stall.*

A neat, organized, and well-supervised stable area is less susceptible to accidents and to petty thievery. Put equipment away and close up trunks when you are through using it; this not only looks neater, but it does not leave your equipment displayed so anyone can walk off with it. Don't leave small, valuable items like cameras or wallets casually out in the open or leave tack at the wash rack or the warm-up ring; this invites theft, and the chances of recovery are very poor. Saddles and good leather items should be marked with your driver's license number on the underside; do not rely on brass nameplates, which are easily removed. Any time you leave the tack room, it should be locked with a chain and combination lock. Trunks that stand outside the stalls should have padlocks, also.

Night security is usually handled either by having one of the grooms sleep in the tack room, or by hiring a horse-watching service. The commercial services check in on the horses several times during the night and will call you at your hotel or call a veterinarian if indicated. Any time you leave a horse stabled away from home, you should post a stall card on his door giving an emergency number where you can be reached. If someone else is checking on him or feeding him for you, essential information on the horse and his habits should also be included.

Public Relations

Horse shows are the shop window of the horse world, whether you are a trainer, instructor, breeder, or dealer in show horses—or a horse owner, proud of your horses and the impression you make on the public. When you are at a show, everything you do will be scrutinized, in the ring and out of it. Those who watch you may be experienced horse people who know what they are looking at when they watch a horse or a handler, or they may be ignorant but interested in horses and what goes on around them. The manner in which you present yourself, your horses, and your stable can make a lasting impression for or against your stable, yourself, and your breed or type of horse.

Your stable area should be as attractive as possible, without being inefficient or needlessly ornate. Neatness makes the greatest difference. Stalls should be kept well bedded and picked out, aisles swept, trash picked up, and equipment neatly hung up when not in use. Clean, shiny tack hung up neatly looks nicer and is ready for the next class; blankets and bandages should be freshly laundered and neatly folded or rolled up and hung on their racks. Naturally, your horses should be properly trimmed and well groomed.

The dress and attitude of the stable's personnel are important, too. It is incongruous to see a beautifully appointed stable area and tack room, immaculate horses, and the stable help looking like bums in grubby tee shirts and filthy jeans. Naturally, you don't wear your best clothes to muck out stalls, but you should take pride in the impression *you* make, and you can look neat, clean, and professional. Many stables supply shirts, jackets, or caps with the stable's logo and colors; this looks much more professional, especially when you are out in the public eye. Your language and behavior also reflect on your stable as well as yourself; foul language and rude behavior create a very bad impression and will turn people off.

A horse show is not the place to train horses or to settle a serious behavior problem with a horse. Discipline is necessary at times, but a violent altercation with whip or shank is seldom worth the adverse reaction it will cause from spectators, other horsemen, and even show officials. People are put off by anything that smacks of cruelty, callousness or rough handling. By preparing your horses properly at home and avoiding public problem sessions or questionable methods, you will avoid distressing incidents and give a better impression of your stable, your horses, and your horsemanship.

Be helpful and friendly to spectators whenever possible. It might be easier to close off your aisles and warn off all strangers with an unfriendly glare, but you will not commend yourself, your stable, or even your sport to people that way! You sometimes hear comments like "Those snobbish horse show people. . . ." Unfortunately, some people have the impression that all horse people, or at least all horse show people, are snobs. An unfriendly attitude is what starts and perpetuates petty divisions and feuds and can even create enemies for all horse people. Remember that the person you are rude to today could be tomorrow's client, or may someday vote on whether or not horses will be zoned out of your neighborhood. If you are too busy to answer questions at the moment or if your horse has had about all the petting he can stand, say so in a polite manner and suggest that the person stop back later, or tell him when he can watch one of your horses in a class. Spectators love to have someone special to root for; they are interested in the people and horses behind the scenes, and it is no more trouble to be civil than to be unpleasant. You'll make a lot of friends this way also.

Lastly, leave your stable area cleaner than you found it. If you have parked your trailer on the host stable's grounds all day, clear away the manure your horse has left around it and pick up all your trash, bottles, and cans. Make a last check of the area before you leave—you never know what you'll find that would have been forgotten.

Appendix A: Trimming Styles by Breed

BREED	MANE	BRIDLE PATH	TAIL	OTHER NOTES
American Saddle Horse				
3-Gaited	Mane and forelock roached off cleanly.		Set tail, top of dock trimmed, clipped, or feathered but not long hair. Tail braces, wigs, or switches are permitted.	Legs, head, and ears trimmed closely. Ears trimmed inside and out, with points left on.
5-Gaited and Fine Harness	Long mane. First lock and forelock braided with satin ribbon.	6"–8"	Set tail with long hair at top of dock. Tail braces, wigs and switches are permitted.	As above.
Pleasure	Long mane, braided	As above.	Long natural tail, unset, without brace or artificial appliances.	As above.
Andalusian (and Lusitano)	Long, full, and natural mane and forelock. French braid with traditional bullfighting ribbon puffs may be used for special occasions, but not for dressage competition. French braid or Continental braid optional for dressage classes.	No more than 1"	Long, full, and natural tail, unset and unbraided.	As above. Legs, head, and face trimmed. Ears may be trimmed inside or edges only. In Europe, ears and whiskers are seldom trimmed. Dyes, coloring, and addition of hair to mane or tail is prohibited.

BREED	MANE	BRIDLE PATH	TAIL	OTHER NOTES
Appaloosa				
Western	Pulled to 3½"–4½"; should fall evenly to left side. Mane usually banded. Long performance mane acceptable. Roached mane permissible but uncommon.	6"–8"	As long and full as possible. Tail extensions permitted; tails may be lengthened by hair-to-hair attachment only.	Sparse mane and tail hair are a breed characteristic. Clear hoof polish should be used as striped feet are a breed characteristic and should be visible. Legs, head, and ears trimmed closely.
English / Hunter style	Pulled to 3½"–4½". Hunter braids with conservative colored yarn, braided on right. Forelock braided if mane is braided.	1". Longer if shown Western	As long and full as possible. Tail may be hunter braided if mane is braided. Mud knot or braided stick may look better if tail is short. Tail extensions Permitted (as above).	As above.
Arabian (Half-Arabians)	Long, full, and unbraided. Braiding prohibited except in Hunter or Dressage classes.	6"–8"	Long, full, and free. Set tail, ginger or any artificial appliances prohibited.	Head, ears, and legs trimmed closely. Ears trimmed inside and out, with points left on.

continued

BREED	MANE	BRIDLE PATH	TAIL	OTHER NOTES
Buckskin (usually shown western)	Pulled to 3½"–4½", falls to left; Pulled mane may be banded. Long performance style mane acceptable. Roached mane permissible but seldom seen.	6"–8"	Long and natural; no artificial appliances.	As above.
Connemara	Pulled to 3½"–4" as for Hunter. Hunter braids with yarn or sewn-in button braids with thread. Forelock braided.	1"	Long and natural. May be hunter braided if mane is braided. May be pulled as for sport horses.	As above. Ears need not be trimmed on inside.
Friesian	Full, natural mane, as long as possible.	Not to exceed 2"	Long, full, natural tail.	Tail setting, ginger, artificial appliances, and addition of hair to mane or tail prohibited. Only guard hairs to be trimmed on ears.
Gypsy Vanner (Gypsy cob)	Full, natural mane, as long aspossible.	2"	Long, full, natural tail.	May be shown body clipped or in natural coat, including full facial hair.
Hackney (horses and ponies)	Pulled to 3"–3½". For formal classes, sewn-in button braids with yarn in conservative color to match livery.	1"–2"	Docked and set. End of tail hair banged off square.	Head, ears, and legs trimmed closely. Ears trimmed inside and out, with points. White legs are booted up.

BREED	MANE	BRIDLE PATH	TAIL	OTHER NOTES
Haflinger				
English and Western Pleasure and Performance	Long, full, and natural; unbraided.	5"–6"	Long, full, and natural	Head trimmed. Ears trimmed (trimming outside only is acceptable). Legs may be trimmed, booted up, or left with natural fetlocks.
Pleasure or Carriage Driving	Long, full, natural mane Pulled mane (4"–5")	4"–5"	As above.	As above, but Marathon horses are not booted up.
Dressage Hunter, and Jumping classes	Pulled mane unbraided or braided with Hunter braids, button braids, or Euro-style braids. Long natural mane with 5"–6" bridle path acceptable.		As above	As above. Legs usually trimmed or booted up.
Draft type	Long, full, natural mane, may be braided in Draft style French braid with ribbon.	5"–6"	Long, full, and natural or docked and braided in draft style.	Legs may be trimmed, booted up, or left with natural fetlocks.
Icelandic Horse	Long, full, and natural; trimming or braiding.	No bridle path	Long, full, and natural. No trimming, braiding, added hair, or artificial appliances.	Shown with natural and untrimmed hair; ears, facial whiskers , legs, and fetlocks left untrimmed.

continued

BREED	MANE	BRIDLE PATH	TAIL	OTHER NOTES
Miniature Horses	Long, natural mane.	1"–4"	Long, full, and natural.	Head, ears, and legs trimmed closely.
Missouri Fox Trotter (Also Rocky Mountain Horse, Racking Horse, Spotted Saddle Horse)	Long, natural mane. First lock of mane and forelock braided with ribbon.	6"–8"	Long, full, and natural.	Head and legs trimmed closely. Ears clipped out, leaving poins at tips of ears.
Morgan	Long, full, and natural, unbraided. Braiding prohibited except in Hunter, Dressage, or ADS Carriage Driving classes.	6"–8"	Long, full, and natural. Set tails, ginger or artificial appliances prohibited. No hair may be added to tail or mane.	As above.
National Show Horse	Long, full and natural mane. Adding hair to mane prohibited.	6"–8"	Long, full, and natural tail. Set tails, ginger, or adding hair to tail	As above.
Palomino				
Stock type	Pulled to 3½"–4½", falling to left. May be banded. Long, natural mane acceptable.	6"–8"	Long, full, and natural. Artificially changing color of mane or tail prohibited.	As above.
Pleasure type	Long, natural mane.	6"–8"	As above.	As above.

BREED	MANE	BRIDLE PATH	TAIL	OTHER NOTES
Paso Fino	Long, full, and natural mane. No braiding or or artificial hair coloring.	No more than 4".	Long, full, and natural. Look of hair cascading down from tail bone is desired. Tail hair is parted down center of dock. No artificial color or appliances.	Face, ears, and legs trimmed, but natural look is desired. Clipping should not be obvious.
Peruvian Paso	Long, full, and natural. Geldings may have forelock roached and mane cut to ½ inch, standing up, for ¾ length of neck. The coat mane on the last ¼ of the neck is left long.	PPHRNA rules upt to 2". OBPPH rules no bridle path.	Full, long, and natural. Narrow at dock and wide at skirt, with skirt banged.	Natural appearance is desired; obvious close trimming may be penalized. Trim well in advance of show so hair will be back to natural color. Obvious use of cosmetics including sprays, may be penalized. Natural texture of coat is considered in judging. Feet are cleaned but not polished.
Pinto				
Stock type	Pulled to 3½"–4½". Usually banded, on left Long performance mane acceptable.	6"–8"	Long, full, and natural.	Face, ears, and legs trimmed. Legs usually booted up. Ears trimmed inside and out.

continued

BREED	MANE	BRIDLE PATH	TAIL	OTHER NOTES
Pleasure type	Long, full, and natural. Forelock and first lock braided with ribbon for gaited and fine harness.	6"–8"	Long, full, and natural.	As above.
Hunter type	Pulled to 3½"–4½" inches. Hunter braided with matching yarn, on right side. Forelock braided.	1"	Long, full, and natural. May be hunter braided if mane and forelock are braided.	As above.
Paint (APHA)	Pulled to 3½"–4½". May be banded for western classes. May be Hunter braided for hunter seat classes.	6"–8"	Long, full, and natural. May be Hunter braided when mane is braided. Tail extensions permitted, but only hair to hair attachments.	As above.
Pony of the Americas	Pulled to 3"–3½", falls to left. May be banded when shown western. May be Hunter braided when shown English (on right). Roached mane with forelock and wither lock left is acceptable but uncommon.	4"–6"	Long and natural. Hunter braided when mane and forelock are braided. Mud knot or braided stick may look better if tail hair is sparse.	Face, ears, head, and legs trimmed and tail hair are closely. Sparse mane and tail hair are a breed characteristic. Clear hoof polish should be used as striped feet are a breed characteristic and should be visible.

BREED	MANE	BRIDLE PATH	TAIL	OTHER NOTES
Quarter Horse (AQHA)				
Western	Pulled to 3 ½"–4 ½", falls to left. May be banded for western, but no braiding permitted in western classes. Long performance style mane preferred on reining and performance horses.	6"–8"	Long, full, and natural. Tail hair extensions permitted. Only hair to hair attachments.	Head, ears, and legs trimmed closely. Legs may be booted up. Ears clipped clean inside.
Hunter	Hunter braided, on right, with yarn in matching or conservative color. Forelock braided.	1"–2"	Tail hunter braided or unbraided. Tail extensions permitted (as above).	As above.
Shetland Pony	Long, full mane. Forelock and first lock of mane braided with satin ribbon, or shaved forelock with bridle braid.	4"–6"	Long, full tail; may be set but tail braces and all artificial hair (wigs or switches) prohibited. Tail may be tied.	As above.
Tennessee Walking Horse	Long, full mane Forelock and first lock of mane braided with ribbon. Bows may	6"–8"	Long and full. Set tail, with or without tail brace and tail wigs permitted in Show Walking Horse	As above, but leave extra hair on front of pasterns for protection. Permitted lubricants (Vaseline,

continued

BREED	MANE	BRIDLE PATH	TAIL	OTHER NOTES
	be added to braids.		classes. Natural, unset tail in Pleasure Walking Horse classes.	glycerine, or mineral oil) may be applied to pasterns to prevent rubbing by action devices. Horses showing evidence of previous soring of pasterns (scar, callous, or granulation tissue) are barred from showing.
Thoroughbred	Pulled to 3½"–4½", falls to right. Hunter braided onright, with matching or conservative color yarn. Forelock braided (may be left unbraided on jumpers or dressage horses.) Button braids or scallped braids permissible but less common.	1"	Long and full; may be banged or switch tail. Hunter braided tail optional when mane is braided. Mud knot or braided mud tail optional, especially on wet days.	Head, ears, and legs trimmed closely. Legs may not need to be booted up if hair is fine. Quarter marks sometimes used for formal turnout.
Warmbloods	Pulled to 3½"–5", may fall to either side. Braided as for dressage, using flat button, knob, or Euro-style braids. Braids	1"–2"	Pulled or trimmed at top of dock to "turnover" point. May be banged or switch tail. Braiding tail is permitted when mane is braided but	Head and legs trimmed neatly. Legs may be booted up. Europeans seldom trim ears or whiskers; edges of ears may be trimmed with

BREED	MANE	BRIDLE PATH	TAIL	OTHER NOTES
	may be taped for dressage but not for other disciplines. Scalloped braids permissible but unusual. Forelock may be braided or not.		seldom seen.	hair left inside. Quarter marks sometimes used for formal turnout.
Welsh Pony				
Section A	Full, natural mane bridle path. Long, full forelock. Braiding of forelock and first lock of mane with ribbon allowed only in Roadster and Formal Driving classes. Hunter braiding permitted on hunter ponies.	3"–5"	Long, full, and natural. Set tail, ginger, spoon cruppers, and artificial stimulants or appliances prohibited. Hunter braided tail permitted when mane is braided hunter style.	Head, ears, and legs trimmed closely; legs may be booted up. Artificial coloring of mane or tail prohibited.
Section B	Usually mane is pulled to 3"–3½". Hunter braided. Button braids or scalloped braids less common but acceptable. Mane braided on right; forelock braided.	1"	Hunter braided tail optional. Mud knot or braided mud tail looks nice on some ponies.	As above.

Appendix B: Trimming Styles by Type and Event

TYPE OR EVENT	MANE	TAIL	OTHER NOTES
Combined Driving	Trimmed according to breed or type of horse used. Often pulled as for sport horses. May be braided in sewn-in button braids (yarn matching mane color).	According to breed or type of horse, but very seldom braided. Upper hair of dock may be pulled.	Trim bridle path and head as usual, but do not boot up legs on marathon horses. May be body clipped, even in summer, for more efficient cooling.
Dressage	Pulled to 3½"–5"; braided with button, knob, or Euro-style braids, usually taped. Long-maned horses: free mane, French braid, or Continental braid optional. Forelock may be braided or unbraided. Ribbons, bangles, etc., prohibited.	Usually pulled short at top of dock. Banged tail optional. Tail seldom braided.	Head and legs trimmed. Do not wipe foam from mouth. Ears trimmed outside but often not trimmed inside. Bridle path no more than 1"–2". Quarter marks optional.
Eventing	Pulled to 3½"–5". Braided (tape optional) for dressage. Unbraided for cross-country. Braiding (no tape) optional for stadium jumping.	Upper hair of dock pulled (optional). Banged tail optional. Braided tail optional but unusual for stadium jumping.	Head and legs trimmed. Bridle path 1". Quarter marks optional. Sometimes body clipped for three-day events, even in summer, to aid cooling.

TYPE OR EVENT	MANE	TAIL	OTHER NOTES
English Pleasure, Saddle Seat	Long, full, and natural. Bridle path 6"–8". Some breeds use braided forelock and first lock, but some prohibit braiding (see breed standards).	Long, full, and natural. Most breeds prohibit tail setting and addition of tail wigs, etc.	Head and legs trimmed closely. May be booted up. Ears clipped clean, with points.
English Pleasure, Hunter Seat	Hunter braided or unbraided. Mane may be left free. Long manes may be braided hunter style or in a French braid, but not Continental.	Hunters often left unbraided.	Head and legs trimmed as for hunters or for breed.
Equitation, Hunter Seat	Pulled to 3½"–4½" and hunter braided with matching yarn. Forelock braided. Bridle path no more than 1". Mane always braided on right side.	Hunter braided tail optional, but preferred for formal classes. Natural or pulled tails are acceptable.	Head and legs trimmed. Booted up if necessary. Quarter marks optional for formal turnout.
Equitation, Saddle Seat	*Three-Gaited Saddle Horse:* mane and forelock roached off. *All others:* Long, natural mane; forelock natural or first lock braided with ribbon, according to breed.	*Three-Gaited:* set tail, with dock trimmed or feathered. Wigs and tail braces permitted. *All others:* Tail long, full, and natural, according to breed.	Head and legs trimmed, often booted up. Ears clipped clean, with points.

continued

TYPE OR EVENT	MANE	TAIL	OTHER NOTES
Equitation, Stock Seat/Western	Pulled to 3½″–4½″, with 5″–6″ bridle path. Mane should fall on left side. Banding optional but usual. Long performance style mane also acceptable.	Long, full, and natural. Tail extensions permitted according to breed rules.	Head and legs closely trimmed; ears clipped clean. Often booted up.
Fine Harness	Long and full; 6″–8″ bridle path. First lock of mane braided with ribbon. Forelock braided or shaved off with bridle braid.	Set or may use spoon crupper or tail brace (some breeds require natural tail). Long hair at top of dock. May use tail switch or wig.	Head and legs closely trimmed; ears clipped clean. Often booted up.
Gymkhana	Long natural performance mane with 6″ bridle path, or pulled to 3½″–4½″.	Long, full and natural.	Head and legs trimmed closely. May be booted up.
Hunters and Pony Hunters	Pulled to 3½″–4½″. Hunter braided with yarn in color to match mane or conservative color. Sewn-in button braids or scalloped braids optional but seldom seen today. Mane is always braided on right.	Long and full. Braided tail is optional but preferred for formal classes. If tail is braided, mane must also be braided. Banged tail or switch tail optional. Mud knot or braided mud tail optional on wet days.	Head and legs trimmed closely. Show hunters may be booted up, but not field hunters. Bridle path no longer than 1″. Forelock but quarter marks optional for formal turnout.
Jumpers	Pulled to 3½″–4½″. Hunter braids optional. Forelock may be braided or not.	Long and full. Pulled top of dock optional. Braiding tail optional, but only if mane is braided. Mud tail optional on wet days.	Head and legs trimmed closely. Bridle path no more than 1″.

TYPE OR EVENT	MANE	TAIL	OTHER NOTES
Parade Horses	Long, full and natural. Bridle path 6"–8". Forelock and first lock braided with ribbon; may be metallic or have added bows. Forelock may be shaved and bridle braid used.	Long, free, and full. Some breeds permit set tails, tail braces, and tail wigs or switches. Ribbon braids sometimes attached to top of dock to fall with tail hair.	Head and legs trimmed closely; legs booted up. Ears trimmed clean, with points. Glitter on hooves, face, and dusted over croup.
Park Horses	Long, free and full. Bridle path 6"–8". No braiding.	Long, free, and natural. No braiding or pulling. Most breeds prohibit tail setting, ginger, or any artificial appliances.	Head, legs, and ears trimmed closely. Ears clipped clean, with points. Legs booted up.
Pleasure Driving	Long, free, and full. Bridle path 6"–8". Some breeds require natural, unbraided mane; some permit braiding forelock and first lock with ribbon.	Long, full, and natural. Most breeds prohibit tail setting, ginger, tail braces or tail wigs, or other artificial appliances.	Head, legs, and ears trimmed closely. Ears trimmed clean with points. Legs usually booted up.
Reining and Western Performance	Long, full and natural; bridle path 6"–8". Mane may be pulled to 3½"–4½" and left free or banded. Forelock usually free; may be braided.	Long, full and natural. Shortened tail out of style.	Head, legs, and ears trimmed closely; legs may be booted up.
Roadsters	Long, free, and full. Bridle path 6"–8" inches. Forelock shaved; first lock and bridle braid braided with ribbon in stable colors.	Long, free, and full. Some breeds permit tail braces and tail wigs; others require tail free and natural.	Head, ears, and legs trimmed closely; legs booted up. Ears trimmed clean with points.

continued

TYPE OR EVENT	MANE	TAIL	OTHER NOTES
Saddle Horses (3-gaited)	Roached mane and forelock.	Set tail with top of dock trimmed or feathered. Tail usually tied. Tail braces, wigs, and switches are permitted.	Head, ears, and legs trimmed closely. Legs booted up. Ears clipped clean, with points.
Saddle Horses (5-gaited)	Long, full mane; bridle path 6"–8". First lock and forelock braided with ribbon or forelock shaved with bridle braid.	Tail set and may be tied braced. Long and full, including hair of upper dock. Tail wigs or switches permitted.	Same as above.
Walking Horses	Same as five-gaited Saddle Horse	Same as five-gaited Saddle Horse, except that set tails are prohibited in Plantation Pleasure divisions.	Same as above.
Western (Pleasure and Performance, also Halter)	Pulled to 3½" – 4½". 6"–8" inch bridle path. Pulled mane usually banded. Performance mane (long natural mane) optional. Mane usually falls on left forelock sometimes braided.	Long, full and natural. May have tail hair extensions, according to breed rules.	Head, ears, and legs trimmed closely. Legs may be booted up. Ears clipped clean, with points.

$\mathcal{I}$ndex

American pony breeds, 273–274
anti-sweat sheet, 104, 105
Apron clip, 148–149
azoturia, 14–15

bandage
    exercise, 123–124
    leg, 30, 115–124, 125
    materials, 117
    padding under, 118
    removing, 178
    shipping, 120–123, 306
    stable or standing, 118–120
    tail, 94–96
banging, 68, 113, 233–234
bathing, 37, 38, 105–110
bedding, 303, 311
biting horses, 48–49
blanket, 163–167, 170–174
blanket clip, 151, 152
body brush, 51, 63, 65
body clip, 149–158, 166
booting up, 141–142
boots, 30, 124, 126–127, 306
bots, 54–55
braiding strips, 89–90
braids
    banded, 224–225, 247–249
    button, 201, 226–227
    continental (lattice), 231–232
    equipment for, 191–192
    forelock, 199–201

French, 199–201, 208–211, 228–231
knob style, 197–198, 222–223
maintaining, 206
mane, 78–79, 85, 87, 190–206,
    222–232
for pleasure horses, 259=260
protecting, 216–219
with rubberbands, 203–204, 212
saddle and harness horses, 279–282
scalloped mane, 201–202
sewn-in, 201
tail, 88–90, 91, 207–219
taking out, 206
taped, 222–223
tips for, 204–206, 212
tying off, 196–198
yarn-braid method, 193–196
bridle path
    pleasure horse, 258–259
    trimming, 129, 145–146, 147
    trimming styles by breed, 324–333
    western horse, 245
brush
    material types, 62
    quality of, 61
    types of, 63–68
    using, 50–51

cactus cloth, 63–64, 66, 103
cavaletti, 22–23
chorioptic mange, 269
clipper blades, 135, 136–137

clippers
  cleaning, 154–155
  introducing a horse to, 158–162
  parts, 134–135
  types of, 131, 132–134
clipping. *See also* trimming
  body, 149–158
  restraints for, 161–162
  techniques, 138–140
clothing, horse, 16, 163–174, 297–298
coat dressing, 37–38, 107, 109
coat polish, 72, 175, 263
conditioner, 37, 71–72, 87, 93–94,
  106–107, 175
conditioning
  basic program, 24–25
  beginning, 7–10
  exercise, 19–23
  feeding, 10–13
  foot and leg care, 25–30
  health and veterinary care, 13
  mental attitude, 32–33
  organization and planning, 4–7
  problems, 14–16
  process, 17–19
  skin and hair coat, 30–31
  stabling, 3–4
  turnout, 16–17
condition scale, 8
cooler, 104, 105, 108, 165, 169–170
cooling out, 102–105
cosmetic products, 72
cramps, muscle, 14–15
cross-ties, 44–46, 47, 48
Culicoides gnat, 97–98
currycomb, 49–50, 60–61

dandy brush, 50, 63, 64
dehydration, 11
dental care, 15–16
detangling, mane and tail, 72, 75–76
deworming, 15
dock, 39, 74, 235–236

dressage
  mane, 222–232
  tail, 233–236
  trimming, 221
driving, 21, 240–241

ears, trimming, 144–145
electrolytes, 11
equine rhabdomyelosis, 14–15
equipment, show, 292–303
eventers, 237, 239
exercise, 20–25

face, trimming, 262–263
face brush, 63, 65
face clip, 147–148, 149
farrier, 10, 25–26
feather, 266–269
feeding, 10–13, 38, 303, 307
feet. *See also* hoof
  cleaning, 55
  daily care, 26–27
  evaluation of, 10, 25–26
  final touches, 180–182
  packing, 59
  picking up, 55–58
  thrush, 58
  western show horse, 253–254
filling, leg, 27, 29
final touches, 175–186
finishing bandage, 96
finishing brush, 63, 64
first aid kit, 295–296
fly control, 4, 16, 37, 73, 91, 175
fly sheets, 37, 168
forelock, 146, 199–201, 250, 259, 279
Friesians, 266–268, 326
full clip, 151–152
full head clip, 148

galls, preventing, 31
gnats, 97–98
groom, horse show, 304–305, 308–312,
  315–320

grooming
    basic procedures, 49–53
    bathing, 37, 38
    benefits of, 41
    bot egg removal, 54–55
    injuries, care for, 53
    mutual between horses, 41, 42
    products, 70–73
    safety, 43–49
    sensitivity of horse to, 42–43
    timing of, 37
    for yourself at show, 305–306
grooming block, 66, 68
grooming tools. *See also specific tools*
    brushes, 50–51, 61–68
    caring for, 68–69
    checklist, 299–300
    currycomb, 49–50, 60–61
    vacuum cleaners, 69–70
Gypsy cobs, 266–267, 326

hair coat
    cleaning, 36–40
    conditioning, 30–31
    final touches, 175
    protecting, 37–38
    rubbing, 51
    shedding, 39
    staring, 35
    structure, 36
halter
    breakaway, 16
    cross-ties and, 44–45
    pleasure horse show, 264–265
    shipping, 306
    western show, 254–255
handling a horse, 46–49
hard wisping, 68, 113
hay net, 309–311, 314
head, trimming, 142–143, 244–245, 276, 278
head down command/signal, 159
health care, 13
heel mites, 269

highlighting, 175–177, 263
high trace clip, 151, 152
hood, 169
hoof
    daily care, 26–27
    grooming products, 73
    saddle horse, 278–279
    safe conditioning, 19
    trimming, 10, 25–26
hoof dressings, 27, 58–59, 73, 180, 253–254
hoof packing, 59, 73
hoof pick, 63, 66
hoof polish, 73, 180–182, 253–254, 263–264, 279
horse show
    assisting in grooming, 318–320
    duties at, 315–318
    equipment, 292–303
    grooming for yourself, 305–306
    planning and preparation, 290–292
    public relations, 321–323
    schedule, 316–317
    security, 320–321
    setting up at, 308–311
    shipping your horse, 306–308
    show grooms, 304–305
    tack stall, 312
    trailer or van, showing from, 313–315
hot oil treatment, 72, 87, 93, 158
hot toweling, 108–109
hunter
    formal turnout, 187, 188
    mane, 188–189, 190–206
    tail, 189–190, 207–219
hunter clip, 151, 152, 153

Iberian horses, 270–272
Icelandic horses, 272–273, 327
inoculations, 5, 13

jowl strap, 111, 112

kicking horses, 47

leading a horse, 47–48
legs
    booting up, 141–142
    evaluation of, 25, 27–28
    feather, 266–269
    lifting safely, 55–58
    problems, 28–29
    protection of, 30
    rubbing, 112, 114–115
    structure, 26
    wraps and bandaging, 115–124,
      125
leg trimming, 140–141, 253, 263
lice, 98
longeing, 21
long-maned breeds, 266–269

makeover, one-day, 184–186
mane
    banded, 224–225, 247–249
    braiding, 78–79, 85, 87, 188–189,
      190–206, 222–232
    crimping, 249–250
    detangling, 75–76
    dressage horses, 222–232
    dressing, 82–84
    final touches, 179
    grooming, 53
    growth of, 40
    hunter, 188–189, 190–206
    Iberian horses, 270–271
    long-maned breeds with feather,
      266–269
    pleasure horse, 256–258, 259–260
    problems, 84–87, 97–98
    protecting, 40, 78–79
    pulling, 80–82, 246
    saddle horse, 279–282
    scalloped, 201–202
    training to one side, 84–87
    trimming, 77
    trimming styles by breed, 324–333
    washing, 107
    western show horse, 245–250
mane comb, 66, 68
mane-trimming comb, 82, 84
massage therapy, 43, 112
mental attitude, horse's, 32–33
mitt, 65, 66, 68
moisture magnet, 65
mud fever, 269
mud knot, 217–218
muscle cramps, 14–15

neck covers, 169
neck sweating, 110–112

packing feet, 59
parade horse, 288–289
parasites, 2, 15, 54–55, 97–98
Paso Fino, 272, 329
periople, 58–59, 253, 263
Peruvian Pasos, 272, 329
pinworm, 51, 97
pleasure horse
    bridle path, 258–259
    forelock, 258
    mane, 256–258, 259–260
    polish, 263–264
    show halter, 264–265
    tail, 256–257, 260–262
    trimming, 256, 262–263
polo wrap, 117, 123–124, 178
ponying, 21
proud flesh, 53
public relations, 321–323
pulling, mane, 80–82
pulling comb, 66, 68, 80
pulse, 19, 20

quarter marks, 182–184
quick-release knot, 44, 46

racing clip, 151, 152
razor trimmer, 84
records, keeping, 5–6
recovery rate, 19
Recurrent Summer Dermatitis, 97–98
rest, balancing work with, 18
restraint for clipping, 161–162
riding, exercising horse by, 20
roundpenning, 21
rubbing
    coat, 51
    by horse, 97
    legs, 112, 114–115
rub rags, 64

saddle horses, 275–282
saddle patch, 151, 153, 158
safety
    blanket, 171
    in conditioning, 18–19
    grooming, 43–49
    handling horses, 46–49
    picking up feet, 55–58
    turnout, 16
    tying horses, 44–46
salt, 11
Scotch comb, 50, 67
scurf, 36, 41, 51
sebum, 35
security, stable area, 320–321
set-tail horses, 283–288
shampoo, 38, 70–71, 92–94, 106–107
sheath cleaner, 73, 109–110
shedding blade, 66, 67
sheets, 37, 166–168, 170, 173
shipping your horse, 306–308
shoeing, 6, 10, 25
show jumpers, 237, 238
silicone coat spray, 72, 93, 107, 153
skin
    cleaning, 36–37
    conditioning, 30–31

    preventing sores and galls, 31
    structure and function, 34–36
skirt, braiding, 88–90, 91
smegma, 109
sores, preventing, 31
sponge, 65, 67, 107
sport horses, 220–221
stable blankets and sheets, 166, 167
stabling, 3–4
stain remover, 71
stains, 37, 53, 93, 177
stall
    grooming, 43, 44
    setup at horse show, 308–311
    tack, 312
stall screen, 308
stocking up, 28, 29
strapping, 68, 113
strip clip, 151, 152, 153
sunscreen, 17, 73
supplements, 11–12, 38
sweat, 35–36, 37
sweat scraper, 66, 67
sweep brush, 63, 64
swimming, 23

tack, 184, 298–299, 302–303
tack stall, 312
tail
    bandages, 94–96
    banging, 233–234, 260
    braiding, 88–90, 91, 207–219
    covers, 90–92
    dressage, 233–236
    extensions, 99–101, 251–253
    final touches, 179–180
    grooming, 53
    growth of, 40
    hunter, 189–190, 207–219
    Iberian horses, 271–272
    as indicator of mental state, 39, 74
    long-maned breeds, 268

pleasure horse, 256–257, 260–262
problems, 97–98
protecting, 40
pulling, 234
rings in, 260–262
set-tail horses, 283–288
trimming styles by breed, 324–333
washing, 92–94, 107
western show horse, 250–253
white, 92–93
tail brace, 283, 286
tail brush, 68
tail set, 283–288
tail wig, 286, 287
tail wrap, 216–219, 306
Tennessee Walking Horses, 275–276, 331–332
thatching, 105, 165
thrush, 58
ticks, 53, 98
toe hold, 161, 162
trace clip, 151, 152, 153, 158
trailer, showing from, 313–315
tranquilizers, 162
traveling tail bandage, 94–95
treadmill, 23
trimming
    all-purpose basic trim, 129–130
    apron clip, 148, 149
    body clip, 149–158
    booting up, 141–142
    bridle path, 129, 145–146, 147
    clippers, 131–137
    clipping techniques, 138–140
    cosmetic changes, 130–131
    dock, 236–237
    dressage horses, 221
    ears, 144–145
    face clip, 147–148, 149
    forelock, 146
    full head clip, 148
    head, 142–143

legs, 140–141
long-maned breeds, 267–268
pleasure horse, 256, 262–263
saddle horse, 276–279
styles by breed, 324–333
western horse, 244–246
whiskers, 144
turnout, 16–17
turnout rugs, 168
twitch, 161–162
tying horses, 44–46, 47, 48, 313–314
tying-up syndrome, 13, 14–15

udder, cleaning, 109
ulcer, gastric, 15
underclothing, 167

vacuum cleaner, 69–70
veterinary care, 13

walkers, automatic, 23
water, 11
water brush, 63, 64, 65
waterless cleaner, 71
weight, assessment of, 7–8
western show horse
    description, 242–244
    forelock, 250
    head, 244–245
    legs and feet, 253–254
    mane, 245–250
    show halters, 254–255
    tail, 250–253
wet coat, drying, 164–165
whisk brush, 50
whiskers, trimming, 144
white markings, 177–178
windpuffs, 28, 29
winter coat, 38–39, 149–150, 164
wisping, 68, 113–114

yarn, braiding, 191, 193–196